THE FRICK COLLECTION

VOLUME VIII · ENAMELS, RUGS AND SILVER

ENAMEL ROOM · THE FRICK COLLECTION

THE
FRICK COLLECTION

AN ILLUSTRATED CATALOGUE

VOLUME VIII · ENAMELS, RUGS AND SILVER

*Limoges Painted Enamels,
Oriental Rugs and English Silver*

THE FRICK COLLECTION · NEW YORK · 1977

DISTRIBUTED BY PRINCETON UNIVERSITY PRESS

Versus

1/86
1.16.87

PHILIPPE VERDIER

ASSISTED BY

JOSEPH FOCARINO

———

LIMOGES PAINTED ENAMELS

Sixteenth and Seventeenth Centuries

MAURICE S. DIMAND

———

ORIENTAL RUGS

Sixteenth and Seventeenth Centuries

KATHRYN C. BUHLER

———

ENGLISH SILVER

Eighteenth and Nineteenth Centuries

TABLE OF CONTENTS

LIMOGES PAINTED ENAMELS

PHILIPPE VERDIER assisted by JOSEPH FOCARINO

ORIENTAL RUGS

MAURICE S. DIMAND

ENGLISH SILVER

KATHRYN C. BUHLER

PAUL STORR

BENJAMIN and JAMES SMITH

INDICES

PREFACE

With this volume, the complete new quarto edition of *The Frick Collection: An Illustrated Catalogue,* launched in 1968, makes another significant advance. As with all the books in this projected nine-volume series, the present one is indebted in part to the folio *Illustrated Catalogue of the Works of Art in the Collection of Henry Clay Frick* published by Miss Helen C. Frick in memory of her father, specifically to the comments of Joseph Breck on enamels published in 1955 and to Maurice S. Dimand's first studies of the Collection's rugs published in 1956, along with brief notes on the English silver prepared by David J. Way.

The union in the present volume of texts concerning enamels, rugs, and silver reflects the founder's interests during his late years. With the grand range of his picture collecting already established, Mr. Frick turned to other domains, in all three of the present cases to areas long favored by distinguished collectors who preceded him and whose example he sought to emulate.

Indeed, the architecture of the new Fifth Avenue residence he had built in 1913–14 was modified specifically to accommodate the important collection of painted enamels he acquired beginning in 1915, most of them from the estate of J. Pierpont Morgan. The handsome panelled gallery in which they have always been displayed was identified on early plans of the building simply as "Mr. Frick's Room," but on a subsequent drawing it appears as the "Limoges Gallery." The latter plan specified, incidentally, that the architectural ornament of the room was based on Italian and Flemish models. The small but distinguished group of Oriental rugs in the Collection was shown originally, as now, across the expanse of the West Gallery and in the Living Hall. The examples of English silver continue to complement the English decorative style of the Dining Room and the British portraits it contains.

We have been fortunate in being able to engage as the authors of the present volume three noted specialists in their respective fields: Philippe Verdier, Professor of Art History at the University of Montreal and one of the world's leading authorities on Limoges enamels; Maurice S. Dimand, Curator Emeritus of Islamic Art at the Metropolitan Museum of Art, New York, who restudied our rugs and expanded his earlier entries concerning them; and Kathryn C. Buhler, Fellow for Research in the Department of American Decorative Arts at the Boston Museum of Fine Arts, who contributed much new material on our silver. The authors have acknowledged separately in their texts the individuals who assisted them. I should like to add here an expression of our gratitude to Richard Ettinghausen, Consultative Chairman of the Islamic Art Department at the Metropolitan Museum of Art, for his generous and friendly assistance; to Rostislav Hlopoff for his role in the preservation of the Collection's enamels; and to Svetoslao Hlopoff for his opinions on technical matters concerning the silver.

Members of The Frick Collection staff have with unfailing cooperation contributed in their various ways to this publication. Edgar Munhall, Curator, and Bernice Davidson, Research Curator, shouldered the complex responsibilities of dealing with authors, photographers, and printers. Joseph Focarino exercised his familiar editorial skills so far beyond the customary limits that, with Mr. Verdier's generous agreement, he is justly listed as assisting that author. David Monroe Collins, Business Administrator, dealt ably with the myriad practical details a publication of this type entails. The black-and-white photography was the work of Richard di Liberto, the Collection's accomplished staff photographer, and of former staff members Francis Beaton and Peter O'Sullivan. The color photographs were done by Geoffrey Clements and Mr. O'Sullivan.

It is a pleasure to acknowledge here the unhesitating assistance that members of the Collection's staff provide daily throughout such undertakings as the quarto catalogue. I should also like to take this opportunity to thank our friends at Conzett and Huber, who have once again succeeded in meeting the high production standards set at the beginning of the catalogue project by the Trustees of the Collection, through their Publications Committee. The Trustees' continuing support for this scholarly endeavor is especially appreciated at a time when serious financial burdens have reduced other Collection projects and programs.

EVERETT FAHY
DIRECTOR
THE FRICK COLLECTION

XX

EXPLANATORY NOTE

A few remarks may be useful regarding the methods of presentation within each entry of this catalogue.

AUTHORSHIP: For those objects in enamel and silver that cannot with certainty be assigned to specific artists, the following classifications are used: *Attributed to,* implying that there is some doubt as to the author of the piece; and *Workshop of,* suggesting that the design may have been the master's but the execution was, in part at least, by an assistant.

SIGNATURE, MEDIUM, AND DIMENSIONS: All legible enamellers' signatures and silversmiths' marks are reproduced except those that are repeated on two or more pieces in the same group. Materials are specified only for the Oriental rugs, which are of varying composition; all of the Limoges pieces in The Frick Collection are of painted enamel on copper, and all the English silver is sterling. In the dimensions, height (H.) precedes width (W.); the abbreviation L. indicates length; and D. indicates diameter when referring to objects that are circular in plan, and depth when applied to pieces of other forms. The dimensions given for enamelled plaques are exclusive of frames, which can be assumed to be later additions unless otherwise specified; where enamels could not safely be removed from their frames, the dimensions are those of the visible surface.

DESCRIPTION: The terms left and right refer to the spectator's left and right unless otherwise indicated.

CONDITION: While most of the enamels in The Frick Collection are uncommonly well preserved in view of their age and fragility, virtually all of them show some damage; generally the larger losses described have been repaired unless otherwise specified. The Persian rugs, though they too are well preserved relative to their age and function, have all been restored to one degree or another. The

Mughal rugs, both of them fragmentary, show considerably more wear. The condition of the silver is on the whole very good apart from the loss of much original gilding.

BIBLICAL REFERENCES: In the description and discussion of enamels decorated with Biblical subjects, quotations and the spellings of proper names follow the usage of the King James version.

EXHIBITIONS AND COLLECTIONS: References to exhibitions and provenance are taken for the most part from purchase records and inventories and from Volumes VII and XI of the folio *Illustrated Catalogue of the Works of Art in the Collection of Henry Clay Frick,* published in 1955 and 1956 respectively. The great majority of the enamels were formerly in the collection of J. Pierpont Morgan and were lent by him for varying durations to the Victoria and Albert Museum, London; after his death in 1913 these pieces were lent by his estate to the Metropolitan Museum of Art, New York, from 1914 to 1916.

LIMOGES PAINTED ENAMELS

INTRODUCTION

The history of enamelling during the Middle Ages and the Renaissance alternates between a preciousness characterized by the use of gold or silver as supports for the enamel and a more expeditious technique based on copper.[1] From its appearance in Langobard-Byzantine Italy through the end of the Romanesque period, Western European enamelling had constituted merely a branch of the goldsmith's art, inheriting the cloisonné process on gold from Byzantine enamels. Champlevé enamels on copper replaced the cloisonné in the middle third of the twelfth century in the Mosan region and Cologne, migrating rapidly to Saint-Denis, Champagne, and southern England—that is, to the cradles of Gothic art. They were executed by itinerant workshops and could be built into vast iconographic programs. In the south of France, particularly in the region of Conques, and along the pilgrimage routes to Santiago de Compostela,[2] a parallel evolution led gradually from the cloisonné technique and art form to the champlevé. Within the political framework of the Plantagenet empire and in the radiance of the nearby abbey of Grandmont, then a European center of monastic reform, the production of champlevé enamels eventually became concentrated at Limoges in central France. Before the death of Richard the Lion-Hearted in 1199, Limoges enamels had already invaded the international market.[3]

During the reign of Philippe IV (1285–1314) a new foyer arose in Paris.[4] It revived in a purely decorative fashion the cloisonné enamels on gold of Byzantium, in precious artifacts produced for secular as well as ecclesiastical use. The fourteenth century was dominated, however, by a variety, not quite so luxurious, of translucent enamelling: the *basse-taille* enamels on silver, or more rarely on gold. After experimental attempts at applying enamel to silver in the champlevé technique, the *basse-taille* enamels received their decisive launching from Tuscany. Thence they spread to Catalonia, Aragon, Montpellier, the Rhine valley, northern France, Paris, and England.[5] In the last decades of the fourteenth century an aristocratic refinement took place in Paris, followed in the fifteenth century by Burgundy, that led to the design of costly three-dimensional secular and religious objects in gold encrusted with opaque and semiopaque enamels.[6] This new technique did not discard the *basse-taille* enamelling on gold, and both would coexist in the goldsmith's art of the Renaissance.

Beginning around 1420, an attempt was made in the Netherlands at painting in gold *camaïeu* and white enamel impasto over a dark blue ground previously enamelled on silver. Surviving examples of this "niederlenndisch Schmelzwerch," as it still was called in a late sixteenth-century inventory, are very rare. They include a medallion—possibly by the youngest of the Limbourg brothers who worked for Jean, Duc de Berry—now in the Walters Art Gallery, Baltimore, and the famous Monkey Cup at the Cloisters in New York.[7] The Netherlandish type of enamelling branched off to the Alpine countries and struck root in Venice. Its derivatives are characterized by wild animals and birds painted in white impasto enamel on a translucent blue or amethyst enamel ground encrusted with silver sunbursts, stars, and rosettes.[8] A variety of Venetian enamelling, the so-called Turkish enamels, adorned utilitarian objects wrought in copper.[9] In another family of painted enamels, found in Lombardy with outposts in Tuscany, a copper support was again substituted for silver.[10] Toward the turn of the fifteenth century enamelled vessels with white floriated decoration became the specialty of Venice, while elsewhere in northern Italy chalices and paxes were decorated with enamelled plaques executed in a mixed technique: translucent and painted enamel on a silver support into which the design had first been scratched and on which foils were occasionally laid to heighten the brilliance of the translucent enamel.[11]

At Limoges, a century intervened between the ruin of the enamellers' workshops during the storming of the city by Edward, the Black Prince, in 1370, and the revival of enamelling—this time in the form of painted enamels on copper—during the reign of Louis XI (1461–83). The latter issued a series of edicts restricting through the right of descent the rank and title of guild master within privileged families. The lucrative business of enamelling was thus contained, from the end of the Middle Ages through the eighteenth century, within a limited circle of Limoges families, including those of Pénicaud, Limousin, Reymond, Court, Courteys, Noylier, Laudin, and Guibert, the last revealed thanks to a signature of initials on a pair of saltcellars in The Frick Collection (see p. 226).

Until the first quarter of the sixteenth century the production at Limoges remained largely that of an anonymous craft. The incunabula amount to about fifty plaques attributed to the so-called Monvaerni Master—Monvaerni being probably a coded name, following the practice in use toward the end of the Middle Ages. Up to about 1530, these and some 150 additional plaques comprise the known early production of the Limoges painted enamels of the Renaissance. The adoption of the new technique at Limoges had been anticipated in France by a few scattered attempts: the two well-known roundels enamelled about 1450 by Jean Fouquet in a gold *camaïeu* technique,[12] and a pair executed in colored enamels with gilt scrolls on a black ground, also from about 1450, now at Poitiers.[13]

The so-called Monvaerni derived his inspiration from French painting (the Avignon *Pietà* in the Louvre, Nicolas Froment's *Raising of Lazarus* in the Uffizi) as well as from the colored woodcuts that, as of the middle third of the fifteenth century, were disseminated from the Rhine valley to central France. Prints by the Master of 1446, the Master of the Nuremberg Passion, the Master of the Playing Cards, the Master of St. John the Baptist in the Desert, and the Master E. S. began to be substituted for the pattern books previously used as models by painters, illuminators, and goldsmiths. The emergence of engravings as transmitters of subjects and of forms, whether acting independently or reciprocally, also was felt in North Italian painting before the end of the fifteenth century. This phenomenon had an overwhelming impact throughout Europe and was a primary factor in reshaping the cultural and religious mentality of the Renaissance. In their subservience to prints, six generations of Limoges enamellers, from the end of the Middle Ages well into the seventeenth century, were to concentrate on the "praxis"—or execution—leaving the "idea"—the invention itself—to their graphic models.[14] Indeed, the painted enamels of Limoges can be viewed as a digest of European art from the Late Gothic in the North and the first arrival of decorative Italian formulas, on to Dürer and to the followers of Raphael led by Marcantonio Raimondi, and through the two Schools of Fontainebleau with their grafting of Flemish elements on Italian and French Mannerism. They also incorporate a compendium of book illustration from the Books of Hours of the early sixteenth century to the woodcuts published in Lyon after the middle of the century. The influence of Lyon book illustration after the third quarter of the sixteenth century was predominant, and with reason. Lyon was then among the most cosmopolitan cities in Europe; its printers, booksellers, bookbinders, and type founders are said to have numbered some three thousand in the Renaissance.[15]

The process of imitating prints was gradually extended from the adaptation of forms to the actual technical execution of the Limoges enamels. At first the guidelines suggested by woodcuts were followed in the delineation of color areas. Afterward, the methods used by engravers in designing by cutting and in modelling by crosshatching were assimilated.

The copper plate, flat and rather thick in the earliest painted enamels of Limoges, was soon thinned and slightly domed up from the edges. The concave underside was brushed over with a counterenamel made of the sediments left after successive washings of the powdered enamels in water. The counterenamel was fired at the same time as the priming laid on the obverse of the plate, in order to counteract the tensions and shrinkages resulting from the successive firing and cooling processes; the protective layer it afforded also prevented oxidation.[16] The thick, irregular, and motley counterenamels of the first period of Limoges painted enamels appeal to modern eyes in their chance resemblance to twentieth-century abstract painting. Sometime around 1530 the opaque counterenamel was replaced by a clear flux or frit, the same base from which colored enamels were made. Only during the seventeenth century were the Limoges enamellers to revert to opaque counterenamelling.[17]

The colored enamels were obtained by adding about three percent of various metallic oxides to a flux composed of silica, soda ash, potash, lead oxide, and borax. The principal colors were transparent tan (iron) and transparent green (copper) added to lead glass; mulberry red (manganese), transparent dark blue and turquoise blue (copper), mustard yellow (antimony), and dark yellow (iron, uranate salts) added to leadless alkaline glass; and opaque white (tin), black (cobalt, iron, manganese), and russet red (iron) added either to leadless alkaline or lead glass. The lumps of enamel were broken up and ground to a granular powder in a mortar filled with water. They were cleaned repeatedly in fresh water and kept submerged in covered vessels until these vitreous substances were ready to be fused onto their copper support.

The design could be established in three ways: on a black background, on a white one, or on the copper itself.[18] If the last method was followed, care had to be taken to lay first an area of white enamel where blue or green was to be applied, in order to prevent a direct contact of copper oxide with the copper plate. The system of laying an undercoat of black enamel was mainly that of the so-called

Monvaerni. A secondary ground of white enamel was applied on top of the black one and was scraped through, after it had dried but not yet been fired, in order to lay bare the black contours and to model shadows. The white background method was the one most frequently followed, notwithstanding all sorts of qualifications and nuances. Essentially, the contours were delineated in broad blue or russet lines on the ground of white enamel previously fired, and they were themselves then fired. The network of lines thus stabilized functioned, *mutatis mutandis,* like the *cloisons* screening off areas of various colors in the cloisonné and champlevé techniques. This process made it easier for the enameller to visualize the subsequent laying of harmonious and complementary colors side by side on the plate. Because enamels of different colors had to be fired at different temperatures, successive firings were necessary—or at the least, a color area applied as wet enamel had to dry before a contiguous area of another color was laid. Nevertheless, two adjacent colors on a painted enamelled plate, when seen under magnification, overlap slightly across their common border line. Having taken over the technical approach observed in the *basse-taille* enamels, the Limoges craftsmen went further by omitting the metal divisions altogether.[19]

The handling of white enamel for modelling flesh and rendering garments and other details had a precedent in the technique of encrusting enamels on gold, but an important difference occurred in the case of painted enamels: the white enamel was now laid on a surface resembling the primed board or canvas of an easel painting instead of being applied to a three-dimensional object. In the Monvaerni enamels the white of the flesh tones is brushed on thickly, forming outcrops on the corrugated surface, and is pointed up with red washes, producing an effect of hectic fever. Much later at Limoges the faces painted by the enamellers Pierre Courteys and Jean de Court also look flushed, though more swarthy. The flesh tones in the enamelled production of the Master of the Baltimore and Orléans Triptychs resulted from the application of white over a ground of transparent blue superposed on russet enamel. That method remained exceptional. It achieved a beautiful tinge of grayish beryl, over which the half-tones were added in a reddish glaze. Usually until about 1530 the flesh tones were painted in a lilac that was obtained through the admixture of manganese to white, over which was then applied a white glaze.

The *enlevage* (scraping away) technique was a diversified one. Either the *enle-*

vages were worked out with a spatula or brush handle in order to establish the hardest contours and structural outlines, or they were delicately stippled with a needle for modelling the intermediate areas and underlining curves.[20] A parallel may be drawn to the technique of painting on stained glass, making allowance for the fact that when black enamel and grisaille washes were used for designing and modelling on glass the *enlevage* technique produced highlights, whereas on painted enamels the network of lines laid bare by a similar technique would be not light but dark.[21]

When the method for rendering the flesh tones was applied to the entire surface of the plaque, the result was a grisaille enamel. Though the Late Gothic and Early Renaissance periods at Limoges are marked exclusively by the polychrome style, grisaille enamels invaded the production in the middle third of the sixteenth century. The Story of Psyche after engravings by the Master of the Die and Agostino Veneziano was first enamelled in grisaille by Léonard Limousin in 1535 before he reproduced the series in color in 1543. Jean II and Jean III Pénicaud were, with Pierre Pénicaud and the mysterious monogrammist who signed KIP (Jean Poillevé?), the virtuosi of the grisaille and its sfumato effects. A similar pendular hesitation between grisaille and color can be seen in French illumination during the revolution brought about by Jean Pucelle in the first third of the fourteenth century and its aftermath during the reign of Charles V (1364–80). Apart from exemplifying the cyclical returns often observed in art history, the preference given to grisaille enamels reflects the sober Spanish taste that provided the keynote of fashion during the Mannerist period in Europe, as well as the somewhat gloomy mood with which the Reformation pervaded the atmosphere in the wake of the bright optimism of the Early Renaissance. The dark grisailles of the enameller who signed M. D. PAPE (Martin Didier?) are built on an abstract structure of straight lines as if they were etchings, and are in fact in advance of the most daring achievements in the etchings of the School of Fontainebleau itself. The same nightly splendor is cast on the grisailles of Jean Court *dit* Vigier, of which a small number are dated between 1555 and 1558. The production of Pierre Courteys, like that of Pierre Reymond and Jean de Court, is well balanced between color and grisaille. In his late years Pierre Reymond returned to his early preference for the polychrome manner. The reaction against grisaille evidenced by the intense coloring in the work of Suzanne Court and Jean I, Jean II, and Joseph Limousin is in

10

keeping with the incipient Baroque taste and the kind of worldly art favored by the Jesuits in the footsteps of the Counter-Reformation. Nevertheless, the grisailles experienced a revival of popularity at Limoges under the Laudins in the middle third of the seventeenth century.

The grisaille technique demonstrates how dominating an influence prints exerted on painted enamels not only as sources of iconography but also as guidelines for execution. The wiry contours in Pierre Reymond's enamels and his strict discipline in modelling with a regular network of crosshatchings betray his subservience to the constructive methods of his engraved models. Even in the colored enamels of the Mannerist period at Limoges, the polychromy appears to be less painting in its own right than color added to transposed engraved design. A similar process can be noted in book illustration. Gillet Hardouin is held responsible for the thin films of color pointing up the woodcuts printed in books bearing his publisher's imprint in the early sixteenth century.[22] To signal another case, in 1586 the illuminator Guillaume Richardierre was paid the rather extravagant sum of 140 écus for having with two helpers added gouache overlays to seven engraved plates, 252 vignettes, 302 initial letters, sixty-one majuscule letters and 232 minuscule, plus the title page and colophon, of a *Missale romanum* published by Jaques Kerver in 1583.[23] When looked through as if they were transparencies, the gouached engravings of the seven plates unmistakably recall contemporary enamels by Jean de Court or Jean I Limousin.

In medieval times an enameller had customarily been a goldsmith or bronze sculptor. The first mention made of Nardon Pénicaud, in a Latin document of 1493, designates him as "aurifaber"—that is, a goldsmith. Jean II Pénicaud, his workshop, and the master who signed KIP, as well as the one who signed IC with a crown, stamped the backs of their enamels with goldsmiths' marks. For over a century foils of silver or gold were inserted under layers of enamel in order to reinforce the sparkling effects of reflected light, thus perpetuating at Limoges a device wistfully reminiscent of the luminous beauty of the translucent medieval enamels. "Jewels"—drops of enamel laid on foil and often set in collars of imitation pearls—were lavishly used until about 1530 for adorning orphreys and haloes and even for studding landscapes with flowers.

Progressively the Limoges enamellers of the sixteenth century won their independence and formed a body of craftsmen distinct from the goldsmiths, though the ties were never completely severed. Their progress in autonomy can be measured by the increasingly frequent use of signatures, which throughout the century were reserved for pieces that had been specifically commissioned as opposed to those produced in the workshop by craftsmen under the supervision of the master and his family associates. The one enamel signed by Nardon Pénicaud is a Crucifixion dated April 1, 1503, in the Musée de Cluny, Paris, made to commemorate the renunciation by Louis XII of his claims to the throne of Naples. In contrast there are eight known works by Jean I Pénicaud bearing his name or initials. Léonard Limousin, after having been introduced to the court at Fontainebleau, was in 1548 named by Henri II *valet de chambre,* a title accompanying the designation of an official painter.[24] In *The Incredulity of St. Thomas,* a painting he executed in 1551 for the church of Saint-Pierre-du-Queyroix in Limoges, he proudly inscribed on the book held by an Apostle presumably intended as his self-portrait: LEONARD LIMOSIN ESMAILEIVR PEINTRE VALET DE CHAMBRE DV ROY. Léonard II Limousin also became enameller to the King and inserted the fleur-de-lis between his initials. The enameller Jean de Court probably is identical with the Jean de Court who was painter to Mary Queen of Scots and who later succeeded François Clouet as painter to Charles IX. Apparently he shared his time, like Léonard Limousin, between directing his firm in Limoges and carrying out commissions for the monarchy and the court.

It was indeed through Fontainebleau, that leading art center in Europe during the middle third of the sixteenth century, that the Limoges enamellers won international recognition. No knowledge of Fontainebleau art can be complete without the supplementary chapter afforded by Limoges enamels. So much has been destroyed of the stuccoed and painted decoration of grotesques and scrollwork at Fontainebleau—only the Galerie François I and the Salle de Bal remain substantially what they were—that the backs of enamelled dishes and ewer stands and the insides of tazze provide an invaluable addition to the visual records of the palace preserved in the prints of the first School of Fontainebleau and in the *Petites Grotesques* (1550) and *Grandes Grotesques* (1556) of Jacques Androuet du Cerceau.

The enamels of Limoges retained an almost exclusively religious character until the execution of the *Aeneid* plaques about 1530. But the production afterward centered on luxury ware, in which Christian and pagan subjects are curiously mixed. In their new function, the enamels were on the one hand increasingly incorporated into the decoration of architectural ensembles, while on the other they emerged progressively as art objects in their own right, suitable for the collector's cabinet. According to the testimony of Abbé Guilbert, enamels were set in the framework of the frescoes in the Galerie François I at Fontainebleau; Il Rosso had planned to use more of them, but they reportedly were destroyed after his death in 1540 by the jealous Primaticcio.[25] In the fifteen compartments of the vault of the Galerie d'Ulysse at Fontainebleau (demolished 1738–39) enamels arranged in groups of four were interspersed amid the painted grotesques and mythological cartouches.[26] The legendary figures from antiquity enamelled by Léonard Limousin for his first patron, Jean de Langeac, Bishop of Limoges (1533–41), charming medallion portraits painted within squares poised on one of their angles, were doubtless intended to decorate the wainscoting of a study.[27] Catherine de Médicis had set into the wainscoting of the Cabinet des Émaux of her hôtel in Paris thirty-nine oval plaques and thirty-two portraits, each one foot high; in addition, eighty-three smaller portraits, some of them enamels and others paintings, were mounted in the wainscoting of her Cabinet des Miroirs.[28] The precious character of Léonard Limousin's enamels is evidenced by their having been kept in the Cabinet des Bagues atop the medieval donjon of the palace at Fontainebleau, intermingled with works by Benvenuto Cellini, Matteo dal Nassaro, and other goldsmiths and gem carvers.

The enamelled portraits, mythological compositions, and religious scenes of Limoges have a common denominator: splendor. It was the historical lot of the enamellers of Limoges to translate their themes into brilliant artifacts as difficult to create as goldsmiths' work, aimed like jewelry at magically freezing the beauty of light within colored surfaces. This unforgettable splendor explains why Limoges enamels were so much in demand when the great collections of the nineteenth and early twentieth centuries were constituted. The group of enamels purchased by J. Pierpont Morgan, from which most of the enamels acquired by Henry Clay Frick were culled, ranks as one of the finest selections ever formed of the craft of the Renaissance artists of Limoges. The presentation of the Frick enamels in closely packed rows within tiered cases brings back to life the displays of enamels in the French hôtels and palaces of the Renaissance.

The author began his research for the present catalogue in the summer of 1968 at the Louvre. Thanks to the fine spirit of cooperation of Pierre Verlet, then Chief

Curator of the Département des Objets d'Art, he was given access to the papers bequeathed to the Louvre by the heirs of J.-J. Marquet de Vasselot, a set of notes invaluable to anyone anxious to trace the complicated provenance of Limoges enamels through the sales of the nineteenth and early twentieth centuries. The author used also the equally precious files left to the Musée Municipal at Limoges by the heirs of Louis Bourdery. That museum's Director, Madeleine Marcheix, was for four years kindness incarnate in checking and providing all sorts of information and comparative material. In London, many problems reached their solutions thanks to the collaboration of Hugh Tait, Assistant Keeper in the Department of British and Medieval Antiquities at the British Museum, and Roger Pinkham of the Department of Ceramics at the Victoria and Albert Museum; thanks go to both of them for having authorized the study of many pieces not on exhibition.

The names singled out above represent but a few of those who have been so generous in giving their time and in ordering a great number of reproductions. These photographs have provided the basis of the stylistic analyses and have been useful in selecting the comparative pieces, particularly those from American collections, that are cited in practically every entry of the catalogue.

The present work was to a large extent achieved as the result of a friendly collective research. The author's thanks and gratitude are hereby extended to: Madame P. André, secretary to the late Baronne Édouard de Rothschild, Paris; Raoul de Broglie, retired Director of the Musée Condé, Chantilly; Antoinette Faÿ, Curator at the Musée National, Sèvres; Rosamund Griffin, Assistant Administrator, Waddesdon Manor, Buckinghamshire; Yvonne Hackenbroch, Curator, Western European Arts, the Metropolitan Museum of Art, New York; Katherine Hanna, Director, the Taft Museum, Cincinnati; M. Hébert, retired Curator, Département des Estampes, Bibliothèque Nationale, Paris; William Hutton, Chief Curator, the Toledo Museum of Art; Bertrand Jestaz, Curator, Département des Objets d'Art, Musée du Louvre; the late and deeply regretted Dorothy Miner, former Keeper of Manuscripts, the Walters Art Gallery, Baltimore; Merribell Parsons, Bell Memorial Curator of Decorative Arts, the Minneapolis Institute of Arts; Pierre Quarré, Director, Musée des Beaux-Arts, Dijon; Madeleine Rocher-Jauneau, Director, Musée des Beaux-Arts, Lyon; Francis Salet, Director, Musée de Cluny, Paris; Michel Stettler, Director, Abegg-Stiftung, Bern; Jean Vézin, Curator,

14

Département des Manuscrits, Bibliothèque Nationale, Paris; and Leonie von Wilckens, Chief Curator, Germanisches Nationalmuseum, Nuremberg.

NOTES

1 For a broad study of this theme, see M.-M. Gauthier, *Émaux du moyen âge occidental,* Fribourg, 1972.

2 See W. L. Hildburgh, *Medieval Spanish Enamels,* London, 1936.

3 On the history of Limoges enamels, see E. Rupin, *L'Oeuvre de Limoges,* Paris, 1890. For the Grandmont enamels, see the seven articles by G. Souchal in *Bulletin monumental,* CXX, 1962–64.

4 C. Enlart, "L'Émaillerie cloisonnée à Paris sous Philippe le Bel," *Monuments et mémoires: Fondation Eugène Piot,* XXIX, 1927, pp. 1–97.

5 Gauthier, Chap. 5.

6 T. Müller and E. Steingräber, "Die französische Goldemailplastik um 1400," *Münchner Jahrbuch der bildenden Kunst,* V, 1954, pp. 29–79. U. Middeldorf, "On the Origins of 'Émail sur Ronde-Bosse,'" *Gazette des Beaux-Arts,* LV, 1960, pp. 233–44.

7 H. Kohlhaussen, "Niederländisch Schmelzwerk," *Jahrbuch der Preuszischen Kunstsammlungen,* LII, 1931, pp. 153–69. P. Verdier, "A Medallion of the 'Ara Coeli' and the Netherlandish Enamels of the Fifteenth Century," *Journal of the Walters Art Gallery,* XXIV, 1961, pp. 8–37. E. Steingräber, "Nachträge und Marginalien zur französisch-niederländischen Goldschmiedekunst des frühen 15. Jahrhunderts," *Anzeiger des Germanischen Nationalmuseums,* 1969, pp. 29–39.

8 E. Steingräber, "Studien zur venezianischen Goldschmiedekunst des 15. Jahrhunderts," *Mitteilungen des Kunsthistorischen Institutes in Florenz,* X, 1962, pp. 147–92.

9 E. Steingräber, "Émail," in *Reallexikon zur deutschen Kunstgeschichte,* Stuttgart, V, 1960, col. 44.

10 A. Morassi, *Antica oreficeria italiana,* Milan, 1936, Nos. 179 ff.

11 See for example P. Verdier, *The Walters Art Gallery: Catalogue of the Painted Enamels of the Renaissance,* Baltimore, 1967, No. 9, p. 12, No. 10, p. 13.

12 The roundels are thought to have been set into the frame of Fouquet's diptych *The Virgin and Étienne Chevalier,* formerly in the Cathedral at Melun. One of the medallions, a self-portrait, is now in the Louvre, and the other, which showed the Descent of the Holy Ghost Unto the Jews and Gentiles, was destroyed in the Schlossmuseum, Berlin, in 1945. See G. Ring, *A Century of French Painting: 1400–1500,* New York, 1949, Nos. 124, 125, pp. 210–11, Pls. 89, 90.

13 É. Molinier, *L'Émaillerie,* Paris, 1891, p. 242. There is in the Royal Ontario Museum, Toronto, a curious enamelled pax dated 1434—the year it was presented to the church of Saint-Germain at Rennes—which was executed in a complex technique akin to that of the Netherlandish enamels, with traces of translucent enamels over

foil on the back and an encrusted enamel framework (see W. Buckley, "A 'Limoges' Enamel Plaque of 1434," *Burlington Magazine,* LIX, 1931, pp. 117–18). A copper engraved and enamelled plaque in the Cathedral of Amiens, executed after the death on November 8, 1456, of Bishop Jean Avantage, curiously anticipates Monvaerni's lean and angular style (see: G. Durand, "Note sur une plaque en cuivre émaillé," *Bulletin archéologique du Comité des Travaux historiques et scientifiques,* 1889, pp. 193–98, and *Monographie de l'Église Notre-Dame Cathédrale d'Amiens,* Paris, II, 1903, pp. 433 ff.; E. Panofsky, "Two Roger Problems," *Art Bulletin,* XXXIII, 1951, Fig. 3 facing p. 37, p. 38, note 32).

14 Two interesting exceptions to the traditional pattern of inspiration and duplication may be noted. The first concerns the artist termed by Marquet de Vasselot the Master of the Orléans Triptych. Some of his enamels are close, in their composition, style, and features of execution, to illuminations in a Book of Hours (Limoges Usage) in the Art Institute of Chicago. The conclusion has been drawn, though it is not necessarily foregone, that the illuminator and the enameller were the same person (see M. C. Ross, "The Master of the Orléans Triptych, Enameller and Painter," *Journal of the Walters Art Gallery,* IV, 1941, pp. 9–25). Gauthier (pp. 309–10) would date both the manuscript and the enamels seemingly much too early, to the period 1475–85. For a further discussion of both, see p. 20 and p. 22, note 5, of the present catalogue. The second exception involves the series of plaques reproducing in colored enamels seventy-four of the 143 woodcut illustrations to the *Aeneid* in Sebastian Brant's edition of Virgil's *Opera,* printed by Johann Grüninger at Strasbourg in 1502 (reprinted at Lyon in 1517 and 1529). Each of the *Aeneid* enamels is a unicum, and no enamels are known after woodcuts illustrating other works of Virgil. As a rule Limoges enamels are repetitive. See R. Pinkham, "Attributions to the Aeneid Master," *Apollo,* XCV, 1972, pp. 370–75.

15 L. Romier, "Lyon et le cosmopolitisme au début de la Renaissance française," *Bibliothèque d'Humanisme et Renaissance,* II, 1949, p. 35.

16 H. Maryon, *Metalwork and Enamelling,* New York, 1971, pp. 178, 183.

17 L. Bourdery, *Les Émaux peints: Exposition rétrospective de Limoges,* Limoges, 1888, pp. 217–23.

18 On these processes, see: M.-M. Gauthier and M. Marcheix, in *Les Émaux de Limoges,* Prague, 1962; P. E. Michaels, "Technical Observations on Early Painted Enamels of Limoges," *Journal of the Walters Art Gallery,* XXVII–XXVIII, 1964–65, pp. 21–44.

19 The difficulty of preventing enamels from overlapping when *cloisons* were absent was overcome in the technique of *basse-taille* translucent enamels by adding a little gum tragacanth to each area to be enamelled in one color and allowing it to dry before the next wet batch of differently colored enamel was laid alongside it (Maryon, p. 188).

20 In the champlevé enamels executed around 1200 for the abbey of Grandmont, the guidelines of the design were dotted in the

copper and the flesh tones verge on lilac. The mutation in the enamelling process from the champlevé technique followed in Limoges between about 1170 and about 1370 to the painted technique adopted in the second half of the fifteenth century did not preclude a subcurrent of continuity in the formulas.

21 J. Lafond, *Le Vitrail,* Paris, 1966, pp. 37, 41–42. It should be pointed out that the stained-glass designers drew as heavily as the enamellers on prints for their cartoons (see É. Mâle, in A. Michel's *Histoire de l'art,* IV, Pt. 2, Paris, 1911, pp. 789, 790, 802). The church of Sainte-Foy at Conches, Normandy, can be thought of both as a museum of French Renaissance stained glass and as a repertory of European engraving (J. Lafond, in *Annuaire normand,* Bayeux, 1940–41; R. Fritz, in *Westfalen,* XXXVI, No. 3, 1958, pp. 159 ff.). Possibly Heinrich Aldegrever designed the panel with putti at the bottom of the St. Louis window at Conches. The splendid stained-glass panel representing the Way to Calvary in the Musée de Cluny, Paris, is an accurate copy of a woodcut (F. Perrot, "Un Panneau de la vitrerie de la Chapelle de l'Hôtel de Cluny," *Revue de l'art,* No. 10, 1970, pp. 66–72).

22 See for instance *French Sixteenth Century Books,* Cambridge, Massachusetts, 1964, II, No. 297.

23 E. Picot, *Catalogue des livres composant la bibliothèque de feu Monsieur le Baron James de Rothschild,* Paris, III, 1893, pp. 323–24. The book was executed for the ambassador of Charles Emmanuel of Savoy to the court of Henri III. The magnificent binding *à la fanfare* cost only 15 écus, the missal itself 3 écus.

24 In 1545, during the reign of François I, Léonard Limousin was already referred to as "l'esmailleur de Lymoges, esmailleur pour le roi" (Comte L. de Laborde, *La Renaissance des arts à la cour de France,* Paris, 1850, I, pp. 296, 419).

25 Abbé P. Guilbert, *Description historique des chateau, bourg et forest de Fontainebleau,* Paris, 1731, I, pp. 78–101.

26 *Idem.* See also M. Marcheix, "Plaque émaillée de Léonard Limosin, Limoges, Musée Municipal," *Bulletin de la Société archéologique et historique du Limousin,* XCVIII, 1971, pp. 204, 205.

27 F. Bodin, "Jean de Langeac, Mécène et humaniste," *Bulletin…du Limousin,* LXXXVI, 1955, pp. 91–94. Marcheix, 1971, *loc. cit.*

28 E. Bonnaffé, *Inventaire des meubles de Catherine de Médicis en 1589,* Paris, 1874, Nos. 842, 843, 848.

MASTER OF THE BALTIMORE AND ORLÉANS TRIPTYCHS

Late Fifteenth Century–Early Sixteenth Century

The anonymous enameller generally known as the Master of the Orléans Triptych might better be termed the Master of the Baltimore Triptych, inasmuch as the more accomplished, and probably the earlier, version of the Annunciation triptych from which his title derives is the one now in the Walters Art Gallery, Baltimore. Around his name between twenty-five and thirty enamels have been grouped on the basis of style. His work is still free from Italian influence, but toward the end of the fifteenth century he began to show an interest in German prints.

Triptych: The Crucifixion; St. Barbara; St. Catherine of Alexandria (18.4.1)

Central plaque $8\frac{1}{8} \times 6\frac{5}{16}$ in. (20.7 × 16.1 cm); wings $8\frac{1}{8} \times 2\frac{9}{16}$ in. (20.7 × 6.5 cm).

Description: In the central panel, Christ, draped in a loincloth of turquoise blue and wearing the crown of thorns, has "yielded up the ghost" (Matthew 27:50). His head rests on His right shoulder. At upper left an angel receives the soul of the Penitent Thief, whose head is bowed toward Christ, while at right a devil snatches the soul of the Unrepentant Thief, who is turned away from Christ with his head thrown back over the crossbar. The thieves are not nailed or bound to their crosses but hang suspended by their broken, bleeding arms. The three bodies are set off against the red-violet walls and towers of Jerusalem. At the foot of Christ's cross to the left, the Virgin, clad in a blue mantle, is supported by St. John and Mary Magdalene,

who wear red-violet, blue-violet, and green. Between the Penitent Thief and Christ appear the heads of two holy women, one in a turban. To the right of the cross, the Centurion, garbed in fantastic robes and a miter-like hat, raises his right hand to testify that "Truly this was the Son of God" (Matthew 27:54). His rich blue mantle is adorned with an ermine collar, a gold chain, a green purse, jewelled orphreys, and a corded belt which he holds with his left hand. The paunchy figure beside him, a representative of the Sanhedrin, has been given the towering headgear with upturned brim worn by the prophets in late medieval iconography and in mystery plays.[1] No less extravagantly dressed, he holds with both hands his low belt, in the stance of a prosperous burgher. Soldiers in armor and two standard-bearers throng behind them.

The blue enamel of the sky was applied progressively over a white preparation, so that the horizon is clear and the color darkens toward the zenith. In the left wing stands St. Barbara wearing a blue mantle over a red-violet gown trimmed with ermine, both richly jewelled and highlighted with gold. Her left hand rests on her symbolic emblem, a tower, painted in turquoise blue, and in her right she holds a palm. The niche behind her, hung with a red-violet curtain decorated with jewels and gilded roundels, culminates in a vault edged with gold cusps and painted to resemble the sky in the central panel. Above the niche is an architectural framework supported by a crocketed ogee arch springing from two columns. The right wing shows St. Catherine wearing a costume similar to St. Barbara's. She reads from a book, her attribute as patron of philosophers, and holds a sword, the instrument of her martyrdom. She stands over Maximin (Maximinus), the emperor who ordered her death; he is clad in blue and tur-

quoise. The architectural framework repeats that on the left wing.[2] The drawing throughout is strong, even harsh, and the coloring takes on a metallic brilliance. The flesh tints are warm, verging on violet, with their modelling puffy at the eyes and lips. Their distinctive tinge, coupled with the red-violet keynote of the palette, characterize the technique of an enameller who combined blue and red preparations and sometimes finished the flesh tints with a red glaze.[3]

Condition: The triptych is in very good condition. There is a small chip at the upper right corner of the central plaque, repaired losses appear in the mantles of the Virgin and St. Catherine, and the white preparation is exposed in spots on the sleeves of St. Catherine and St. Barbara. The gilding has faded in some of the stars on the central plaque, in the superscription of Christ's cross, in the arch above St. Barbara, in the curtain behind St. Catherine, and, most notably, in the row of cusps across the tops of both wings.

The Crucifixion scene reappears as the central plaque of a triptych in the former Czartoryski collection at Cracow[4] and, what is exceptional, in an illuminated Book of Hours (Limoges Usage) of about 1511 at the Art Institute of Chicago.[5] Other illustrations in the Book of Hours also compare closely with enamels by the Master of the Baltimore and Orléans Triptychs and raise the question of their relationship. Did the same artist who painted them execute the enamels? Which works were originals and which copies? Or did they simply derive from common sources?[6]

The St. Catherine and St. Barbara are close to figures similarly framed in the margins of a Book of Hours (Roman Usage) published by Gillet Hardouin in 1503 and of a *Hore dive Virginis Mariae* published by Gillet and Germain Hardouin about 1511.[7] Furthermore, the Frick St. Catherine—like the simplified version on a plaque in the Wallace Collection, London,[8] formerly the right wing of a triptych from the same workshop—strongly resembles a stained-glass window in the Li-

20

mousin church of Eymoutiers.[9] A common prototype may be the St. Catherine window in the Cathedral of Moulins, dedicated at the end of the fifteenth century by Catherine d'Armagnac, second wife of Jean II, Duc de Bourbon.[10]

The Frick triptych was in Spain until the end of the nineteenth century. Many Limoges Renaissance enamels were commissioned in Spain, renewing a commercial trend of the Middle Ages when the production of Limoges champlevé enamels was at its peak.[11]

Exhibited: Paris, Hôtel Sagan, Exposition d'objets d'art du Moyen Âge et de la Renaissance, 1913, No. 235, lent by Paul Garnier.

Collections: Paul Garnier, Paris.[12] His sale, December 18–23, 1916, Hôtel Drouot, Paris, Lot 54. Duveen. Frick, 1918.

NOTES

1 Isaiah wears a similar hat, with a flap falling over the forehead, on the left wings of the Annunciation triptychs by the same master in the Musée Historique, Orléans (J.-J. Marquet de Vasselot, *Les Émaux limousins,* Paris, 1921, No. 51, Pl. XVIII), and the Walters Art Gallery, Baltimore (P. Verdier, *The Walters Art Gallery: Catalogue of the Painted Enamels of the Renaissance,* Baltimore, 1967, No. 17, pp. 26–29). He shows the same accented Semitic features in a Book of Hours (Roman Usage) published by Antoine Vérard (P. Lacombe, *Livres d'heures imprimés au XVè et au XVIè siècle, conservés dans les bibliothèques publiques de Paris,* Paris, 1907, No. 21, pp. 19–20).

2 The summary treatment of the tops and bottoms of the wing compositions derives from the borders of Books of Hours illustrated with strips of figures within niches.

3 P. E. Michaels, "Technical Observations on Early Painted Enamels of Limoges," *Jour-*

nal of the Walters Art Gallery, XXVII–XXVIII, 1964–65, pp. 26–29. Michaels demonstrates that when models by the Baltimore and Orléans Master were copied by an assistant or in another shop, the flesh tints became lilac—a mulberry-red glaze applied over, or mixed with, the white of the flesh tones modelled on an underlayer of blue, or rarely of mulberry red. Such was the practice in the Pénicaud workshop and in that of the Master of the Louis XII Triptych.

4 Marquet de Vasselot, No. 54, Pl. XIX; for the Frick triptych, see No. 53.

5 M. C. Ross, "The Master of the Orléans Triptych, Enameller and Painter," *Journal of the Walters Art Gallery,* IV, 1941, pp. 9–25. Compare the illuminations in the Book of Hours with: the Crucifixion in the Frick and Cracow triptychs; the Crucifixion in the center of a triptych by the same master in the Hermitage Museum, Leningrad (Marquet de Vasselot, No. 55); the

22

right wing of the latter, representing the Way to Calvary; and an isolated wing in the Musée des Arts Décoratifs, Paris, done from the same cartoon as the right wing of the Hermitage triptych (*idem,* No. 58). Katherine Gentille, wife of Martial Dubois, consul of Limoges in 1510, had her arms painted in the Chicago Book of Hours, which she once owned (see F. Delage, "Les Beaux Livres d'Heures limousins," *Nos Pays du Centre-Ouest,* 1947, I, pp. 4–6). Certain details of the Crucifixion plaques in the Frick, Cracow, and Hermitage triptychs could have been borrowed from a Crucifixion in a Book of Hours published by Antoine Vérard about 1488 (Lacombe, No. 12; Vélins 1631 in the Réserve of the Bibliothèque Nationale, Paris); that Crucifixion was copied in a 1498 Book of Hours (Roman Usage) printed for Simon Vostre, with the mark of Philippe Pigouchet.

6 Christ, the two thieves, Jerusalem, and the figures at right in the Frick, Cracow, and Hermitage triptychs were copied in the workshop of Nardon Pénicaud on a triptych now in the museum at Bourges (Marquet de Vasselot, No. 105, Pl. XXXIV). The two thieves are very close to those in a paste-print of Calvary in the Guildhall, London (see p. 66 and p. 70, note 6).

7 A. Alès, *Bibliothèque liturgique: Description ...de la bibliothèque de S. A. R. Mgr. Charles-Louis de Bourbon,* Paris, 1878–84, Nos. 183, 184.

8 Marquet de Vasselot, No. 57, Pl. XX. *Wallace Collection Catalogues: Objects of Art (Illustrations),* London, 1924, pp. 49, 239, 241.

9 Photograph, Monuments Historiques, Paris, No. 224.486.

10 The Cathedral was then the collegiate church. See: *Bulletin du Comité historique des arts et des monuments,* IV, 1853, pp. 76–80; M. Huillet d'Istria, *Le Maître de Moulins,* Paris, 1961, notes 216–19. Curiously, the Master of the Louis XII Triptych combined the figures of St. Barbara and St. Catherine into a single figure of St. Catherine, who, reversed and transferred to the left wing in a series of triptychs, lost her book and received the palm; see Marquet de Vasselot, No. 136 (now in the Metropolitan Museum of Art, New York), No. 137, Pl. LIV, No. 138, and Verdier, No. 31, pp. 56–60. In an intermediate stage —on the right wing of a triptych signed MONVAERNI in the Taft Museum, Cincinnati (No. 1931.268; Marquet de Vasselot, No. 29, Pl. X)—St. Catherine appears with both book and sword and simultaneously presses the palm against her bosom with the hand holding the sword.

11 The triptych in the Museo Lázaro Galdiano, Madrid, in which the same Crucifixion is inserted between the Mocking and the Flagellation of Christ is a modern work (see F. Torralba, "Esmaltes en el Museo Lázaro Galdiano," *Goya,* No. 55, 1963, p. 15).

12 G. Migeon, "La Collection de M. Paul Garnier," *Les Arts,* May 1906, repr. p. 23.

23

NARDON PÉNICAUD

c. 1470 (?) – 1541

Léonard Pénicaud—called, in the Limousin dialect, Nardon—was elected consul of Limoges in 1513, served twice as tax collector and twice as captain of the guards for his district, and owned property of value both within the city and in its environs. Between thirty-five and forty enamels attributed to his shop have survived, among them his only signed and dated work, a Crucifixion of 1503 in the Musée de Cluny, Paris. During his forty-year career the style of Nardon Pénicaud underwent no fundamental changes, but remained characterized by impassive and monumental figures and by simple compositions typical of the Late Gothic period in France. Only gradually did Renaissance features enter his work in the form of architectural elements and furniture. He evinced an increasing interest in book illustrations and in prints, particularly those of Israhel van Meckenem after compositions by Martin Schongauer. At his death Nardon left three sons, Jean, Léonard, and Pierre.

Double Triptych: Scenes from the Passion (16.4.3)

Signed, by a modern hand, on the sword of the recumbent soldier in the lower central plaque: N PENICAVLT (see *Condition*). Upper central plaque 5½ × 10⅞ in. (14 × 27.7 cm); upper wings 5½ × 5 in. (14 × 12.7 cm); lower central plaque 9¹³/₁₆ × 11⁵/₁₆ in. (24.9 × 28.7 cm); lower wings 9¹³/₁₆ × 5 in. (24.9 × 12.7 cm).

Description: The triptych consists of three arched plaques over three rectangular ones mounted in a gilt-copper frame. The colored enamels are golden-brown, green, blue, turquoise, purple, and red-violet, their effect enhanced by liberal gilding (see *Condition*). The flesh tints tend toward violet, the result of their having been applied over a layer of

dark blue. The blue delineations appear almost black where they are juxtaposed to white. The plaque at upper left, the Way to Calvary, shows Christ bearing the cross and returning to Veronica the veil she had offered Him to wipe His face; on the veil are impressed His features.[1] Soldiers surround Christ, one of them holding the three nails of the Crucifixion and leading Christ by a rope tied around His waist. The Virgin and three holy women follow. The procession is just outside the gate of Jerusalem. In the plaque at upper center, the Crucifixion, Christ and the two thieves are dead, and the blind Longinus, guided by an attendant, pierces Christ's side with a spear. The Centurion, on

horseback to the right of the cross, raises his forefinger to proclaim Christ's divinity. Mary Magdalene, on her knees, embraces the shaft of the cross and gazes upward. The Virgin turns away in despair, her left hand grasping her lowered right wrist; a holy woman and St. John support her, and another holy woman in a turban looks on from far left. The sponge-bearer, Stephaton, stands to the right of Christ's cross. Before the cross of the Unrepentant Thief is a figure on horseback seen from behind, identified by the gold inscription on the hem of his mantle as CAIPHAS. Still further to the right stands a soldier holding a shield painted with a devil's head and inscribed CLIPEVS:ANNE:QVIC.SOCER:CAIPHEVS CONC;[2] the mask with flaming hair may have been intended as a portrait of the high priest Annas, the father-in-law of Caiaphas. In the background are the walls and towers of Jerusalem. The scene at upper right is the Harrowing of Hell. Christ, His head radiating light and His five wounds bleeding, stands holding the cross-staff, His naked body wrapped in the imperial purple mantle denoting His victory over death. His left hand is grasped by Adam, behind whom kneel Eve, St. John the Baptist dressed in camel's hair, and the Forebears. The gates of hell are broken, the devils are in rout. Christ tramples the prostrate Satan and pierces him with the cross-staff. On the plaque at lower left is the Deposition. Joseph of Arimathaea, at the top of the ladder, uses a shroud passed across Christ's chest to lower His body into the arms of the Virgin, who is assisted by St. John. Nicodemus, identified by the inscription NICODEME on his sleeve, kneels to extract the nail from Christ's feet. Beyond

him is Mary Magdalene holding a jar of ointment. At the foot of the cross are a hammer, the skull of Adam, and a bone. The lower central plaque, the Entombment, shows Joseph of Arimathaea at left and Nicodemus at right holding the ends of the shroud as they lower Christ's body into the tomb. Beyond the tomb stands the Virgin, in approximately the same attitude as in the Crucifixion panel above, supported by St. John. A holy woman grasps the Virgin's left forearm while gesturing toward Christ with her left hand. A turbaned holy woman at left holds the crown of thorns, and Mary Magdalene stands with her ointment jar at right, wiping away a tear with the end of her veil. In the foreground are two sleeping soldiers in armor. Joseph of Arimathaea's sleeve is inscribed IOSEP:AR, and the hem of his robe repeats the letters IO. Nicodemus' robe carries the inscription NICODEMVS:QVI:VENERAT:ADIHESVM:NOCTE:SCIMVS:QVIA:ADEO:VE,[3] and again the letter N. The sleeping soldier at left, dressed in a cuirass and chain mail and holding a halberd, lies on a shield inscribed ITE:CVSTODITE:SICVT:SCITIS.[4] The shield of the soldier at right, who wears plate armor and carries a mace, bears a devil's head and the inscription CIGILLVM IMPERATORIS.[5] The arch above the tomb recess carries the wording CRISTVS:PASSVS:ET:SEPVLTVS:EST:ET:RESVREXIT:TERCIA:DIE.[6] The ground is strewn with plants and flowers.[7] Tiny foils were used to give a glittering effect to the panels of the tomb, enamelled in imitation of purple and green porphyry. In the scene at lower right, the Resurrection, Christ stands before the foot of the tomb, which is set in perspective. Over

26

His naked and stigmatized body He wears the mantle of His triumph. His right hand is raised in benediction, and in His left He holds the cross-staff with a banner. An angel pulls aside the lid of the tomb. In the foreground are two slumbering soldiers. The one at left, on whose raised knee Christ appears to rest His right foot, leans on a German shield inscribed MANDATA:TVA:DIDI:CVSTOD.[8] A third soldier is dazzled by the luminous apparition of Christ Resurrected. In the background the three Marys approach, and beyond them looms Jerusalem. These last details are rendered in a particularly painterly manner. Two of the Marys are depicted within the gold radiance of Christ's halo, while the third merges with the transparent blue shadow of the rock at left. The slope of the rock is green at the bottom but gradually brightens to gold near the top.

Condition: The triptych is in generally good condition. Its brilliant appearance results from its having been carefully regilt during restoration. The signature on the sword in the Entombment plaque is not old and looks spurious, though it may have been regilt, like the other inscriptions, over faint traces of an original. Repairs are visible at the corners of the Deposition, near Christ's right elbow in the Entombment, and in the sky on several of the plaques. Chips occur along the top of the Way to Calvary, and there is rather serious crazing in both upper corners of the Resurrection.

The Way to Calvary and the Harrowing of Hell are copied from engravings by Martin Schongauer,[9] though in his rendering Nardon Pénicaud blunted the expressionistic quality of his models. In the Way to Calvary he took pains to render both the profile of Veronica, which is largely concealed in the engraving, and the full face of Christ imprinted on the veil. The two subjects after Schongauer reappear infrequently in enamels from the workshop of Nardon and Jean I Pénicaud.

The Crucifixion reproduces two other plaques from the Pénicaud workshop—one forming the center of a triptych in the Museo Sacro at the Vatican, the second an isolated plaque in the Walters Art Gallery, Baltimore[10]—but with a few simplifications. The stylized sun and moon above the cross are omitted here, and the naked little souls of the thieves are no longer carried away by an angel and a devil. Also missing are the drops of raised enamel over foil used to ornament the ground.

In the Deposition there may be a recollection of an engraving by Mantegna or his workshop,[11] though the shroud used by Joseph of Arimathaea to lower the body of Christ could also have been suggested by Dürer's woodcut in the series of *The Small Passion* (1509–11) or by the Deposition in the *Horae deiparae Virginis Mariae* published in Paris in 1520 by Thielman Kerver.[12]

In an earlier plaque of the Entombment from the workshop of Nardon Péni-

28

caud,[13] the model followed was Schongauer's engraving in his series of *The Passion*. For the present Entombment, however—and again for the central plaque of a triptych in the British Museum, London,[14] which includes the same Deposition and Resurrection—Nardon Pénicaud took direct inspiration from a carved Holy Sepulchre in Limoges. Of the Holy Sepulchre in the Limoges Cathedral all that survives is the framework, done in the Flamboyant style with ogee arches and angels holding scrolls, and of that at Saint-Pierre-du-Queyroix there is only a brief description.[15] But a fairly accurate idea of their composition and style may be gathered from other Entombments, or Holy Sepulchres, carved in the Rouergue and in the regions of Albi and Toulouse, one of which, in the Cathedral at Rodez, is dated 1523.[16] The majority of these Entombments seem to date from the third decade of the sixteenth century, which makes it quite unlikely that the present plaque was executed much before about 1525. On one point Nardon Pénicaud departed from his models: he adapted the central group of the Virgin, St. John, and the holy woman behind Christ's tomb from the same group in various Crucifixion plaques enamelled in his workshop, including that of the present triptych, transposing the holy woman and St. John and directing the gazes of all three toward Christ's corpse. The putti holding shields at the springing of the arch above the tomb recess derive ultimately from Italian tomb sculpture.[17]

The Resurrection is based on an engraving by Israhel van Meckenem,[18] who copied several details, including the motif of the angel pulling away the lid of the tomb, from Schongauer.[19] The three soldiers are after Dürer's *Resurrection* of 1512, but their locations have been changed and the figures are reversed.

Exhibited: London, Victoria and Albert Museum, 1902–12, lent by J. Pierpont Morgan. New York, Metropolitan Museum, Morgan Collection, 1914–16, lent by J. Pierpont Morgan.

Collections: Said to have been bought in Italy in the eighteenth century by an ancestor of the Marqués de Ferraz, Barcelona, from whom it was acquired by J. Pierpont Morgan, London and New York.[20] Duveen. Frick, 1916.

NOTES

1 Veronica's veil had been venerated at St. Peter's in Rome since the pontificate of Boniface VIII (1294–1303) and was in France an object of particular devotion in the Gironde region and in Normandy.

2 "Shield of Annas, the father-in-law of Caiaphas [who conspired with him]."

3 "We know that Nicodemus, who came by night to remove the body of Jesus, was sent by God." Inscriptions similar to those on the Frick triptych were embroidered on the costumes of characters performing mystery plays of the Passion. The composition of the Entombment itself recalls the staging of the mystery plays, and the garments are characteristic of those worn in them.

4 "Go and watch as you have been instructed."

5 "Seal of the emperor."

6 "Christ suffered, was buried, and rose from the dead on the third day."

7 The unifying effect of grass and flowers along the bottoms of the three lower plaques of the triptych is the same as that found in Brussels tapestries.

8 "I have been instructed to execute your orders."

9 A. Bartsch, *Le Peintre-graveur,* Vienna, 1803–21, VI, Nos. 16, 19, pp. 126–27. The Harrowing of Hell is also found on the right wing of a triptych that figured in the Edward Steinkopff sale, Christie's, May 22–23, 1935, Lot 37.

10 J.-J. Marquet de Vasselot, *Les Émaux limousins,* Paris, 1921, No. 108, Pl. XXXVI; for the Frick triptych, see No. 109, Pl. XXXVII. F. Stohlman, *Gli smalti del Museo Sacro Vaticano,* Vatican City, 1939, No. S 111, p. 50, Pl. XXVIII. P. Verdier, *The Walters Art Gallery: Catalogue of the Painted Enamels of the Renaissance,* Baltimore, 1967, No. 25, pp. 42–45. In all three Crucifixions the upper portion above the spectators was copied after a Crucifixion by the Master of the Baltimore and Orléans Triptychs known in two examples, one of which is in The Frick Collection (see p. 21; compare also p. 20). The figures of Christ and Mary Magdalene reproduce those on Nardon Pénicaud's Crucifixion plaque of 1503 in the Musée de Cluny, Paris (Marquet de Vasselot, No. 77, Pl. XXVII), which comes from the priory of S. Pietro in Rogliano, Calabria (C. Tonnelier, "La Véritable Destination de l'émail dit 'de Saint-Pierre de Royan,'" *Revue du Bas-Poitou et des provinces de l'Ouest,* March–April 1965). The Cluny Crucifixion is symbolical, displaying the *Arma Christi*—the instruments of Christ's Passion—as objects of mystical contemplation. Among them is a Veronica's veil which superseded the veil in Schongauer's print as the model for the veil in the Way to Calvary of the present triptych. The same veil appears in a Way to Calvary after Schongauer included in a group of twelve plaques of the Passion from the Workshop of the Large Foreheads (Marquet de Vasselot, No. 107); for these see p. 56 and p. 58, note 9.

11 T. Borenius, *Four Early Italian Engravers,* London—Boston, 1923, No. 7, p. 34. The engraving was well known to the artists of the Northern Renaissance; see for example the painting by Hans Muelich in the Musée Marmottan, Paris.

12 Marquet de Vasselot, p. 131. However, the Deposition on fol. M 8 vo. of the *Horae* shows Joseph of Arimathaea with his back turned and the shroud passed over his shoulders. The group of Joseph of Ari-

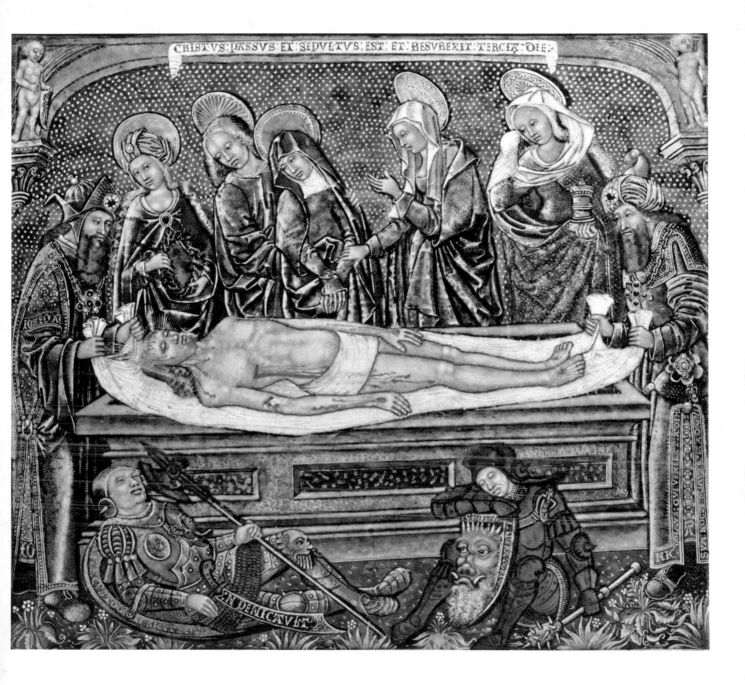

mathaea on the ladder, Nicodemus holding the ends of the shroud, which passes over the transverse bar of the cross, and the figure of Christ was copied by Jean I Pénicaud on the right wing of a triptych in the Kunstgewerbemuseum, Berlin (Marquet de Vasselot, No. 160, Pl. LXIV; see also p. 189). In the Berlin Deposition, St. John occupies the place of Nicodemus, the Virgin clasps her hands, and Mary Magdalene holds the ointment jar in her right hand. Many elements of the Berlin composition had been used previously, but in reverse, on the Frick Deposition.

13 Marquet de Vasselot, No. 106, Pl. XXXV.

14 *Idem,* No. 110, Pl. XXXVIII.

15 A. Lecler, "Étude sur les Mises au Tombeau," *Bulletin de la Société archéologique et historique du Limousin,* XXXV, 1888, pp. 511–30. W. H. Forsyth, *The Entombment of Christ: French Sculptures of the Fifteenth and Sixteenth Centuries,* Cambridge, Massachusetts, 1970. The heads of two holy women from a carved Entombment are preserved in the Musée Municipal at Limoges, where they are dated—perhaps too early—to about 1500 *(Musée Municipal, Limoges: Collection archéologique,* Limoges, 1969, Nos. 217, 218, p. 101, repr.). One of them wears a wimple, as does the Virgin in the present enamel, and the other wears a turban like that of the enamelled

holy woman holding the crown of thorns, though beneath the turban she too wears a wimple.

16 M. de Bévotte, *La Sculpture à la fin de la période gothique dans la région de Toulouse, Albi, Rodez,* Paris, 1936, Pl. XXIX. The carved Entombments of central and southern France follow the tradition of the fifteenth-century Entombments of Burgundy. See the comments of Marquet de Vasselot, p. 49, note 2, on two Entombment plaques enamelled by the so-called Monvaerni (No. 18, Pl. V, No. 19).

17 An arched enamelled plaque from Nardon Pénicaud's workshop showing analogous heraldic putti was sold with the collection of Bey Paul Adamidi, Hôtel Drouot, Paris, March 1, 1971, Lot 84.

18 A. Shestack, *Fifteenth Century Engravings of Northern Europe from the National Gallery of Art,* Washington, 1967, No. 193. Compare the *Resurrection* forming the right wing of a triptych by Dieric Bouts in the Capilla Real, Granada.

19 Shestack, No. 62.

20 C. H. Read, "The Nardon Pénicaud triptych belonging to Mr. J. Pierpont Morgan," *Burlington Magazine,* April 1904, p. 98, repr. p. 101. A triptych in the Museo Lázaro Galdiano, Madrid, captioned "Triptico de Morgan," is modern (see F. Torralba, "Esmaltes en el Museo Lázaro Galdiano," *Goya,* No. 55, 1963, p. 14).

34

Workshop of
NARDON PÉNICAUD

Triptych: The Death, Assumption, and Coronation of the Virgin (16.4.2)

Central plaque $8^{15}/_{16} \times 7^{9}/_{16}$ in. (22.7×19.2 cm); wings $8^{15}/_{16} \times 3^{3}/_{8}$ in. (22.7×8.6 cm).

Description: In the central panel, the Virgin, dressed in a hooded blue mantle, lies on a bed set on a golden-yellow dais and draped in red-violet. Her head is propped against a pillow and her eyes are closed, but in her joined hands she holds a burning candle, aided by a kneeling Apostle. Above the bed is a tasselled green canopy enriched with jewels; between its red-violet curtains hangs a cloth of honor. Beyond the bed, St. Peter, in the capacity of a priest administering the last rites, wears a stole and sprinkles holy water with an aspergillum. The holy-water vessel is held by St. John. An Apostle to Peter's left holds an open prayer book, another reads the Office of the Virgin, and a young Apostle prepares to swing a censer as his companion blows to kindle the flame of the incense. In the foreground, four Apostles sit or kneel in awkward and contorted postures. The floor, tessellated in white, green, and mulberry red, gives the illusion of cubes seen in perspective. The golden-yellow wainscoting on the far wall is inset with slabs of variegated marble in the Italian manner. An arched doorway at right opens onto a landscape and a sky speckled with tiny clouds. Along the arch runs a scroll twined around a torus and inscribed AVE MARIA. The same scroll and torus run along the coved ceiling, with the inscription O MATER DEI A[ET]ER[N]A VIRGO PVERPERA V[IR]GVLA IESSE NŌ: SINE CORPORE S[ED] SINE TEMPORE TĒD (final letters missing).[1] In the left wing, the Virgin ascends to heaven attended by six angels. The angel at lower right is about to drop her sash to St. Thomas, who had arrived too late to witness the Assumption and doubted it, but came to believe after he received the sash. He kneels in adoration. The Virgin wears a blue mantle over a red-violet dress, the angels' garments are green and red-violet, and Thomas wears a red-violet mantle over a blue robe. The sky is speckled with tiny clouds like those in the central plaque. A walled Limousin town rises at the horizon, beyond flowers in the foreground and trees in the middle distance. In the right wing, the Virgin is crowned by the Trinity. God the Father, wearing the closed imperial crown symbolizing Godhead une and triune, blesses the Virgin. Christ, naked but for a loincloth and mantle and exhibiting His wounds, holds with His Father the crown above the Virgin's head. In His left hand is the cross-staff. The Dove of the Holy Ghost hovers above the crown. The kneeling Virgin, her forearms crossed in a gesture of humility,

36

is turned slightly toward Christ but facing the viewer. The low podium is enriched with enamelled jewels, and the tessellated pavement is the same as in the central plaque. Overhead is a canopy with a cloth of honor and a jewelled cornice, again repeating those in the central plaque. Panels of variegated marble are set in the backs of the double throne. God the Father wears a turquoise blue robe and a red-violet mantle with a wide collar studded with pearls and jewels. Christ's mantle is blue, instead of the conventional red, and has a green lining. The Virgin's mantle is blue and is clasped with a brooch identical to the one worn by Christ; her dress is red-violet. The wooden frame is a Spanish work of about 1600.

Condition: The triptych is in good condition. On the central panel, the inscription across the top has been extensively repainted, both upper corners are broken, the bottom is chipped, and the lower right corner is repaired. There are small chips on the left side of the left wing and at the top of the right wing.

The composition of the Death of the Virgin duplicates essentially the central panel of a triptych executed in the workshop of the Master of the Baltimore and Orléans Triptychs.[2] The Assumption wing appears to be unique among the painted enamels of the Early Renaissance. The Coronation of the Virgin by the Trinity is related to a stained-glass window in Saint-Pierre-du-Queyroix, Limoges,[3] and in some details compares also with a window, probably done by Robert Courtois about 1498, in Notre-Dame-des-Marais, La Ferté-Bernard (Sarthe).[4] It conforms with the treatment of that theme in the printed Books of Hours,[5] where it derives from models in the International Gothic style—thus differing from the Trinitarian Coronations by the Master of the Louis XII Triptych, which remain more in line with the French iconographical tradition.[6] Other Coronations of the Virgin by the Trinity were executed in the workshop of Nardon Pénicaud or in a studio imitating his manner.[7]

Exhibited: London, Victoria and Albert Museum, 1902–12, lent by J. Pierpont Morgan. New York, Metropolitan Museum, Morgan Collection, 1914–16, lent by J. Pierpont Morgan.

Collections: Faustino Alonso Nueva, León, until about 1897. J. Pierpont Morgan, London and New York. Duveen. Frick, 1916.

NOTES

1 "Oh Mother of God, who gave birth and forever remained virgin, sprout of the tree of Jesse, ascending in body to eternity...."

The sense is obscured by damages at the end of the inscription, but the conclusion would presumably have been "TĒDIT AD

38

COELUM." The reference is undoubtedly to Mary's Assumption, both in soul and in body.

2 J.-J. Marquet de Vasselot, *Les Émaux limousins,* Paris, 1921, No. 67; for the Frick triptych, see No. 104 and pp. 124–26. Marquet de Vasselot's unpublished notes in the Louvre mention a duplicate of the Orléans Master's triptych in the Henri Heugel collection, Paris. Compare the Death of the Virgin in Vélins 1631 at the Bibliothèque Nationale, Paris. The composition remains very much the same in an oval enamelled plaque inscribed M DV FORT 1581 in the Musée de Cluny, Paris (No. 11.287).

3 Photograph, Monuments Historiques, Paris, No. 238.062. In the window, the Coronation is performed by Christ Pantocrator, who rests His left hand on the Globe, and God the Father, who holds the Book. Though their gestures differ, the two are united in the act of crowning.

4 This window and another representing the Raising of Lazarus show German iconographical features. The possibility of some influence from tapestries should not be discarded; compare, for example, the Death of the Virgin in the tapestry at Notre-Dame, Beaune, attributed to Pierre Spicre (J. Bacri, "Pierre Spicre, peintre bourguignon du XVᵉ siècle," *Gazette des Beaux-Arts,* XIII, 1935, p. 219).

5 See Marquet de Vasselot, p. 124, note 2.

6 See the two in the Louvre (Marquet de Vasselot, No. 142, Pl. LVII, No. 143) and one in the Musée des Beaux-Arts at Dijon (Trimolet Collection; *idem,* p. 181, note 4). The crown in these works is brought by an angel, as in Vélins 1647 at the Bibliothèque Nationale, dated about 1500, with the mark of Thielman Kerver. In a roundel at the Louvre, Christ alone crowns the Virgin, as in thirteenth-century iconography (Marquet de Vasselot, No. 126, Pl. XLVIII). The early fifteenth-century aristocratic formulation in which angels crown the Virgin, whom the Father and Son bless, was followed in an enamelled diptych of the Last Judgment and the Coronation auctioned at the van Gelder sale, Hôtel Drouot, Paris, June 24–25, 1953, Lot 291, attributed to the workshop of the Master of the Baltimore and Orléans Triptychs.

7 These include: one in the M. Boy sale, Galerie Georges Petit, Paris, May 15–24, 1905, Lot 191; one in the Charles Mannheim sale, Paris, 1910, Lot 75; a plaque mounted as a pax in the former Baronne Édouard de Rothschild collection, Paris; a rounded plaque for a pax, Minneapolis Institute of Arts (No. 37.7.13); and a plaque in the collection of Dr. Giraud, Marseille. An enamelled Coronation of the Virgin by the Trinitarian God, who wears the imperial crown and holds the Globe, was in the Jules S. Bache collection (*Loan Exhibition of Religious Art,* Seligmann Galleries, New York, March–April 1927, Pl. XXXV). A plaque from approximately the same period was auctioned at the Edward Joseph sale, Christie's, May 6 *et seq.,* 1890, Lot 505.

Triptych: The Way to Calvary; The Crucifixion; The Deposition
(18.4.8)

Central plaque 10½ × 9⁷/₁₆ in. (26.7 × 24 cm); wings 10½ × 3¾ in. (26.7 × 9.5 cm).

Description: In the central plaque, Christ's body is shown not frontally and vertically, as in the Crucifixions reproduced on pp. 21, 25, and 53, but turned toward a three-quarter view, with the silhouette slightly broken.[1] An angel and a devil receive the souls of the two thieves, one of whom faces Christ while the other glances over his shoulder at the devil. Immediately to the left of Christ's cross, Longinus, mounted on a dappled horse and still holding his spear, points to his eyes, miraculously healed of their blindness by the blood that issued from Christ's pierced side. The Virgin stands in the left foreground, her head turned away, her hands lowered and tightly pressed together in despair. Behind her are St. John and two of the Marys. All three women wear white wimples under their hooded mantles. Mary Magdalene kneels at the right of the cross and embraces its shaft, staring toward the left, lost in grief. She wears a red-violet mantle lined with green, a blue skirt, a green blouse trimmed with jewels, and a red-violet turban the end of which flutters above her left shoulder. On the ground before her is her ointment jar, which resembles Venetian glass. In the right foreground is a magnificent rider seen from behind, his face turned in profile away from the cross. He is richly dressed in a blue cloak over a jewelled golden-brown doublet and wears a double gold chain. He converses with another horseman at extreme right who gestures toward Christ. Beyond this group, the Centurion,

wearing a turban and a jewelled collar, makes with his right forefinger the traditional gesture testifying that Christ was truly born of God. In the background, soldiers wearing helmets or military caps hold aloft lances, a fork, and a banner. Jerusalem is set off against a light blue sky which abruptly turns cobalt blue toward the zenith. The colors of the garments are predominantly cobalt blue in the foreground and light blue interspersed with yellow-gold in the middle distance; zones of violet-red and yellow-brown intervene, and areas of emerald green are distributed at the periphery. The spectrum is spread in an impressive concentricity. The flesh tones verge on lilac in Christ's body but are paler and more corpse-like in the modelling of the thieves' figures. In the left wing, Christ is shown wearing a robe of red-violet and carrying the cross over His left shoulder. The Virgin follows between St. John and a holy woman. To the right stand helmeted soldiers, one of whom holds aloft a club. Beyond are the gate, walls, and buildings of Jerusalem. In the right wing, Joseph of Arimathaea, standing atop a ladder set behind the cross, lowers the body of Christ to Nicodemus. The Virgin has sunk to the ground in agony and is comforted by St. John. The garments are enamelled blue and turquoise, with passages of green and red-violet. Flowers growing in the foreground establish a decorative unity among the three panels.

Condition: Both wings are in good condition except for chips and repaired losses along the tops and in the upper corners. The blue

42

of the Virgin's mantle in the Deposition has been dulled by pitting, the result of blisters that have been removed. The central plaque is in excellent condition aside from repaired losses in the upper and lower right corners, some pitting, and a blister in the enamel on the back of the horseman in the right foreground.

The central panel is copied from a woodcut in the *Hore dive Virginis Marie, secundum verum usum romanum* published in Paris by Thielman Kerver in 1505, with subsequent editions.[2] The woodcut in turn borrowed the majestic rider seen from behind, with his horse raising its shod right hind hoof and its tail twisted around its left hind leg, from Martin Schongauer's large engraving *Christ Bearing the Cross*. Schongauer's print, which was copied by Israhel van Meckenem, Wenzel von Olmütz, and the monogrammist I. C.,[3] records a lost painting by Jan van Eyck, which was also interpreted by Hans Memling in his *Passion of Christ* at the Galleria Sabauda, Turin.[4]

An earlier version of the Frick triptych, including the same wing compositions, is in the Walters Art Gallery, Baltimore,[5] and another close variant is in the Louvre.[6] In those works the skull of Adam and some bones appear at the foot of the cross in both the Crucifixion and the Deposition panels, and the delineation is stronger. The lines of the *enlevages* in the Frick triptych are more broken than firm, due perhaps to the shakier hand of Nardon Pénicaud, already aging and working with the assistance of Jean I, or perhaps to the copy's having been reproduced with the help of tracings after the master model. The coloristic effect, allowing for minor modifications in the palette, is very much the same.

Exhibited: London, Victoria and Albert Museum, 1904–12, lent by J. Pierpont Morgan. New York, Metropolitan Museum, Morgan Collection, 1914–16, lent by J. Pierpont Morgan.

Collections: Johannes Paul sale, October 16–24, 1882, Cologne, Lot 632.[7] J. Pierpont Morgan, London and New York. Duveen. Frick, 1918.

NOTES

1 A return to the Gothic tradition of depicting Christ's body in slightly broken silhouette is observable in the Crucifixion painted around 1505 by Jean Bourdichon for a Book of Hours now in the Pierpont Morgan Library, New York (M. 732; see R. Limousin, *Jean Bourdichon,* Lyon, 1954, p. 72, Fig. 147), and on an oval medallion in gold with

44

translucent enamel, a Flemish work of the early sixteenth century, in the former Baronne Édouard de Rothschild collection, Paris.

2 The woodcut was re-used in Guilielmus Lyndewode's *Provinciale seu constitutionis Anglie,* published in Antwerp by Christophe van Ruremunde in 1525 (A.-J.-Delen, *Histoire de la gravure dans les anciens Pays-Bas,* II, Paris, 1934, p.43, Pl.XI). The composition also appears in an illumination for a French Book of Hours of about 1515 in the Walters Art Gallery, Baltimore (W 452, fol. 94 vo.), where it introduces, as in the printed Book of Hours, the psalm "Domine labia mea aperies." The group of the Virgin and St. John appears in Vélins 1636 at the Bibliothèque Nationale, Paris, with the mark of Germain Hardouin and an almanac for 1500–20 (P.Lacombe, *Livres d'heures imprimés au XVè et au XVIè siècle, conservés dans les bibliothèques publiques de Paris,* Paris, 1907, No. 92). The latter Book of Hours is interesting also for its combination of copies of Dürer's *Apocalypse* with architectural frameworks in the Italian taste.

3 J.-J. Marquet de Vasselot, *Les Émaux limousins,* Paris, 1921, p. 338, Pl. LXXXIV.

A. Bartsch, *Le Peintre-graveur,* Vienna, 1803–21, VI, Nos. 21, 23, 18, 13. On copies of the print in German painting and sculpture, see A. Schmid, "Kopien nach Kupferstichen von Schongauer," *Repertorium für Kunstwissenschaft,* XV, 1892, pp. 19–25.

4 R.A.Koch, "Martin Schongauer's Christ Bearing the Cross," *Record of the Art Museum: Princeton University,* XIV, 1955, No. 2, pp. 22–30. G.J. Kern, *Die verschollene Kreuztragung des Hubert oder Jan van Eyck,* Berlin, 1927. See also: E. Panofsky's review of Kern in *Kritische Berichte,* I, 1927, pp. 74–83; C. Aru and E. de Geradon, *La Galerie Sabauda de Turin,* Antwerp, 1952, pp. 14–20, Pl. XXXI.

5 P. Verdier, *The Walters Art Gallery: Catalogue of the Painted Enamels of the Renaissance,* Baltimore, 1967, No. 26, pp. 46–50.

6 Marquet de Vasselot, No.178, Pl.LXXII; for the Frick triptych, see No.180. The composition of the Crucifixion panel also reappears, with modifications, in an isolated plaque (*idem,* No.179).

7 A page printed in Spanish is affixed with wax to the back of the central panel, indicating that the triptych was in Spain before it entered the Paul collection.

Workshop of the
MASTER OF THE LARGE FOREHEADS

Late Fifteenth Century–Early Sixteenth Century

The anonymous Master of the Large Foreheads may have begun his career under the Master of the Baltimore and Orléans Triptychs, from whom he took over—and exaggerated—the high, rounded foreheads, slanting eyes, and puffy eyelids that characterize his production. He further stylized his figures by emaciating their features and dwarfing their ears into insignificance. Elaborate architectural settings are typical of his enamels.

Plaque: The Adoration of the Magi (16.4.4)

$10^3/_{16} \times 9^3/_{16}$ in. (25.9 × 23.4 cm).

Description: The Virgin, dressed in a blue mantle over a red-violet gown and holding the naked Child on her knee, sits on a richly carved and jewelled bench. She extends her left hand to accept the cup presented by the elderly king who kneels before her. The latter, dressed in a golden-yellow robe with a blue purse hanging from its belt, has respectfully set his jewelled cap on the pavement, which is made of green tiles with jewelled centers. Joseph stands behind the Virgin, his green hood lowered over his shoulders; he tucks up his red-violet robe with his right hand. The middle-aged king standing at center wears a crown and holds a covered cup. The more deferential young king at right, smartly dressed in a justaucorps, open cape, and high stockings, has bared his head, freeing his flowing fair hair touched with gold. He also holds a covered cup. The garments of the two standing kings are blue, yellow, and red-violet. In the background at left is a ruined structure representing the stable, the architecture of which displays features of both the Late Gothic and the Early Renaissance styles. Six doves roost in its eaves. Toward the right are a ruined Romanesque tower and a Gothic gateway. The kings' three attendants are shown on horseback at upper right. Angels look on from the stable.

Condition: The plaque is in fairly good condition. The enamel is worn at both upper corners, and nearly all of the raised enamelled jewels have been lost, including the Star of Bethlehem at the top. The surface is covered with many bubbles formed during the cooling process after firing.

The composition is adapted from an Adoration of the Magi enamelled twice by the Master of the Baltimore and Orléans Triptychs.[1] The triptych by that master in the John Herron Art Institute, Indianapolis, has the Nativity and the Circumcision represented on its wings. The same tripartite program was enamelled three times in the Workshop of the Large Foreheads: on a triptych in the Cathedral at Saragossa which must be slightly earlier than the Frick plaque; on a triptych in the Hermitage Museum, Leningrad, a later work which introduces in its central panel and left wing various Renaissance architectural features; and on a triptych which originally consisted of the Frick plaque and two wings formerly in the Hainauer collection, Berlin.[2] All three times the second enameller made the same error in copying the Adoration by the first: in each case it is no longer the Child who reaches for the cup proffered by the oldest king, but His mother. A fourth triptych from the Workshop of the Large Foreheads, in the Musée de Cluny, Paris, follows a different model for the Adoration.[3]

If the central subject was partly misunderstood, it was on the other hand rendered more complex by other borrowings. Many details are after a print by the Netherlandish Master I. A. M. of Zwolle (active about 1470–90).[4] The horse shown in front view with one leg raised is copied, in reverse, from a Crucifixion enamelled by the so-called Monvaerni,[5] and the horse seen from behind derives—as does that in the Crucifixion panel of Frick triptych No. 18.4.8 (see p. 45)—from Martin Schongauer's engraving *Christ Bearing the Cross*.

The Adoration of the Magi enamelled by the Master of the Baltimore and Orléans Triptychs was adapted at least three times in the workshop run by Nardon and Jean I Pénicaud.[6] The above-mentioned error was never committed there, and the composition remained closer to the earlier and simpler scheme.

In copying the production of the Master of the Baltimore and Orléans Triptychs, the Master of the Large Foreheads was unable to imitate the difficult technical handling of the flesh tones modelled in white over a layer of russet red glazed with transparent blue. Instead, his flesh tones are made up essentially of a mixture of opaque white and semitranslucent mulberry red thinly applied over a layer of blue, or sometimes red; the result is a pinkish-violet hue more hazy than that obtained through a similar method by the Master of the Louis XII Triptych and in the workshop of Nardon Pénicaud.[7] The Master of the Large Foreheads also added dots of white to point up the highlights, and a single dot of white was invariably juxtaposed to the pupils of the eyes.

48

Exhibited: London, Victoria and Albert Museum, 1902 and 1908–12, lent by J. Pierpont Morgan. Glasgow, Kelvingrove Art Gallery, 1903–08. New York, Metropolitan Museum, Morgan Collection, 1914–16, lent by J. Pierpont Morgan.

Collections: J. Pierpont Morgan, London and New York. Duveen. Frick, 1916.

NOTES

1 J.-J. Marquet de Vasselot, *Les Émaux limousins,* Paris, 1921, No. 69, Pl. XXV. P. Verdier, "An Enamelled Triptych by the Master of the Orléans Triptych," *Bulletin: John Herron Art Institute,* XLIV, 1957, pp. 42–46.
2 Marquet de Vasselot, No. 114, No. 117, Pl. XLIII, No. 115; for the Frick plaque, see No. 116, Pl. XLII. Compare two plaques in the Beaucousin collection in 1853 which match the height of the Frick panel (*idem,* pp. 284–85). Marquet de Vasselot's No. 124 is a rough duplicate, on a smaller scale, of the central panel of the Hermitage triptych.
3 *Idem,* No. 125.
4 A. Shestack, *Fifteenth Century Engravings of Northern Europe from the National Gallery of Art,* Washington, 1967, No. 136.
5 Marquet de Vasselot, No. 15, Pl. IV.
6 *Idem,* No. 123 (wrongly attributed to the Workshop of the Large Foreheads). L. Cottreau sale, Galerie Georges Petit, Paris, April 28–29, 1910, Lot 48 (*idem,* p. 147, note 1). Marczell von Nemes sale, Munich, June 16–19, 1931, Lot 481, Pl. 80 (formerly Alfred Pringsheim collection).
7 P. E. Michaels, "Technical Observations on Early Painted Enamels of Limoges," *Journal of the Walters Art Gallery,* XXVII–XXVIII, 1964–65, pp. 29 ff. Michaels' analysis proves that many enamels loosely attributed to the Master of the Baltimore and Orléans Triptychs are actually closer to the production of the Workshop of the Large Foreheads, though they lack some characteristic mannerisms of the latter, in particular the porcelain-doll aspect of its figures.

Triptych: The Way to Calvary; The Crucifixion; The Deposition
(16.4.5)

Central plaque 9⅛ × 8 in. (23.2 × 20.4 cm); wings 9⅛ × 3½ in. (23.2 × 8.9 cm).

Description: In the central panel, Christ is nailed to a high tau-shaped cross and the thieves are suspended by their broken arms from crosses set at angles. An angel receives the soul of the Penitent Thief while a devil carries away the frightened soul of the Unrepentant Thief. Above a rolling landscape and beneath a blue sky speckled with wispy gold clouds are delineated the crenellated walls and towers of Jerusalem. Mary Magdalene, wearing a brown mantle lined with blue and a red-violet robe with blue sleeves, kneels at the foot of the cross and embraces its shaft, looking up at Christ. Behind her is the swooning Virgin, aided by St. John; she is dressed in two shades of blue, he in red-violet. Two holy women complete the group, one looking up at the cross, the other turning away from it toward the Virgin. To the right of the cross, the Centurion, dressed in blue and brown and mounted on a white horse, testifies with his raised right hand to the divinity of Christ. Beyond him are two other horsemen and a detachment of soldiers. The compositions of both wings are nearly identical to those of Frick triptych No. 18.4.8 from the workshop of Nardon Pénicaud (see p. 43). In the Deposition panel, however, a different figure has been substituted for Nicodemus, and the enameller has added the figure of Mary Magdalene, who holds an ointment jar and wipes away a tear with the hem of her red-violet mantle. Once again, foreground flowers establish a decorative unity among the three panels.

Condition: The triptych is in generally good condition. There is a prominent repair near the center of the left wing, and additional repairs are visible at the corners of all three panels and across the upper section and along the margins of the central plaque. Many of the flowers and jewels appear to have been retouched.

The three crosses, Jerusalem, and the detachment of soldiers in the central panel derive from a Crucifixion by the Master of the Baltimore and Orléans Triptychs known in two examples, one in The Frick Collection (see p. 21), the other in the former Czartoryski collection at Cracow.[1] But the two thieves betray a knowledge of Flemish art: the Penitent Thief is represented as young and turned toward Christ, whereas the Unrepentant Thief is bearded and faces away from Christ, with his head no longer jerked back over the crossbar as in the original versions.[2] The body of Christ was carefully copied after a composition by Nardon Pénicaud,[3] who had himself adapted the Baltimore and Orléans Master's Crucifixion. In that adaptation, now in the museum at Bourges, Nardon Pénicaud completely changed the foreground figures, borrowing his Virgin and his standing Centurion from a print by Lucas van Leyden in the series *The Life of Christ* (1521).[4] In turn, the enameller of the Workshop of the Large Foreheads introduced in the present plaque three figures taken from Nardon Pénicaud's Crucifixion in the Museo Sacro at the Vatican[5]—the two horsemen in the foreground and the bearer of the shield painted with a devil's mask—and incorporated reminiscences of the carousel-like steeds found in much earlier Crucifixion enamels by the so-called Monvaerni.[6] The piecemeal arrangement of the present Crucifixion is rendered more conspicuous by the curious absence of the lance- and sponge-bearers in a composition already crowded enough to have integrated them.

Both wings, the Way to Calvary and the Deposition, closely resemble those of three triptychs in which Jean I Pénicaud may have collaborated with Nardon, including the above-mentioned triptych in The Frick Collection, another in the Louvre,[7] and the third in the Walters Art Gallery, Baltimore.[8] However, in the Depositions forming the right wings of those triptychs, as again in the left wing of the triptych at Bourges where the same composition is reversed, the figures number only five. The weeping Magdalene added to the Frick Deposition derives probably from a carved Entombment, a model also used once by Jean I Pénicaud.[9]

Exhibited: New York, Metropolitan Museum, Morgan Collection, 1914–16, lent by J. Pierpont Morgan.

Collections: J. Pierpont Morgan, London and New York. Duveen. Frick, 1916.

NOTES

1 J.-J. Marquet de Vasselot, *Les Émaux limousins,* Paris, 1921, No. 53, No. 54, Pl. XIX.
2 Compare, for instance, a Brussels tapestry of about 1510–30 in the Metropolitan Museum of Art, New York (*The Middle Ages: Treasures from the Cloisters and the Metropolitan Museum,* exhibition catalogue, Los Angeles County Museum of Art and Art Institute of Chicago, 1970, No. 115).
3 Marquet de Vasselot, No. 105, Pl. XXXIV.
4 Compare a plaque of the Crucifixion in the Victoria and Albert Museum, London, an early work of Jean I Pénicaud done when he was still painting in the manner of Nardon (*idem,* No. 176; repr. in R. Pinkham, "Attributions to the Aeneid Master," *Apollo,* XCV, 1972, p. 371, Fig. 2).
5 Marquet de Vasselot, No. 108, Pl. XXXVI.
6 *Idem,* No. 15, Pl. IV, No. 29, Pl. X.
7 *Idem,* No. 178, Pl. LXXII.
8 P. Verdier, *The Walters Art Gallery: Catalogue of the Painted Enamels of the Renais-*

sance, Baltimore, 1967, No. 26, pp. 46–50.

9 On the left wing of a triptych in Linares (Marquet de Vasselot, No. 182, Pl. LXXIII). The gesture of Mary Magdalene wiping away a tear is seen frequently in carved Entombments. To the examples repertoried by W. H. Forsyth (see p. 34, note 15), add R. Didier, "Mises au Tombeau de l'Entre-Sambre-et-Meuse et Saints-Sépulcres disparus," *Bulletin de la Commission Royale des Monuments et des Sites,* Brussels, 1970–71, No. 1, pp. 177 ff., Figs. 1, 7, 8.

54

JEAN I PÉNICAUD

c. 1480 (?) – After 1541

Of the three Limoges enamellers named Jean Pénicaud, Jean I is assumed to have been the younger brother of Nardon mentioned in a document of 1541. His style forms a transition between the Late Gothic as it was still practiced at Limoges in the early sixteenth century and the new Renaissance idiom associated with the reign of François I. He was the first enameller to make ample use of the prints of Albrecht Dürer, which he adapted freely. Also found in his production are compositions and motifs derived from Martin Schongauer and other German and Netherlandish masters, as well as elements from illuminated manuscripts and printed books.

Plaque: The Agony in the Garden (16.4.6)

Signed, on the rock in the foreground at center left: IP (much effaced; see *Condition*). 10¾ × 9⁵/₁₆ in. (27.3 × 23.7 cm).

Description: Christ kneels at center, dressed in a violet robe. An angel bearing a gold cross appears to Him in a cloud, and a gold chalice symbolic of His sacrifice hovers before Him, outlined against a tall rock. Droplets of blood are visible on Christ's forehead. His turquoise blue halo retains traces of gilt cusps and of a cross terminating in fleurs-de-lis. In the foreground at right are the sleeping figures of St. Peter, weakly holding his sword; St. John, with hands folded over a book beneath his chin; and St. James, hooded in his cloak. Peter is dressed in blue, the other two Apostles in crimson. In the background at left, Judas and a troop of soldiers enter the garden through a wooden gate in a wattle fence. The landscape is blue-green and yellow-green, the sky is blue studded with gold stars, and the rocks are painted in opaque white enamel. The drawing and crosshatchings visible through the translucent enamels appear as they would in an engraving. Gilding was used profusely. The counterenamel is a cloudy brick red.

Condition: The plaque shows extensive damage and repair, most notably at the corners, in the mantle of Judas from the right shoulder to the right leg, in the jaw and left cheek of James, in Peter's right temple and mouth, in the book held by John, and in the background above Christ's head. At upper left, a repaired crack runs through the gateposts and the city beyond, turning upward into the sky toward the center. Other repaired cracks follow the upper contour of Peter's right leg and the lower contour of his right sleeve. When the plaque appeared in the Odiot sale of 1889, the white rock in the foreground was still clearly painted with an elaborate device, described in the catalogue as "les lettres I. P. en or, liées ensemble par une sorte de cordelière." Writing in 1921, Marquet de Vasselot,[1] who evidently had not seen the plaque for some years, described "la signature (très effacée) formée des lettres I et P réunies par une cordelière," and this information was repeated in 1955 by Breck.[2] Today, nothing of the signature remains but for some isolated dots and faint indications of the loops of the cord.

The Frick plaque is one of eight known enamels signed with the name or initials of Jean I Pénicaud (see *Condition*). The composition compares with a plaque from his workshop in the Victoria and Albert Museum, London;[3] with another, one of a series of seven, in the former Blumenthal collection;[4] and with the left wing—taller in relation to its width—of a triptych in the former Michel Boy collection, Paris.[5] A composition identical except for the arrangement of the three Apostles, who retain the same poses but are no longer huddled together, appears on a plaque attributed to Couly Noylier in the Musée Municipal at Limoges.[6]

The most direct source of the subject is an engraved *Agony in the Garden* of about 1480 by Martin Schongauer, the first in his series of twelve prints of *The Passion*.[7] But other models intervened, such as Dürer's *Agony* in the two cycles of *The Small Passion* and *The Large Passion* and, for Judas and the soldiers entering the garden, an engraving by the Master A. G.[8] Schongauer's prints, together with variations after the Master B+S, Wenzel von Olmütz, the Master H+R, and Johann von Kulmbach, were copied by the Workshop of the Large Foreheads in a set of twelve enamelled plaques formerly in the collections of Thomas Fortune Ryan and Clendenin J. Ryan.[9]

Exhibited: Paris, Exposition Universelle, 1878. London, Victoria and Albert Museum, 1910–12, lent by J. Pierpont Morgan. New York, Metropolitan Museum, Morgan Collection, 1914–16, lent by J. Pierpont Morgan.

Collections: Ernest Odiot, Paris. His sale, April 26–27, 1889, Hôtel Drouot, Paris, Lot 52, repr. Calvet-Rognat and de Lariboisière sale, April 10–11, 1891, Paris, Lot 27. L. Cottreau, Paris. His sale, April 28–29, 1910, Galerie Georges Petit, Paris, Lot 49. J. Pierpont Morgan, London and New York. Duveen. Frick, 1916.

NOTES

1 J.-J. Marquet de Vasselot, *Les Émaux limousins,* Paris, 1921, No. 156.

2 J. Breck, in *The Frick Collection Catalogue,* VII, 1955, p. 11.

3 Salting Bequest 1909, No. 2111 (Marquet de Vasselot, No. 175).

4 S. Rubinstein-Bloch, *Catalogue of the George and Florence Blumenthal Collection,* Paris, 1926–30, III, Pl. XXI.

5 Marquet de Vasselot, No. 188, Pl. LXXVI.

6 No. 181 a.

7 A. Shestack, *Fifteenth Century Engravings of Northern Europe from the National Gallery of Art,* Washington, 1967, No. 51. Of course, the subject of the Agony in the Garden had been so multiplied in late medieval art and so frequently represented in mystery plays that it hardly needed a model. However, the grouping of the three Apostles in one corner of the composition is rather rare. It is met with in the *Agony in the Garden* of a retable painted by Gaspard Isenmann in 1462–65 for the collegiate church of Saint-Martin, Colmar (now in the Musée d'Unterlinden, Colmar); in an engraving of 1521 by Lucas van Leyden; and in an early sixteenth-century Book of Hours (Paris Usage) in the Pierpont Morgan Library, New York (M. 380, fol. 10).

8 For the Master A. G., an imitator of Schongauer, see: Shestack, No. 121; A. Merckling, "Meister Anton Gerbel," *Jahrbuch der elsässischen-lothringischen Wissenschaftliche Gesellschaft zu Strassburg,* VIII, 1935, pp. 106 ff. Schongauer's *Agony in the Garden* would have appealed to Jean I Pénicaud on account of the sense of breadth and depth it conveys; as in the engraver's *Resurrection,* particular emphasis was placed on spatial recession. See also G. Fiensch, "Versuch die Kupferstichpassion Martin Schongauers zeitlich zu ordnen," in *Festschrift Werner Hager,* Recklinghausen, 1966, pp. 44–53, and the qualifying comments of Shestack on the succession of the *Passion* prints (Shestack Nos. 51–62).

9 Marquet de Vasselot, No. 107. Sold at the American Art Association—Anderson Galleries, New York, November 23–25, 1933, Lot 385 A-M, and Parke-Bernet, January 19–20, 1940, Lot 264 A-M. The twelve plaques had been arranged in a triptych when they belonged to Ferdinand II of Portugal. They passed subsequently into the collection of Heinrich Wencke, Hamburg, and were bought by Charles Mannheim at the Wencke sale, Cologne, October 27–28, 1898, Lot 133, attributed in the catalogue to the Pénicaud workshop. Until recently they were exhibited in the wainscoting of the church at Wye, Maryland.

Triptych: The Kiss of Judas; Christ Mocked and Crowned with Thorns; The Flagellation (16.4.7)

Central plaque 10½ × 9³/₁₆ in. (26.7 × 23.4 cm); wings 10½ × 4 in. (26.7 × 10.2 cm).

Description: In the central plaque, Christ, crowned with thorns, is seated on a yellow bench. He wears a white loincloth, and over His shoulders is a purple mantle secured by a jewelled brooch. At left kneels a man dressed in yellow hose, a mulberry-rose shirt, a blue mantle decorated with a jewelled collar and sunburst, and a blue justaucorps inscribed on the hem with the name MARC (for Malchus); having removed his violet cap in mock reverence, he presents Christ with a reed in lieu of a scepter. Just beyond him a bald man dressed in green makes an obscene gesture toward Christ, and in the right foreground a barefoot boy wearing blue and violet and holding a fool's *marotte* whistles at Christ through his fingers. Christ's tormentors use sticks to beat the crown of thorns into His scalp. The two at right are in heavy shirts of blue and turquoise, open at the chest, and a third at left wears a yellow shirt, yellow hose, and a blue justaucorps enriched with jewels and a sunburst. In the left background are two dignitaries, one in a blue robe and violet cap, the other in a violet cloak and a conical blue hat with jewels and an upturned brim. The floor is tessellated with a *trompe-l'oeil* design of cubes set in perspective, reminiscent of contemporary Limousin stained glass; the pattern is identical to that found in the Death

and Coronation of the Virgin plaques on Frick triptych No. 16.4.2 from the workshop of Nardon Pénicaud (see p. 37). An unusual coloristic effect results from the widespread areas of yellow, of the same hue as the pot-metal yellow of stained glass and complementary to the deep blue, turquoise, and violet enamels of the garments and to the lavender-gray modelling of the flesh tones painted over a layer of blue. In the left wing, Judas, wearing a blue mantle and a gown of yellow, a color associated with treachery, approaches Christ and kisses Him. In his hand is a green purse. Peter holds a drawn sword, and Christ is about to graft back the severed ear of Malchus, the recumbent foreground figure in jewelled armor. Soldiers throng before the garden entrance. The sky is filled with clouds. In the right wing, Christ, naked but for a loincloth, stands bound to a column. Three tormentors dressed in blue, yellow, and green scourge Him in the presence of three dignitaries. At right hangs a curtain enriched with jewels executed in drops of enamel over foil. The tiled pavement is green. Beyond is a public square.

Condition: The triptych is in good condition. In the central plaque, the mulberry-red enamel used on the four columns in the background has deteriorated and shows repairs; a discolored repair is also visible below Christ's right foot. Both wings show pitting in the mulberry-red enamel.

The figures in the central plaque are closely copied from an engraving in Martin Schongauer's series *The Passion.*[1] The youth mockingly whistling through two fingers recurs in another pose in Schongauer's *Way to Calvary,* which served as model for the upper left wing of the Frick double triptych by Nardon Pénicaud (see p. 27). A whistling youth is also encountered in a Mocking and Crowning of Christ in the Victoria and Albert Museum, London, for which Jean I Pénicaud followed a different model.[2] Schongauer succeeded in integrating the Mocking and the Crowning in a unified composition, but not Jean I, who cramped his copy and replaced the airiness of the ciborium-like ribbed vault in the print with a row of heavy columns in the Italianate taste adopted in France under Charles VIII, interspersing them with panels imitating variegated marble.[3]

The composition of the Kiss of Judas is close to the illustration of that subject in a Book of Hours completed for Simon Vostre by Philippe Pigouchet on August 22, 1498.[4]

The composition of the right wing compares with the *Flagellation* in Dürer's *Large Passion* and with the *Christ at the Column* engraved on gouached vellum in a Book of Hours (Roman Usage) published by Germain Hardouin in Paris in 1518.[5] A similar Christ appears in a Flagellation forming the left wing of a triptych from the workshop of Nardon Pénicaud in the Museo Sacro at the Vatican.[6] The right wing of the Vatican triptych is adapted from the same Schongauer print as the central plaque of the present triptych.[7]

The treatment in the Frick triptych of Christ and various other figures—Peter, the bystanders—recalls the calm facial types of Nardon Pénicaud, but the greater vividness of their attitudes is characteristic of the style of Jean I.

Exhibited: London, South Kensington Museum, 1862, No. 1657, lent by G. H. Morland. Paris, Exposition Universelle, 1900, No. 2632, lent by Madame Chabrière-Arlès. Paris, Hôtel Sagan, Exposition d'objets d'art du Moyen Âge et de la Renaissance, 1913, No. 236, lent by Madame Chabrière-Arlès.

Collections: G. H. Morland, London. Frédéric Spitzer, Paris.[8] His sale, April 17–June 16, 1893, 33 rue de Villejust, Paris, Lot 422. Chabrière-Arlès, Paris. Duveen. Frick, 1916.

NOTES

1 A. Bartsch, *Le Peintre-graveur,* Vienna, 1803–21, VI, No. 13, p. 125. Compare an adaptation by Lambert Hopfer in the Cabinet des Estampes of the Bibliothèque Nationale, Paris (Ec 6d Rés., p. 39). Elements of Schongauer's print were also used on the follow-

ing: a pax enamelled in the workshop of Nardon Pénicaud and set into a Spanish silver frame stamped with the mark of Toledo, now in the Martin d'Arcy Gallery of Art, Loyola University, Chicago (D. F. Rowe, S. J., *Enamels: The XIIth to the XVIth Century,* Chicago, 1970, p. 26); a plaque by a follower of the Master of the Baltimore and Orléans Triptychs, formerly in the collections of Alfred Pringsheim, Munich, and Marczell von Nemes (sale, Munich, June 16–19, 1931, Lot 488); and a plaque in the Walters Art Gallery, Baltimore (P. Verdier, *The Walters Art Gallery: Catalogue of the Painted Enamels of the Renaissance,* Baltimore, 1967, No. 30, pp. 55–56). Hans Leu the Elder, in his *Mocking of Christ* after Schongauer's print (Schweizerisches Landesmuseum, Zurich, Dep. 842), painted the man kneeling before Christ in a yellow garment of the same color as that used by Jean I Pénicaud in the Frick plaque. Leu's painting is from a retable executed for the abbey church of Kappel, Switzerland; a second surviving panel, a *Veronica,* is also after Schongauer.

2 J.-J. Marquet de Vasselot, *Les Émaux limousins,* Paris, 1921, No. 155, Pl. LXIII; for the Frick plaque, see No. 163, Pl. LXVI.

3 The columns imitate the architectural frameworks in woodcuts executed by the printers Jean Dupré and Pierre Le Rouge of Paris and Pierre Gérard of Abbeville about 1490; see for instance the page showing Charles VIII enthroned, reproduced in A. Blum, *Les Origines du livre à gravures en France,* Paris, 1928, Pl. IV. This heavy Gothic Italianate taste is less disruptive in an enamelled plaque of the Flagellation in the Victoria and Albert Museum (Marquet de Vasselot, No. 154, Pl. LXII).

4 P. Courboin, *Histoire illustrée de la gravure en France,* Paris, I, 1923, No. 123.

5 J. Lieure, *La Gravure en France au XVIème siècle,* Paris–Brussels, 1927, pp. 6–7, Pl. VI, Fig. 20.

6 Marquet de Vasselot, No. 108, Pl. XXXVI.

7 Compare the plaque of Christ Crowned with Thorns in the Walters Art Gallery (Verdier, *loc. cit.*) and one formerly in the collections of Thomas Fortune Ryan and Clendenin J. Ryan (see p. 56 and p. 58, note 9). Modern duplicates of the Frick triptych are in the Museo Lázaro Galdiano, Madrid (see F. Torralba, "Esmaltes en el Museo Lázaro Galdiano," *Goya,* No. 55, 1963, p. 16), and the Metropolitan Museum of Art, New York (No. 49.7. ii 2; formerly Bache collection, bought in 1925 from Goldschmidt).

8 C. Popelin, in *La Collection Spitzer,* Paris, 1891, II, No. 6, Pl. II.

Triptych: The Way to Calvary; The Crucifixion; The Pietà
(18.4.9)

Central plaque 10 × 8 ¾ in. (25.5 × 22.2 cm); wings 10 × 3 ¹¹/₁₆ in. (25.5 × 9.4 cm).

Description: The central plaque, the Crucifixion, has many elements in common with the corresponding panel of Frick triptych No. 18.4.8 (see p.45). There are, however, significant differences in composition,[1] and even more in style. The high tau-shaped cross and the slightly broken silhouette of Christ follow closely the earlier treatment, but the facial characterization and the accented anatomy are more progressive. The thieves, both of whom now face Christ, are indiscriminately represented as thugs, though the hair of the Unrepentant Thief here falls over his eye to indicate that he will be deprived of the vision of Christ. Longinus and his horse have become more fully visible. Though the same cartoon was used for the group of the Virgin, St. John, and the two holy women, their relative positions have been modified, and Mary Magdalene, still kneeling at the foot of the cross, wears a much more elaborate mantle patterned with a flower-like motif composed of four clusters of rays around a circle.[2] In place of the majestic officer in the right foreground is an older man mounted on a horse with jewelled trappings. A banner decorated with a displayed eagle, the standard of the Roman Empire, but with its head replaced by the tail of a scorpion, the symbol of the Synagogue, has been introduced to balance the lance of Longinus. The angle of vision is set higher, and though the various groups are still disposed in a rotating pattern around the cross, the articulation is clearer and the psychological emphasis is more on the Passion of Christ and less on the Co-Passion of the Virgin. Many of the characters are curiously Germanic in appearance. The sky shades gradually from light blue enamelled on a white preparation above Jerusalem to a cobalt blue that becomes dark above the transverse bar of Christ's cross. The grass is yellow-green, and spots of green are used as a contrast to the splendid blue and red-violet and to the mustard yellow favored by Jean I Pénicaud. The flesh tones are grayish, tinged with red-violet and occasional russet, and the lips are touched with red. The technique is also more painterly. The gilt clouds are dragon-shaped like those introduced under Chinese influence into Italian *trecento* painting. A dark demon snatches the Unrepentant Thief's soul, which is merely delineated in gold, whereas the Penitent Thief's soul and its conveying angel are fully modelled in gold *camaïeu*. The stones cast shadows on the ground, and the direction of the light is underscored by the treatment of the raised lance and standard-pole, both of which are rendered with a line of gold on the lit side and a line of dark blue enamel on that in shadow. In the left wing, Christ, dressed in a dark red-violet gown with gold highlights, carries the cross, assisted by Simon of Cyrene. Beyond is a detachment of helmeted soldiers led by a man in a turban who aims a blow at Christ with his right fist.[3] A group of followers passes beneath the portcullis of the city gate, led by the Virgin, St. John, and a holy woman. In the right wing, the Virgin, seated at the foot of the cross with her hands joined in sor-

row, contemplates the dead Christ lying before her. She is draped in an ample mantle of cobalt blue over a red-violet dress and wears a white wimple. Christ's head is supported by St. John, who wears a red-violet cloak fastened with a jewelled brooch. At right stand Mary Magdalene, bareheaded and folding her hands across her chest, and Mary Cleophas. Against the cross lean a lance, a ladder, and a reed with a sponge, and from its transverse bar hang two whips. Two scourges are tied to the shaft of the column of the Flagellation at ex-

treme right. On the ground are the dice the soldiers cast for Christ's robe, the coins paid to Judas, and the crown of thorns. These paraphernalia compose the mystical theme of the *Arma Christi*.[4]

Condition: The triptych is in fairly good condition. There are losses at all four corners of the central plaque, and the dark blue enamel is faded and pitted on both wings, particularly the left one. A number of the raised enamel jewels have been damaged, and the gilding has probably been partially renewed.

The models adapted in the Crucifixion plaque are, as noted above, largely the same as those used in the corresponding panel of the Frick triptych from the workshop of Nardon Pénicaud, but other sources were drawn on as well. The two horsemen at right and the turbaned man between them can be traced to a *Crucifixion* engraved by the Netherlandish Master I. A. M. of Zwolle before 1480.[5] The entire foreground—including the four figures to the left of the cross, Mary Magdalene, and the mounted Centurion—is close to that of a paste-print in the Guildhall, London.[6] The same Crucifixion is found in Jean I Pénicaud's triptych in the church of Linares, Spain, where two flying angels gather in chalices the blood of Christ's pierced hands and side, and in a triptych from the Basilewsky collection in the Hermitage Museum, Leningrad.[7] The Frick Crucifixion is undoubtedly the earliest of the three, as the figure of Christ in the other two is drawn more in keeping with the new Renaissance canons of anatomy and proportion.

The Way to Calvary compares closely with the corresponding wings of triptychs by Jean I Pénicaud in the Musée Jacquemart-André, Paris, and the Musées Royaux d'Art et d'Histoire, Brussels.[8] In the Brussels wing, the raised enamel jewels dotting the ground have been replaced by large shaded stones; the composition of the accompanying Crucifixion panel follows a different model and is completely in the Renaissance style. The Way to Calvary is found again on the left wing of a triptych in the Victoria and Albert Museum, London, which has been made up of plaques from two unrelated triptychs.[9]

The Pietà panel is of particular interest. The composition is much the same as

66

on the corresponding wings of the triptychs in Leningrad and Brussels, but with the addition here of Mary Cleophas. A five-figured Pietà is encountered in the right wing of an early double triptych by Jean I Pénicaud in the Museo Arqueológico de la Alhambra at Granada,[10] but the treatment of Christ's corpse and Mary Magdalene in that work is more in the Late Gothic tradition. What is remarkable is that in all four of these plaques, and again in the triptych at Linares, Jean Pénicaud incorporated the *Arma Christi* in the Pietà. The earliest example of this iconographical synthesis is in the right wing of a second triptych by Jean I in the Hermitage.[11] In that Pietà, Christ as Man of Sorrows is supported by an angel in front of the tomb, in accordance with the mystical theme introduced into French art around 1400.[12] The Virgin swoons, and St. John supports her with his right arm while with his outstretched left hand he removes the crown of thorns from Christ's head. The *Arma Christi* are displayed in the background. This extraordinary iconographical motif was twice repeated by Jean I rather late in his career, on plaques stamped on the back with the hallmark that was to become customary in the Pénicaud workshop when it was run by Jean II.[13]

Exhibited: London, Victoria and Albert Museum, 1909–12, lent by J. Pierpont Morgan. New York, Metropolitan Museum, Morgan Collection, 1914–16, lent by J. Pierpont Morgan.

Collections: J. Pierpont Morgan, London and New York. Duveen. Frick, 1918.

NOTES

1 The compositional variations suggest that Jean I may have been familiar with the woodcut opening the "Officium trium filiarum beatae Annae" in Jean Bertaud's *Encomium trium Mariarum,* published in Paris in 1529 (see p. 82, note 6), and with a *Calvary* print by the Master E. S., in which the crowdedness of the composition recalls Dutch paintings (A. Shestack, *Master E. S.,* Philadelphia, 1967, No. 41).

2 The motif derives from the Chinese birds grouped around a rosace used in Italian textiles following Far Eastern models (B. Klesse, *Seidenstoffe in der italienischen Malerei des vierzehnten Jahrhunderts,* Bern, 1967, Figs. 101, 104). It recurs in illuminations from the last decades of the fourteenth century and in the so-called Netherlandish enamels of the fifteenth century (P. Verdier, "A Medallion of the 'Ara Coeli,'" *Journal of the Walters Art Gallery,* XXIV, 1961, p. 29, Figs. 17–19). It is frequently noted on garments in enamels by the so-called Monvaerni (J.-J. Marquet de Vasselot, *Les*

Émaux limousins, Paris, 1921, No. 3, No. 29, Pl. X, No. 34, Pl. XI, No. 40, Pl. XIII, No. 43, Pl. XIV).

3 The ruffian who struck Christ on His way to Calvary was sometimes nicknamed Giovanni Butadeo (John the God-Smiter) in the Italian sources which, from the thirteenth century on, gave birth to the legend of the Wandering Jew, condemned for his offense to remain on earth until the Last Judgment. See G. K. Anderson, *The Legend of the Wandering Jew,* Providence, 1965.

4 See R. Berliner, "Arma Christi," *Münchner Jahrbuch der bildenden Kunst,* 1955, pp. 35–133. The instruments of Christ's Passion were included in devotional images depicting the Mass of St. Gregory, to which an indulgence was granted by Pope Gregory XII (1406–15) and extended by Popes Nicholas V, Calixtus III, and Sixtus IV. See: J. W. Holtrop, *Monuments typographiques des Pays-Bas au XVème siècle,* The Hague, 1868, p. 13; P. Kristeller, *Die Apokalypse,* Berlin, 1916, p. 23.

5 A. Shestack, *Fifteenth Century Engravings of Northern Europe from the National Gallery of Art,* Washington, 1967, No. 134. J. J. McKendry, "Four Fifteenth-Century Crucifixions," *Metropolitan Museum of Art Bulletin,* XXV, No. 1, frontispiece and pp. 1–6.

6 A. M. Hind, *An Introduction to a History of Woodcut,* Boston–New York, 1935, I, Fig. 88, p. 198; compare Fig. 89, p. 200, for a reversed impression printed in relief.

7 Marquet de Vasselot, No. 182, Pl. LXXIII, No. 184, Pl. LXXIV; for the Frick triptych, see No. 183.

8 *Idem,* No. 185, No. 187, Pl. LXXV.

9 *Idem,* No. 186. Both wings were in Lord Amherst's collection (sale, Christie's, December 11, 1908, Lot 75) and were added to the central plaque, a Crucifixion, at the time of the Salting Bequest of 1909. The wings are the same height as those of the Brussels triptych, but the Crucifixion is 1 cm taller. The Crucifixion is reproduced, as a work of the Master of the Louis XII Triptych, in R. Pinkham, "Attributions to the Aeneid Master," *Apollo,* XCV, 1972, p. 372, Fig. 8.

10 Marquet de Vasselot, No. 166, Pl. LXVII.

11 *Idem,* No. 49, Pl. XVI, mistakenly identified with the workshop of the so-called Monvaerni by Marquet de Vasselot, followed by O. Dobroklonskaya in *Painted Enamels of Limoges, XV and XVI Centuries,* Moscow, 1969, p. 1.

12 See for example: *Europäische Kunst um 1400: Kunsthistorisches Museum,* Vienna, 1962, Nos. 400, 466, Pls. 38. 40; M. Meiss, *French Painting in the Time of Jean de Berry,* London, 1967, II, Figs. 326, 433.

13 Marquet de Vasselot, No. 192, Pl. LXXVII, No. 193; see also pp. 198–200. Compare a plaque from the Taillefer collection which shows the *Arma Christi* in conjunction with the Deposition and bears on the back the Pénicaud hallmark (L. Guibert and J. Tixier, *Exposition de Limoges: L'Art rétrospectif,* Limoges, 1886, p. 77, Pl. LXII). L. Bourdery was inclined to recognize that Deposition as a late work of Nardon Pénicaud (*Exposition rétrospective de Limoges: Les Émaux peints,* Limoges, 1888, pp. 28–35).

Plaque: Martyrdom of a Saint (16.4.10)

6½ × 6⅛ in. (16.5 × 15.6 cm).

Description: A man lies naked on the pavement of a porch or loggia, his head and body streaked with blood. Three tormentors beat him with sticks as a fourth, dressed in armor with imbricated brassarts, scalloped épaulières, and an elaborate horned, wreathed, and feathered helmet, kneels to tighten a rope around the victim's wrists. Beyond a balustered opening in the background six men witness the scene, two of them wearing crowns and holding scepters. The bearded tormentor to the right of center is clad in green, and the others wear cobalt blue, turquoise, and red-violet. The hems of the garments of the two tormentors at right bear the gold inscriptions MALCO and GANEL ET [DIA?]VE (see below). The architectural setting, enamelled in golden-brown, is Renaissance in character, with an architrave of gilt ova below a frieze of four cherubim. The tiled pavement is gray-green hatched with gold, and the green note is echoed in the bit of landscape visible through the arched doorway. The sky, bright with gold stars, shades from turquoise to cobalt blue. The enamel is either semitranslucent or translucent except for the flesh areas, which are pinkish-white over a dark blue preparation visible in the delineation by *enlevage*. The hair and eyebrows may have been drawn over with strokes of bister. Though the counterenamel is granular and thick the flux is almost translucent, suggesting that the piece was made some time around 1530.

Condition: The plaque shows considerable restoration in the areas of the left door jamb, the upper left corner, the cherub frieze, the right edge, and the garments of the tormentor at right, including part of the inscription on his skirt. Much of the dark blue and red-violet enamel is dulled, and the gold pattern on the tunic of the tormentor at left has faded. Occasional cracks run through the surface.

In the absence of attributes, the identity of the victim depicted on the plaque must remain in question. He could represent St. Sebastian, who, after he survived the arrows of Diocletian's archers, was finally beaten to death. But a somewhat more likely candidate might be the Apostle St. James the Less, first Bishop of Jerusalem and putative author of the Epistle of St. James. According to tradition, James the Less suffered martyrdom by being thrown from the pinnacle of the Temple at the instigation of the scribes and Pharisees, after which he was clubbed to death. As the Temple was noted for its effigies of cherubim (First Kings 6–8), the frieze of cherub heads across the top of the far wall lends some support to this identification. Further evidence in its favor is the inscription MALCO on the tunic of one of the tormentors, an allusion to Malchus, the servant of the high priest of

Jerusalem mentioned by John (18:10). Malchus frequently appeared as a tormentor in medieval mystery plays.[1]

The inscription GANEL ET [DIA?]VE on the skirt of the figure at right would seem to refer to Ganelon, the traitor in the *Chanson de Roland,* whose name became in time synonymous with treachery. The anachronistic coupling of Ganelon with Malchus could be explained if the two inscriptions, which are clearly meant to be read continuously, were translated as "Malchus, traitor and devil."

The purpose for which this curious plaque was made also is uncertain. It could have formed part of a series on the life of St. Sebastian, but assuming that it represents St. James the Less it may have been commissioned as a devotional image by a fullers' guild. Because of the circumstances of his death, James the Less was patron saint of the fullers, whose business it was to increase the weight and bulk of cloth by shrinking and then beating it.

A similar frieze of winged cherub heads, this time in blue, is found on a plaque depicting the Death of the Virgin enamelled by a follower of Jean I Pénicaud.[2] The architectural setting of the present plaque derives from illuminated manuscripts,[3] and the costume of the tormentor with the elaborate helmet may have been inspired by that of Mercury in Altdorfer's *Dream of Paris,* a woodcut of 1511.[4]

Exhibited: London, Victoria and Albert Museum, 1904–12, lent by J. Pierpont Morgan. New York, Metropolitan Museum, Morgan Collection, 1914–16, lent by J. Pierpont Morgan.

Collections: Karl Thewalt sale, November 14, 1903, Cologne, Lot 999. J. Pierpont Morgan, London and New York. Duveen. Frick, 1916.

NOTES

1 The name of Malchus is found in another variant form—as MARC—in the Crowning and Mocking of Christ panel of the Frick triptych by Jean I Pénicaud (p. 63). On the subject of Malchus, see J.-J. Marquet de Vasselot, *Les Émaux limousins,* Paris, 1921, p. 69; compare his No. 40, Pl. XIII, No. 47, No. 48, No. 49, Pl. XVI, all from the workshop of the so-called Monvaerni, and No.

209, by a follower of Jean I Pénicaud. See also the list of Limoges enamels of the early sixteenth century inscribed with the name of Malchus given by Marquet de Vasselot in *Bulletin de la Société Nationale des Antiquaires de France,* 1911, pp. 125–27.

2 Marquet de Vasselot, *Les Émaux limousins,* No. 200; for the Frick plaque see No. 203.

3 Compare the Book of Hours of Louis de

Laval Chatillon, done about 1480 (Bibliothèque Nationale, Paris, Ms. lat. 920, fol. 96).

4 As Charles Talbot of Yale University has kindly indicated to the author, the motif in the *Dream of Paris* was taken by Altdorfer from some Italian print such as the Florentine engraving *The Judgment Hall of Pilate* (A. M. Hind, *Early Italian Engraving,* London, 1938, II, No. A. II. 9), which shows figures comparable to those on the enamelled plaque. Compare also the illuminations from the workshop of Jean Bourdichon in the *Horae Beatae Mariae Virginis* (Chartres Usage) in the Pierpont Morgan Library, New York (M. 388), and for the background with balusters, an enamelled Last Supper in the former Blumenthal collection (S. Rubinstein-Bloch, *Catalogue of the George and Florence Blumenthal Collection,* Paris, 1926–30, III, Pl. XX).

Workshop of
JEAN II PÉNICAUD

Active c. 1531 – c. 1549

The enameller who sometimes used the signature IOHANNES PENICAVDI IVNIOR *appears to have been the eldest son of Nardon Pénicaud and the nephew of Jean I. His signed works range in date from a portrait of 1531/32 showing Luther at the age of forty-eight to a plaque of St. Luke done in 1549. He may have been the Jean Pénicaud who served as consul in 1540 and in 1548. Though he took much of his inspiration from prints, Jean II managed to evolve a highly personal style in which he reinterpreted the Italian Mannerism of the School of Fontainebleau. Many of his enamels are marked on the back with a stamp in the form of a crowned* P.

Triptych: The Lineage of St. Anne (16.4.12)

Central plaque 11¾ × 7½ in. (29.9 × 19.1 cm); wings 11¾ × 3⅛ in. (29.9 × 8 cm).

Description: In the central panel, the Virgin, clad in a blue mantle over a red-violet dress and identified by a white scroll inscribed LA.V.MARIE, sits holding the naked Christ Child, whose scroll bears the monogram IHS. Above them stands St. Anne (S.ANNA) as a *figura orans,* with her hands uplifted in a gesture of benediction; she wears a red-brown mantle over an orange-gold dress. The three men behind her are designated as Joachim (IOACHIN), Cleophas, and Salomas. The composition is completed by Joseph (S. IOSEPH), dressed in blue and red-violet, and by an old serving-woman in a green robe with yellow highlights who bends over the cradle. Above the figures are two raised curtains

painted in the same green and yellow,[1] and in the lower foreground is a scroll inscribed LA. LIGNEE.DE.S.ANNE. The left wing depicts Mary Cleophas (MARIE.CLEOPHE) and her husband Alpheus (DALPHEVS), she in a blue mantle over a red-violet gown and he in purple and green. With them are two of their four children, wearing green and violet and designated as Simon (S.SYMONNDE) and Joseph the Just (S.IOSSEPH). The right wing shows Mary Salome (MARIE.SALOME), in an orange overdress, a red skirt, and dark green sleeves, and David (DAVI), in a red-violet robe and a blue turban. In the foreground, dressed in blue, are the two children of Mary Salome and Zebedee: James the Greater (S.IAQVES.LE.M) and John the Evangelist (S. IEHAN.LE.VANGELI). The canopies in both

75

wings are green, and the backgrounds of all three panels are dark blue dotted with gold. The warm palette is built on strong complementary tones. The flesh tints are rendered in a grisaille glazed with salmon red. The light source from the left is emphasized by the shading of the scrolls, which are tinted in green or mulberry.

Condition: The triptych is in good condition. The central plaque shows a repair near the lower left corner, crazing in the area of St. Anne and Salomas, and more serious crazing—or perhaps a scratch—running through the head and raised arm of the nurse. Signs of possible additional repairs are visible in the upper right corner of the left wing, in the upper left and lower right corners and between the curtains on the central panel, and in the upper and lower left corners of the right wing. The right wing is also chipped along the edges. The enamel colors overflow their gilt outer borders on the central and right panels.

The New Testament makes no mention of the Virgin's parentage. The only reference to her sister is the statement of John (19:25) that "there stood by the cross of Jesus his mother, and his mother's sister, Mary the wife of Cleophas, and Mary Magdalene." Mary the wife of Cleophas has at times been identified with the "Mary the mother of James the less and of Joses" whom Matthew (27:56) and Mark (15:40) place at the Crucifixion, and she has been assumed by extension to be the mother of the four children whom Matthew (13:55) and Mark (6:3) call Christ's "brethren"—namely, James, Joses, Simon, and Judas. The latter James has in turn been linked with the James who in Acts (1:13) is called "the son of Alpheus."

Salome is added to the witnesses at the Crucifixion by Mark (15:40), and she is sometimes assumed to be the same as the woman identified by Matthew (27:56) as "the mother of Zebedee's children"—that is, of James the Greater and John the Evangelist (Mark 1:19).

The Apocryphal Protevangelium of James goes further in stating that the Virgin was born to a certain Anne and Joachim after they had been married twenty years without issue, and that both parents died after the Virgin had been presented in the Temple. But according to a subsequent legendary development, Anne survived Joachim, married Cleophas when Mary was three years old, and bore a second daughter, Mary Cleophas, who later married Alpheus and became the mother of James the Less, Joseph the Just (Joses), Simon, and Jude (Judas). After the death of Cleophas, the legend continues, Anne married Salomas, the child of that third union being Salome, later called Mary Salome, who became the wife of Zebedee

76

and the mother of John the Evangelist and James the Greater. On the basis of this legend, then, the Frick triptych would represent Anne with her three husbands, her three daughters, two of her three sons-in-law, five of her seven grandchildren, and the prophet David.

In the late Middle Ages the lineage of St. Anne through her three husbands was assimilated to the Tree of Jesse, with its line of Christ's descent beginning with Jesse and culminating in the Virgin and Child enthroned.[2] This assimilation explains why David, the son of Jesse, is substituted for Zebedee beside Mary Salome on the right wing of the triptych. The legendary tradition of the Three Husbands of St. Anne,[3] offensive as it may appear in light of the subsequent dogma of the Immaculate Conception, was a frequent iconographical theme in the waning Middle Ages and is well represented in French stained glass of the early Renaissance.[4]

It was, however, an engraving by Marcantonio Raimondi that served as model for the central panel of the Frick triptych: his *Virgin with the Cradle,* which probably was based on a design by Giulio Romano and descends ultimately from compositions by Leonardo and Raphael and from the type known in German art as the "Anna Selbdritt." Marcantonio's print was in turn copied by Marco Dente and other engravers.[5] The *Virgin with the Cradle* was incorporated by the enameller into the broader subjects of the Three Husbands of St. Anne and the Lineage of St. Anne. He also borrowed from a woodcut in the *Encomium trium Mariarum* of Jean Bertaud de Périgueux: the young St. James holding an open book in the right wing of the triptych is a reversed copy of the same child in the woodcut.[6]

Other enamels inspired by Marcantonio's print or by Marco Dente's copy include: a plaque stamped three times with the Pénicaud mark in the Carrand Collection, Museo Nazionale, Florence;[7] the reverse of a medallion attributed to Jean II Pénicaud in the Walters Art Gallery, Baltimore;[8] and a plaque from the Pénicaud workshop in the Musée des Beaux-Arts at Dijon.[9] A beautiful grisaille in the Louvre attributed to the workshop of Jean II Pénicaud shows St. Anne standing as a *figura orans* above the Virgin nursing Jesus, with Mary's cousin Elisabeth and her son John the Baptist and with Mary Salome and her two children.[10]

A workshop copy, or perhaps a modern replica, of the Frick triptych is in a private collection at Nierstein am Rhein. Joseph, Joachim, Cleophas, and Salomas

78

are represented on a plaque, formerly the left wing of a triptych, in the Musée de Cluny, Paris,[11] and Marquet de Vasselot mentioned in his notes a related plaque, the central panel of a triptych, in the former collection of Dott. A. Collè, Milan. The group of the Virgin and Child is adapted to a different composition on an enamel in the Louvre (Sauvageot Bequest) signed M. PAPE; there it appears between two saints, with God the Father above. On a plaque formerly in the Sir Francis Scott collection, Jean I Pénicaud fused the holy kinship of Mary with an ''Anna Selbdritt'' and set the figures against the chevet of a Renaissance church.[12] The Lineage of St. Anne by Couly Noylier (1545) in the Musée Municipal at Agen owes nothing to Marcantonio's print and may be after a stained-glass window.

Exhibited: London, Victoria and Albert Museum, 1901–12, lent by J. Pierpont Morgan. New York, Metropolitan Museum, Morgan Collection, 1914–16, lent by J. Pierpont Morgan.

Collections: Frédéric Spitzer, Paris.[13] His sale, April 17–June 16, 1893, 33 rue de Villejust, Paris, Lot 439. Charles Stein, Paris. His sale, June 8–10, 1899, Galerie Georges Petit, Paris, Lot 20. J. Pierpont Morgan, London and New York. Duveen. Frick, 1916.

NOTES

1 The raising of curtains, a late Roman and early Christian device for revealing—in the sense of unveiling—a sacred object or a holy person or group, was used by Israhel van Meckenem in an engraving of St. Anne with the Virgin and Child and SS. Catherine and Barbara.

2 See for example the Missal of Chartres printed by Kerver in 1529. A hymn quoted by F. J. Mone (*Lateinische Hymnen des Mittelalters,* III, p. 195) reads: "Anna radix uberrima / Arbor tu salutifera / Virgas producens triplices / Septem onusta fructibus" ("Anne, most fertile root, Tree of Salvation, shooting off three branches laden with seven fruits"). The stained-glass window of the Lineage of St. Anne at Saint-Vincent, Rouen, done about 1525 by a pupil of Arnoult de Nimègue, is patterned as a genealogical tree; it was formerly integrated with the Tree of Jesse into a unified four-lancet window (La Quérière, *Revue de Rouen,* II, 1843). In the *Généalogie de Notre Dame en romans,* the Lineage of St. Anne is shown as a medieval table of consanguinity (H. Martin and P. Lauer, *Les Principaux Manuscrits à peintures de la Bibliothèque de l'Arsenal,* Paris, 1929, Pl. XVII, Ms. 3517).

3 To the literature on this subject summarized by B. Kleinschmidt in *Die heilige Anna: Ikonographie,* II, Düsseldorf, 1930, pp. 110–11, should be added the monograph of P. Séjourné, *Les 4 Maries de l'Évangile,*

80

Bourges, 1930.

4 See É. Mâle, *L'Art religieux de la fin du moyen âge en France,* Paris, 1908, pp. 227–28, Figs. 102, 103.

5 A. Bartsch, *Le Peintre-graveur,* Vienna, 1803–21, XIV, No. 63, pp. 70–73. H. Delaborde, *Marc-Antoine Raimondi,* Paris, 1887, No. 11, p. 94. Compare Altdorfer's print of the *Virgin with the Cradle* (Schmidt No. 178) reproduced in H. Tietze, *Albrecht Altdorfer,* Leipzig, 1923, p. 177.

6 *Encomium trium Mariarum Ioannis Bertaudi Petragorici, iurium licentiati, cum earum cultus defensione,* Paris, 1529. The woodcut of St. Anne's lineage is repeated on fol. vi vo. and fol. xviii vo. of the first part and before the Mass of the Three Marys in the second part (R. Brun, *Le Livre illustré en France,* Paris, 1930, Pl. VI).

7 U. Rossi, *Catalogo del Reale Museo Nazionale di Firenze,* Rome, 1898, No. 1193, p. 284.

8 P. Verdier, *The Walters Art Gallery: Catalogue of the Painted Enamels of the Renaissance,* Baltimore, 1967, No. 51, pp. 103–04. The lady depicted on the obverse of the medallion has since the publication of the Walters catalogue been identified as Guillemette de Sarrebruck, who in 1526 married Robert III de la Marck, Duc de Bouillon and Marshall of France (R. de Broglie, "Les Clouet de Chantilly," *Gazette des Beaux-Arts,* LXXVII, 1971, Nos. 326, 327, p. 326).

9 From the Trimolet collection.

10 No. O. A. 4003. J.-J. Marquet de Vasselot, *Catalogue sommaire de l'orfèvrerie, de l'émaillerie et des gemmes,* Paris, 1914, No. 496.

11 No. 14.742. The right wing, inscribed with the names LIZAREL and ALFEVS, is in a private collection.

12 Scott sale, Sotheby's, April 27, 1965. J.-J. Marquet de Vasselot, *Les Émaux limousins,* Paris, 1921, No. 141, there attributed to the workshop of the Master of the Louis XII Triptych. The square sanctuary and the shell half-domes above the side chapels correspond to the opened curtains and the two hanging canopies in the central plaque and wings of the Frick triptych.

13 C. Popelin, in *La Collection Spitzer,* Paris, 1891, II, No. 33, Pl. V.

MASTER OF THE PASSION, Attributed to

Active First Half of the Sixteenth Century

Plaque: The Seven Sorrows of the Virgin (16.4.11)

Dated, in gold, above the lower left medallion: 1533. 7 × 5⅝ in. (17.8 × 14.3 cm).

Description: Seated at the center of the plaque with her hands clasped is the Virgin as Lady of Sorrows, dressed in a blue mantle and white wimple. Seven swords with silvered blades and gilded hilts point at her breast. The swords issue from silver-and-gold wreaths enclosing roundels in which are depicted her Seven Sorrows. Beginning at upper left they show the Circumcision, the Flight into Egypt, the Loss of the Child in Jerusalem, Christ Falling on the Way to Calvary, the Crucifixion, the Pietà, and the Entombment. Two women kneel at lower left and right, the former wearing a nun's habit painted in purple and black, the latter a rich costume of blue and golden-orange. The background is emerald green with gilt scrolls, the foreground blue-green. Gilding was used extensively to highlight the costumes, and the plaque is bordered by a gilt twisted cord within narrow bands of silver and black. The counterenamel is dark, gritty, and uneven.[1]

Condition: The plaque is in very good condition except for a diagonal crack running through the three upper roundels and for tarnish on the silver overlay.

The roundel of the Flight into Egypt derives from a Dürer woodcut, done before 1506, in the series *The Life of the Virgin.* That of Christ Falling on the Way to Calvary is based on the corresponding subject, dated 1509, from Dürer's woodcut series *The Small Passion.*

The subject of the Seven Sorrows of the Virgin inspired a number of Limoges enamelled plaques, including several attributed to Jean II Pénicaud or to the Pénicaud workshop,[2] at least two by Pierre Reymond,[3] and one by Léonard Limousin.[4] The present plaque recalls certain features in the early work of both the latter painters, but it resembles even more the style of the delicate and elusive master whom Marquet de Vasselot referred to in his unpublished notes now in the Louvre as "le maître fin." In technique and design the plaque is not far from, though much superior to, the few enamels signed by Pierre Vigier (Pierre Callet), who is mentioned in documents between 1523 and 1536 and who married Valérie

Limousin, possibly a relative of Léonard Limousin.[5] It compares with a small, charming plaque in the British Museum, London, where only five Sorrowful Mysteries are depicted, as in the Rosary, against a background of translucent blue enamel and gilt scrollwork.[6] Certain similarities of technique—the thinness of the *enlevages,* the minutiae worked out with the needle, and, in contrast, the vigorous underlying crosshatchings and superimposed gilding—characterize a plaque of the Crucifixion in the Walters Art Gallery, Baltimore.[7] Its maker, who has been termed the Master of the Passion, is not as subtle as the "maître fin," nor can he be identified with the Aeneid Master, who was active in the circle of Jean I Pénicaud and whose broad use of brushwork conveyed to his production a distinct painterly aspect.[8]

Questions of authorship aside, the Frick Seven Sorrows is closely related to a plaque of the Nativity in the Germanisches National-Museum, Nuremberg,[9] where the two kneeling ladies in the foreground are duplicated exactly, even to the details of their costumes. That the ladies belonged to the same family is revealed in the Nuremberg plaque by the coat of arms introduced between them. It is impaled with a heraldic image of devotion displaying the Five Wounds of Christ and the Sacred Heart transfixed by a lance—an emblem corresponding to the heart of the Virgin pierced by the seven swords. The Nuremberg plaque also shows identical gladiolus blades in the foreground and the same gilt scrollwork meandering over the translucent background. This rare type of scrollwork is found again on a small plaque illustrating the Five Sorrowful Mysteries of the Rosary in the Museo Nazionale, Florence, and on the above-mentioned plaque in the British Museum. By the same master are four roundels representing episodes of the Life and Passion of Christ in the City Art Museum of St. Louis.[10]

The devotion of the Seven Sorrows of the Virgin first appeared in French manuscript illuminations toward the end of the fourteenth century. The theme embodied the mystical concept that the Virgin suffered through her compassion a Co-Passion parallel to the Passion of Christ, thus fulfilling the prediction made to her by Simeon when Jesus was presented in the Temple: "Yea, a sword shall pierce through thy own soul also" (Luke 2:35).[11] At the time of the Jan Hus heresy, the Church, identifying itself with Mary, declared that it had been wounded by the heretics, and a new feast commemorating the torments of the Virgin was inscribed in the calendar at the Cologne synod of 1423. The first confraternities of the Seven

Sorrows of the Virgin appeared in Flanders, that of Bruges being approved by Pope Alexander VI in 1495. An illumination in the 1532 Book of Hours of Perrenot de Granvelle shows the hilts of seven swords attached to roundels enclosing the Seven Sorrows,[12] as in the Frick enamel.

Wreaths similar to those bordering the roundels on the present plaque, half silvered and half gilt, appear around the bust portraits of Biblical and mythological characters made by Léonard Limousin for Jean de Langeac, Bishop of Limoges.[13]

Exhibited: London, Victoria and Albert Museum, 1905–12, lent by J. Pierpont Morgan. New York, Metropolitan Museum, Morgan Collection, 1914–16, lent by J. Pierpont Morgan.

Collections: Charles Stein (?).[14] J. Pierpont Morgan, London and New York. Duveen. Frick, 1916.

NOTES

1 J.-J. Marquet de Vasselot (*Les Émaux limousins,* Paris, 1921, p. 185, note 3) wrote that this plaque of 1533 was the last dated instance he knew of with opaque counter-enamel. However, a thick, cloudy counter-enamel still appears on a plaque showing St. Matthew and St. John in the British Museum, London, signed I.P., which has as its counterpart a plaque in the Victoria and Albert Museum, London, representing St. Mark and St. Luke and bearing the date 1549.

2 Among them: one in the former Visconti collection (sale, Paris, March 13–16, 1854, Lot 65); one showing the Virgin in bust length and pierced with only one sword against a background strewn with tears, since 1895 on loan from the Louvre to the Musée Adrien-Dubouché, then to the Musée Municipal, Limoges (see: L. de Laborde, *Notice des émaux, bijoux et objets divers,* Paris, 1852, I, No. 293; A. Darcel, *Notice des émaux et de l'orfèvrerie,* Paris, 1867, No. 211); a similar plaque from the same model, dated 1541, shown in the Exposition Rétrospective at Limoges in 1886 (L. Bourdery, *Les Émaux peints,* Limoges, 1888, pp. 37–38) and subsequently traced to the Brouland collection at Pau, where it remained until about 1966; and a plaque bequeathed by the Rev. A. H. S. Barwell to the British Museum (No. 1913, 12–20, 27) showing seven roundels in grisaille tinted with green and purple, with a counterenamel of brownish flux. See also note 14, below.

3 In the grisaille plaque by Pierre Reymond from the Trimolet collection now in the Musée des Beaux-Arts at Dijon, the roundels lack wreaths, as do those of the Barwell plaque (see note 2, above). Pierre Reymond also painted the Seven Sorrows on the left

wing of a diptych that figured in the Préaux sale, Paris, January 9–11, 1850 (from the Brunet-Denon sale, Paris, February 2–15, 1846, Lot 448).

4 Sir Francis Scott sale, Sotheby's, April 27, 1965, Lot 7 (probably from the M. Boy sale, Galerie Georges Petit, Paris, May 15–24, 1905, Lot 215).

5 On two plaques stamped P.V. in the Musées des Beaux-Arts at Dijon, see P. Verdier, *The Walters Art Gallery: Catalogue of the Painted Enamels of the Renaissance,* Baltimore, 1967, p. 142 and Fig. 13.

6 No. 1913, 12–20, 80. In tinted woodcuts, the Joyful Mysteries were sometimes represented in pink roundels while the Sorrowful Mysteries were set against a black background (A. Schramm, *Der Bilderschmuck der Frühdrucke,* Leipzig, 1920–43, III, No. 518).

7 Verdier, No. 71, pp. 140–42.

8 See R. Pinkham, "Attributions to the Aeneid Master," *Apollo,* XCV, 1972, pp. 370–75.

9 No. KG. 549. See P. Verdier, "French Renaissance Enamels," *Apollo,* XCIII, 1971, pp. 386–88, Figs. 3, 4.

10 No. 466:56. The roundels, which depict the Nativity, Flight into Egypt, Pietà, and Entombment, constitute *disjecta membra* from a composite panel of the type of the Ascension of Christ by Jean II Pénicaud in the Hermitage Museum, Leningrad (O. Dobroklonskaya, *Painted Enamels of Limoges, XV and XVI Centuries,* Moscow, 1969, pp. 18–20). When in the Alfred Pringsheim collection the roundels were attributed to the Pénicaud workshop. They figured as Lot 489 in the Marczell von Nemes sale, Munich, June 16–19, 1931.

11 See O. G. von Simson, "Compassio and Co-Redemptio in Roger van der Weyden's *Descent from the Cross,*" *Art Bulletin,* XXXV, 1953, pp. 9–16. Roger painted his *Descent from the Cross* for the Chapel of the Archers' Guild in Notre-Dame-hors-les-Murs, Louvain. Roger's master, Robert Campin, painted in grisaille the Virgin transfixed by a sword on the reverse of the *Virgin and Child* panel in the Städelsches Kunstinstitut, Frankfurt am Main (M. S. Frinta, *The Genius of Robert Campin,* The Hague, 1966, Fig. 34).

12 É. Mâle, *L'Art religieux de la fin du moyen âge en France,* Paris, 1908, Pl. 121. See also: W. H. Gerdts, Jr., "The Sword of Sorrow," *Art Quarterly,* XVII, 1954, pp. 212–29; "La Vierge aux Sept Glaives," *Analecta Bollandiana,* XII, 1893, pp. 333–52. In some fourteenth-century ivories, a sword or a jet of blood is directed from the pierced chest of Christ on the cross to the heart of the swooning Virgin (P. Verdier, *The International Style: The Arts in Europe around 1400,* Baltimore, 1962, Nos. 118, 119). The Seven Sorrows were first equated with the Seven Stations of Christ's Passion in the *Speculum humanae salvationis.* Numerous Netherlandish engravings designed as models for devotional images and pyxes show a Virgin of the Pietà type transfixed by a sword and surrounded by six roundels framing her other sorrows (F. W. H. Hollstein, *Dutch and Flemish Etchings, Engravings and Woodcuts,* Amsterdam, 1949–, XII, Nos. 147, 154, 217, 219, 272, 288; compare a composition by Hans Burgkmair, F. W. H. Hollstein, *German Engravings, Etchings and Woodcuts,* Amsterdam, 1954–, V, No.

79). The symbolical scheme remained popular in Flemish art—for instance in the paintings of the *Seven Sorrows of the Virgin* by Adriaen Isenbrant at Notre-Dame, Bruges, done between 1528 and 1535; by Wenzel Coebergher at Notre-Dame, Tournai; and by Pieter Pourbus at Saint-Jacques, Bruges. Limoges enamels representing the same subject, either later than those listed above or by different hands, include: one in the Lowengard sale, Hôtel Drouot, Paris, March 3–4, 1911, Lot 33, dated 1541; one showing a monk kneeling before the Virgin of Sorrows, Gilbert sale, Hôtel Drouot, Paris, November 29–December 1, 1927, Lot 95 (compare Bouvier sale, Paris, December 8–16, 1873, Lot 329, and Nielli sale, 1911, Lot 92); and a plaque signed I.C. in the Louvre from the Corroyer Bequest of 1923 (possibly the same as Lot 4 in the Duboulaye sale of 1879).

13 M. Marcheix, "Plaque émaillée de Léonard Limosin, Limoges, Musée Municipal," *Bulletin de la Société archéologique et historique du Limousin,* XCVIII, 1971 pp. 197–206. Verdier, 1967, Fig. 17, p. 172.

14 The Frick Seven Sorrows may be identical with a plaque attributed to the Pénicaud workshop that was exhibited by Charles Stein at the 1888 Exposition du Métal in Paris (No. 129), though it did not appear in the Stein sale of June 8–10, 1899. According to the exhibition catalogue, the seven roundels coincided with those on the Frick plaque, the counterenamel had a violet tinge, and the dimensions were 17.8 × 13.6 cm. The Stein plaque may in turn be identified with one mentioned in the papers bequeathed by E. Lachenaud to the Musée Municipal, Limoges, as having at some time been in the collection of A. Tollin, though it was not included in the latter's sale, Galerie Georges Petit, Paris, May 20–21, 1897.

COULY II NOYLIER

Active 1539–After 1571

The principal production of Couly II Noylier, son of the enameller Couly I, consists of caskets mounted with plaques inscribed with legends in the Limousin dialect or in Latin. He signed with the name COLIN—*patois diminutive for Nicolas—or with the initials* C.N. *His dated works range from 1539 to 1545. Couly II was consul of Limoges in 1567 and was still recorded as an enameller in 1571.*

Casket: Putti with Mottoes of Courtly Love (16.4.14)

H. 4⅝ in. (11.8 cm); W. 7⁵⁄₁₆ in. (18.6 cm); D. 4¾ in. (12.1 cm).

Description: The casket is composed of thirteen plaques mounted in a gilt-copper frame. On the top of the lid, in a roundel bordered with white and flanked by two putti holding leafy scrolls, is a female portrait bust in profile inscribed LVCRESE.SVIS (Lucretia am I).[1] All the remaining plaques are decorated with scenes of naked putti playing musical instruments, engaging in mock battles, and courting scantily draped young girls, in each instance beneath a motto inscribed in gold. On the front of the lid at left, a putto presents a vase of fruit and flowers to a seated girl, and the motto reads DE CVEVR.IE DONNE (From my heart I give); in the scene to the right, one putto carries a spar with a sail and another sits holding a bagpipe, with the motto SVIS.PAR AMOVR IOYEV (I am by love elated). On the back of the lid at left, a putto brandishing an arrow stands over a fallen putto who holds a shield, and the motto is ARDIS.VALLIAN.SVIS (Bold and valiant

am I); to the right, one putto plays a double flute and another a gittern, beneath the motto AMOVR.DONE.IOYE (Love gives joy). The trapezoidal plaque on the left gable shows a putto seated beside a basket of fruit and flowers and supporting a scroll inscribed VITA BREVIS (Life is brief); the motto is EN BONNE FOY (As a token of good faith). On the right gable, a putto reclines beneath a fluttering scroll inscribed FESTINA (Hasten); above is the motto FIDELLE SVIS (Faithful am I). The front plaque at lower left shows a putto with an arrow watching as a seated putto offers a casket to a girl, with the motto LE PRINS DE BONE FOY (Take it in good faith); at right, one putto blows a trumpet as another brandishes an arrow and leads with a rope a captive whose hands are tied behind him, with the motto PAR AMOR VAINCV (By love defeated). The plaque on the back at lower left shows a squatting putto playing a monocord while his comrade addresses a girl who sits on a throne and holds aloft a flaming heart, with the motto PRENNES.EN GRE LE DONE

90

(Kindly accept, I give it); at right, around a flaming altar stand two putti holding palms and a girl holding a flower, with the motto TOVS IOVR.LEAL.SERAY (Forever shall I be true). On the lower left end, a putto holding a bowl of fruit and flowers sits in a chariot drawn by a second putto and accompanied by two others playing a horn and a gittern; the motto is A CVEVR DOLANT.DONE.VIE (To an aching heart give life), intimating that the seated putto is too debilitated to walk. On the lower right end, two putti armed with shields and a spear stand over a fallen putto who has dropped his shield but still holds a sword; as a girl comes to his aid, he points to his motto, ARDIS.VALLANT.COVRAIGE. ARRAY (Bold and valiant, I shall have courage). All of the figures are painted in grisaille, with glazes of light red. The accessories are blue, brown, and violet. The foregrounds are blue-green, the backgrounds a brilliant translucent red.

Condition: The plaques are in very good condition except for some crazing in the ruby backgrounds, occasional chips along the edges, and repairs to the sides of the left gable.

Caskets in this style and technique, decorated with scenes from the life of Hercules[2] or with putti at play, are traditionally given to Couly II Noylier. The models for the putti were available in North Italian engravings,[3] the sources of which, like those of the putti in contemporary Italian illuminations,[4] are to be sought in Roman wall paintings and sarcophagi.[5] The allusions on the Frick casket to the brevity of life and to the transitory delights of love, which should be plucked and savored in the bloom, reinterpret in the epicurean mood of the Renaissance the medieval tradition of courtly love reserved for the brave and the fair. Such themes were represented on ivory and leather caskets beginning about 1300.

The present casket must have been intended as a marriage gift, since the representation of Lucretia on the lid functions as an emblem of chaste fidelity. Some twenty-four enamelled caskets displaying putti in more or less allegorical contexts are known.[6]

Exhibitions: London, Victoria and Albert Museum, 1901–12, lent by J. Pierpont Morgan. New York, Metropolitan Museum, Morgan Collection, 1914–16, lent by J. Pierpont Morgan.

Collections: J. Pierpont Morgan, London and New York. Duveen. Frick, 1916.

NOTES

1 Compare stylistically the scrollwork and two putti holding a wreath enclosing the arms of France on a folio dated 1539 in a Book of Hours of François I (British Mu-

seum, London, Loan Ms. 58; reproduced in *British Museum Quarterly,* XXXI, Nos. 3/4, Pl. XXX).

2 For these see P. Verdier, *The Walters Art Gallery: Catalogue of the Painted Enamels of the Renaissance,* Baltimore, 1967, No. 67, pp. 132–37.

3 Putti at play appear frequently in engravings by Nicoletto da Modena, Zoan Andrea, Giovanni Antonio da Brescia, the early Master of the Otto Prints, the Master of the Sforza Book of Hours, the monogrammist F. B., the monogrammist NA. DAT, Jacopo Francia, and Giulio and Domenico Campagnola. The motif passed from Italy into German and Netherlandish engravings—for example, the prints of Israhel van Meckenem and Lucas van Leyden.

4 Swarms of putti appear in Italian illuminations dating from the last third of the fifteenth century. They were painted, for example, by Martino da Modena, dancing and playing instruments, in a *Missale romanum* made by Cosimo Tura for Ercole I, Duke of

Ferrara and Modena, or for his son Ippolito (C. Santoro, *I codici miniati della Biblioteca Trivulziana,* Milan, 1958, No. 65, Pl. LII).

5 On Roman sarcophagi, putti often engage in adult activities. See: G. Rodenwaldt, in *Journal of Hellenic Studies,* LIII, 1933, pp. 181–213; R. Stuveras, *Le Putto dans l'art romain,* Brussels, 1969, Figs. 28, 35, 94, 96, 102, 131; Madame Turcan-Deleani, "Contribution à l'étude des amours dans l'art funéraire romain: Les Sarcophages à courses de chars," *Mélanges de l'École Française de Rome,* I, 1964, pp. 43–49. At other times putti symbolize by their sport the bliss awaiting in the afterlife those who have been initiated into the Dionysiac mysteries. See: *Syria,* X, 1929, pp. 217 ff.; E. R. Goodenough, *Jewish Symbols in the Greco-Roman Period,* London, 1958, VIII, pp. 6–21; R. Turcan, *Les Sarcophages romains à représentations dyonisiaques,* Paris, 1966; Stuveras, Figs. 12, 17. On Dionysiac sarcophagi, the spar rigged with a sail is a symbol of the life to come.

6 Those in public collections include: Museo

Nazionale, Florence, Carrand Collection, No. 1197; British Museum, No. 1913, 12–20, 90; Hermitage Museum, Leningrad (A. Darcel, *Collection Basilewsky,* Paris, 1874, No. 319); Badisches Landesmuseum, Karlsruhe, No. 65/34; Musée Municipal, Limoges (*Bulletin de la Société archéologique et historique du Limousin,* 1912, *Chronique,* p. 29); Victoria and Albert Museum, London, eight plaques and a casket, Salting Bequest, Nos. 912–3, 2161; Wallace Collection, London (É. Molinier, *La Collection Wallace* [*Objets d'art*], Paris, 1903, I, No. 256). Those in private collections include: Adda sale, Paris, November 29–December 3, 1965, Lot 182 (South Kensington Loan Exhibition of 1862, No. 1663); Antocolsky sale, Hôtel Drouot, Paris, June 10, 1901, Lot 56; M. Boy sale, Galerie Georges Petit, Paris, May 15–24, 1905, Lots 209, 210; E. Dreux sale, Galerie Georges Petit, Paris, December 5–6, 1911, Lot 169; Eugen Felix sale, Cologne, October 25–30, 1886, Lot 370; M. Heckscher sale, Christie's, May 4–6, 1898, Lot 172, repr.; A. Pringsheim sale, Munich, Lot 39; Charles Stein sale, Galerie Georges Petit, Paris, June 8–10, 1899, Lot 26; E. Vaïsse sale, Paris, May 5–8, 1885, Lot 163, repr.; former Baronne Édouard de Rothschild collection, Paris, three caskets.

Casket: Heads of the Caesars within Wreaths (16.4.15)

H. 4³/₁₆ in. (10.7 cm); W. 6¾ in. (17.2 cm); D. 4⁷/₁₆ in. (11.3 cm).

Description: The casket is mounted with twelve enamelled plaques, ten rectangular ones showing profile heads of the Caesars within wreaths held by winged putti and two trapezoidal gable plaques decorated with putti and mottoes. Each of the Caesars is identified by a vertical inscription in gold (see *Condition*). Of the two plaques on the front of the lid, that at left is inscribed IVLIVS CESAR and that at right OTAVIANO; on these plaques only, the wreaths are entwined with white ribbons (for the purple *lemniscus* or fillet of honor) and the ribbons carry in black the legends IVLIVS.CESAR PERMIER AN-PERVES (Julius Caesar, first emperor) and OTAVIANO SEGOVNDVS INPERA (Octavian, second emperor). The plaques on the back of the lid are inscribed DOM[I]TIANO (Domitian) at left and TIBERIO (Tiberius) at right. The lower end plaques each show two facing heads within a single oval wreath, that on the left end inscribed VESPASIANVS (Vespasian) and TITO (Titus), that on the right end reading NERO and DEBAVOLA (Caligula). The four lower plaques on the front and back of the casket are all inscribed VICELLIO (Vitellius); only that at front right is original (though it should be mounted at the left), and the others are rather weak modern copies. The gable plaques show similar scenes of a reclining putto leaning on a skull beneath a scroll inscribed MEMENTO.MORI.DICO (Remember that you must die, I say).[1] The gilt-copper frame, in the same style as that of the preceding casket, is inscribed on the top DEVM TIME (Fear God).[2] The plaques are painted in grisaille and color, with touches of gold, on a black ground. The flesh tints are rendered with a pink glaze over the grisaille modelling, and the lips are heightened with red. The hair is glazed blue or light brownish-red, the putti's wings are blue-green and reddish-purple or brown, and the wreaths are blue-green with red-violet berries.

Condition: The gold inscriptions on all but the three modern plaques are almost obliterated, and the lower corners of the Julius Caesar and Domitian plaques are damaged. Apart from its missing elements, the casket is otherwise in good condition.

The profile heads are after a series of the *Twelve Caesars* engraved by Marcantonio Raimondi.[3] In the prints the emperors are crowned with laurel wreaths tied by ribbons at the nape of the neck, but the enameller was not entirely consistent in rendering his models: Julius Caesar's crown has no ribbon, and in place of a crown Augustus wears a headdress of leather straps. The pairing of imperial profile heads face to face on the lower end plaques of the casket follows Roman models found on cameos and intaglios.[4]

When in the Soltykoff collection the present casket was attributed to Jean Péni-

98

caud. It was described in the South Kensington Loan Exhibition of 1862 as "probably by Pierre Reymond" and in the Spitzer catalogue as "from the Atelier of the Pénicauds," an attribution continued in the Burlington Fine Arts Club Exhibition of 1897. In the catalogue of the Gibson Carmichael sale it was classified as "in the manner of the Pénicauds." It seems clearly to be the work of an enameller who specialized in the production of caskets and who is known for his interest in historical portraits—that is, Couly II Noylier. However, depictions of the Twelve Caesars were not to become fashionable among the Limoges enamellers until well after the period of Couly's dated works (1539–45).

Exhibited: South Kensington Loan Exhibition, 1862, No. 1666, lent by George Attenborough. London, Burlington Fine Arts Club, 1897, No. 144, lent by Sir Thomas D. Gibson Carmichael. London, Victoria and Albert Museum, 1906–12, lent by J. Pierpont Morgan. New York, Metropolitan Museum, Morgan Collection, 1914–16, lent by J. Pierpont Morgan.

Collections: Soltykoff sale, April 8–May 1, 1861, Hôtel Drouot, Paris, Lot 350. George Attenborough, London. Frédéric Spitzer, Paris.[5] His sale, April 17–June 16, 1893, 33 rue de Villejust, Paris, Lot 461. Sir Thomas D. Gibson Carmichael, Salisbury. His sale, May 12, 1902, Christie's, Lot 75, sold to Durlacher for £700. J. Pierpont Morgan, London and New York. Duveen. Frick, 1916.

NOTES

1 The skull as a reminder of death appears among putti at play on a casket from the same workshop in the former Baronne Édouard de Rothschild collection, Paris. Compare the putto with a skull on the reverse of a medal dated 1458 by Giovanni Boldù (G. F. Hill and G. Pollard, *Renaissance Medals from the Samuel H. Kress Collection,* London, 1967, Fig. 142) and the putto with a skull, an hourglass, and the motto VIVE MEMOR LETHI in the *Emblemata* of Nicholas Reussner (Frankfurt, 1581, I, No. 37).

2 The frame, with its grotesques in the style of nielli by Peregrino da Cesena, its pilasters with cherub-head capitals, and its inscription, reproduces a type discussed in P. Verdier, *The Walters Art Gallery: Catalogue of the Painted Enamels of the Renaissance,* Baltimore, 1967, No. 67, pp. 132–37. Compare also the putti on the gables of the Walters casket.

3 H. Delaborde, *Marc-Antoine Raimondi,* Paris, 1887, Nos. 216–27, repr. p. 249. The reproduction of idealized portraits of the Caesars was initiated by the interest in numismatics that developed in humanist and archaeological circles in fifteenth-century Italy, as evidenced, for example, in the carvings on the façade of the Carthusian

church at Pavia. The new taste struck roots in Florence and spread from there and from Lombardy to England and France. Cardinal Georges d'Amboise, Archbishop of Rouen, one-time governor of Lombardy, and prime minister under Louis XII, imported through his agents in Italy three series of "imagines clipeatae" (medallion portraits) of Roman emperors and other ancients for his château at Gaillon (R. Weiss, "The Castle of Gaillon in 1509–10," *Journal of the Warburg and Courtauld Institutes,* XVI, 1953, pp. 1–12; M.-G. de La Coste-Mompère, "Les Mé-

daillons historiques de Gaillon," *La Revue des arts,* VII, 1957, pp. 65–70). The Twelve Caesars were painted within blue roundels by an assistant of Jean Bourdichon (A. Blum and P. Lauer, *La Miniature française aux XVème et XVIème siècles,* Paris, 1930, p. 86, Pl. 62), and fifteen roundels of emperors decorate a French translation of Julius Caesar's *Commentarii de bello gallico* (Bibliothèque Nationale, Paris, fr. 13429), a manuscript formerly in the library of François I at Fontainebleau. Andrea Fulvio's *Illustriū Ymagines,* first printed in Rome,

was published in Lyon in 1524, and iconographical repertories of emperors were issued in the mid-sixteenth century by Gesner
and Goltzius.

4 See: E. Babelon, *Catalogue des camées an-
tiques et modernes de la Bibliothèque Nationale,* Paris, 1897, Nos. 249, 294, 300; H. B.
Walters, *Catalogue of the Engraved Gems
and Cameos…in the British Museum,* London, 1926, No. 3619; G. M. Richter, *Engraved Gems of the Romans,* London, 1971,
Nos. 516, 543, 577–79, 592, 594a, 596, 623,
624, 774. A Roman cameo with facing bust

portraits of Julius Caesar and Augustus,
Tiberius and Germanicus, was mounted by
Étienne Delaune for Henri II between 1552
and 1559 (Babelon, No. 249; Y. Hackenbroch, "New Knowledge on Jewels and Designs after Étienne Delaune," *Connoisseur,*
CLXII, 1966, pp. 82–95). In Roman funer-
ary art, portrait heads enclosed in wreaths
carried by genii were usually intended to
suggest that the subject had been wafted
to immortality.

5 C. Popelin, in *La Collection Spitzer,* Paris,
1891, II, No. 45, Pl. VII.

LÉONARD LIMOUSIN

c. 1505–1575/77

The greatest exponent of the School of Fontainebleau in enamel painting, Léonard Limousin transposed into his production the Italian Mannerism and decorative formulas brought to the French court by Il Rosso, Primaticcio, and Nicolò dell'Abate. Trained probably in the workshop of Nardon and Jean I Pénicaud, he appears by the mid-1530s to have been introduced at court by his protector Jean de Langeac, Bishop of Limoges and counsellor to François I. In 1536 he signed "Leonardus Lemovicus inventor" on a covered cup decorated with subjects relating to the reconciliation of the King and the Emperor Charles V, and that same year he enamelled a portrait of François' wife, Eleanor of Austria. Among his major works are twelve large plaques of the Apostles enamelled in 1547, now in the church of Saint-Pierre at Chartres, and two reredoses of the Crucifixion and the Resurrection commissioned by Henri II in 1552 for the Sainte-Chapelle, Paris. Though he is best known for his portraits, some 130 of which have survived, over a thousand enamels of widely varying forms emanated from his shop, including tableware, vases, candlesticks, inkwells, mirrors, saltcellars, caskets, hunting horns, a famous backgammon board of 1537, and a fountain made in 1552 for Diane de Poitiers. Léonard Limousin was unusual among the enamellers of Limoges in that he occasionally invented his own compositions and also worked as an engraver and a painter—witness his painting of The Incredulity of St. Thomas *in the Musée Municipal at Limoges. He signed with his name in full or with his initials, sometimes flanking a fleur-de-lis or crowned by a vase containing a lily. The relationship of Léonard Limousin to the numerous other enamellers with the same surname has yet to be clearly established.*

Plaque: Guy Chabot, Baron de Jarnac (16.4.20)

9⅜ × 7¹/₁₆ in. (23.8 × 18 cm).

Description: Chabot is represented in bust length against a blue background, his face turned three-quarters to the left. He wears a black coat enriched with gold embroidery and tassels, a black cap with similar tassels, a white frill, and the badge and collar of the Order of Saint-Michel.[1] The flesh tones are

pinkish shading to brownish-red, the beard and moustache are chestnut turning to gray, and the eyes are brown.

Condition: The plaque is in good condition.

The corners have been damaged and repaired, and further repairs are visible along the right side, including part of the shoulder. There is considerable crazing in the blue background.

Plaque: Louise de Pisseleu, Madame de Jarnac (16.4.21)

$9\,\frac{1}{8} \times 6\,^{13}/_{16}$ in. (23.2 × 17.3 cm).

Description: Madame de Jarnac is shown in bust length against a blue background, her face turned three-quarters to the right. She wears a black headdress over a white coif, a black dress outlined with gold, and a white collar. The flesh tones are pinkish shading to gray and brown, the hair and eyes are brown.

Condition: The plaque is in very good condition, though the gold outlines of the costume have largely disappeared.

The identification of the subjects is due to de Montégut, who published the portraits in 1910.[2] They were recorded by a member of the Roullet family and two notaries in an inventory of the Château de Jarnac dated November 29, 1762, at which time they were described as two small paintings enamelled in blue (in reference to their backgrounds) mounted in an old frame. They remained in the family's possession until the death in the late nineteenth century of Mademoiselle Roullet, the last heir. The old frame has not survived.

Guy Chabot, Baron de Jarnac, was named Seneschal of Périgord in 1545 and served as Governor of La Rochelle in 1561–62. He is best remembered for his duel with François de Vivonne La Châtaigneraie, fought in 1547 before Henri II, Diane de Poitiers, and the court at Saint-Germain-en-Laye. Seeking to avenge his honor, Chabot hamstrung his opponent with an unexpected—and perhaps unpremeditated—blow, an incident that gave rise to the term "coup de Jarnac," descriptive of a sudden and decisive stroke against an adversary. Chabot converted to Protestantism in 1560. In that same year Hubert Goltzius visited him at Amboise and mentioned him as one of the great art collectors of his time. Chabot died in 1584.

Louise de Pisseleu was the daughter of Guillaume de Heilly and was related to Anne de Pisseleu, Duchesse d'Étampes, the mistress of François I.[3] She married Chabot in 1541 and died before 1560.

Various disparities between the two plaques suggest that they may not have been

executed at the same time. Their dimensions differ slightly, and in the portrait of Madame de Jarnac the scale is conspicuously larger, the blue background is considerably darker, and the technique is broader and more summary. Furthermore, the portraits do not follow the traditional treatment for pendants of husband and wife, in which the former usually is turned toward the viewer's right and the latter toward the viewer's left. For these reasons it seems quite possible that the portrait of Jarnac—which, like the other four male portraits by Léonard Limousin in The Frick Collection, shows the subject facing left—was executed as an independent work, and that the pendant was done at some later date.

Exhibited: London, Victoria and Albert Museum, 1901–12, lent by J. Pierpont Morgan. New York, Metropolitan Museum, Morgan Collection, 1914–16, lent by J. Pierpont Morgan.

Collections: Roullet family, Château de Jarnac, Angoumois. Charles Stein, Paris. His sale, June 8–10, 1899, Galerie Georges Petit, Paris, Lots 18, 19. J. Pierpont Morgan, London and New York. Duveen. Frick, 1916.

NOTES

1 The Order of Saint-Michel was created by Louis XI on August 1, 1469, for a limited number of knights of noble birth. Chabot wears the collar and badge of the order but not the costume donned by the knights for their chapters.

2 H. de Montégut, "Deux Émaux attribués à Léonard Limousin de la collection Pierpont Morgan," *Chronique des arts et de la curiosité* (supplement to the *Gazette des Beaux-Arts*), December 31, 1910, pp. 315–17. In a letter to J.-J. Marquet de Vasselot written January 3, 1911, and preserved among the latter's papers at the Louvre, Louis Dimier, who had a hypercritical mind and a low opinion of Léonard Limousin, stated that de Montégut's identification lacked corroboration and that it was in fact rendered impossible by the costumes, which he said

did not date beyond 1540. He apparently was unaware that Chabot and his wife were married in 1541.

3 Beauchet-Filleau and de Chergé, *Dictionnaire historique et général des familles du Poitou,* II, pp. 187 ff. The features of Madame de Jarnac are recorded in a drawing done by Jean Clouet after 1539, showing her dressed "à la mode de la reine" (R. de Broglie, "Les Clouet de Chantilly," *Gazette des Beaux-Arts,* LXXVII, 1971, No. 280, p. 318; compare No. 287, p. 319, and note the family resemblance in the portrait of Perrone de Pisseleu, No. 228, p. 309). Raoul de Broglie, former Director of the Musée Condé at Chantilly, has kindly written the author that the identification proposed by de Montégut is likely to be correct.

108

Plaque: Portrait of a Man (16.4.16)

Signed and dated, in gold, at lower right: LL · 1542. 5¹/₁₆ × 4⁵/₁₆ in. (12.9 × 11 cm).

Description: The subject is shown in half length behind a table covered with a light blue cloth, his face in three-quarter view to the left, his hands clasped before him around a white scroll. He wears a black coat and doublet, a white collar and cuffs, and a flat black cap. His features display a prominent aquiline nose, a thin moustache, sideburns, and a stubbly beard. The flesh tints range from pinkish-white in the light to pale red and gray in the shadows; the eyes are blue, the hair is brown. The background is cobalt blue speckled with gold, and the composition is framed by a black enamel band outlined in gold, with a narrow white stripe at the border.

Condition: The plaque is in good condition. Some enamel is missing from the lower left corner, and repairs are visible along the edges, in the upper forehead, and in the adjacent parts of the hat and hair. The blue background shows considerable crazing and has lost most of its gold flecks.

In the catalogue of the Hollingworth Magniac sale, the subject of the present portrait was thought to resemble Antoine de Bourbon, King of Navarre (1518–62).[1] That identification would be in keeping with the date on the plaque. However, the likeness is not strong, and an equally convincing case might be argued in favor of other notables of the period. One such candidate would be Antoine de Bourbon's father-in-law, Henri d'Albret, King of Navarre (1503–55), assuming that the portrait was done after a somewhat earlier model.[2]

Exhibited: London, South Kensington Loan Exhibition, 1862, No. 1696, lent by Hollingworth Magniac. London, Victoria and Albert Museum, 1901–12, lent by J. Pierpont Morgan. New York, Metropolitan Museum, Morgan Collection, 1914–16, lent by J. Pierpont Morgan.

Collections: Irisson sale, March 14 *et seq.*, 1850, Paris, Lot 150. Hollingworth Magniac, London. His sale, July 2 *et seq.*, 1892, Christie's, Lot 395, sold to Goldschmidt for £231. Charles Mannheim, Paris (1898). J. Pierpont Morgan, London and New York. Duveen. Frick, 1916.

NOTES

1 For portraits of Antoine de Bourbon, see pp. 118–20 of the present catalogue. The indication in the Magniac catalogue that the enamel had formerly been in the collection

of Horace Walpole at Strawberry Hill is incorrect. The confusion stems from the fact that Lots 397 and 398 in the Magniac sale, enamelled portraits of Marguerite, Queen of Navarre, and of Antoine de Bourbon (roundel, D. 3¼ in.), were at Strawberry Hill (Walpole sale catalogue, Strawberry Hill, April 25–May 24, 1842, Lot 33, p. 198, as "Henry [d'Albret], King of Navarre, and his wife, Queen Margaret, enamels by Laudin"; compare Lots 39 and 40, and see pp. 118 and 120 of the present catalogue, notes 1 and 2).

2 Among the supposed portraits of Henri d'Albret enamelled by Léonard Limousin are: one in the Louvre, Baronne Salomon de Rothschild Bequest, 1922; one in the Wallace Collection, London; one dated 1548 in the former Pourtalès and Baron Gustave de Rothschild collections (L. Bourdery and E. Lachenaud, *Léonard Limosin,* Paris, 1897, No. 89, repr. facing p. 228); one dated 1556 in the Jules S. Bache Collection at the Metropolitan Museum of Art, New York (O. Raggio, "Decorative Portraits by Léonard Limousin," *Metropolitan Museum of Art Bulletin,* X, 1951, repr. p. 103); and one in the Musée Condé at Chantilly (Soltykoff sale, Hôtel Drouot, Paris, April 8–May 1, 1861, Lot 1044, sold for 17,700 francs to the Duc d'Aumale; South Kensington Loan Exhibition, 1862, No. 1697, as a portrait of Jean de Bourbon, Comte d'Enghien, who died in 1557).

Plaque: Guillaume Farel (?) (16.4.17)

Signed and dated, in gold, at lower right: LL · 1546 (much effaced). 7⁹/₁₆ × 5⅝ in. (19.2 × 14.3 cm).

Description: The head and shoulders of a bearded man, his face turned three-quarters to the left, are seen behind a table covered with a green cloth. The flesh tones are pink shading to gray, the eyes are brown, and the beard and moustache are grayish-brown, originally touched with gold. The hat, fur-trimmed coat, and doublet are black with traces of gilding, and the collar is white. The background is blue, and the composition is framed by a dark violet band, almost black, outlined in gold and bordered at the outside by a white stripe.

Condition: The plaque is in good condition except for varying degrees of damage at the corners, crazing in the blue background, and some fading of the gold, most notably in the signature and date.

In *The Frick Collection Catalogue* of 1955,[1] Breck proposed a resemblance between the subject of the present portrait and that of an enamel showing an unidentified man in a furred robe, signed with the same initials and date, in the former Czartoryski collection.[2] However, the man in the latter plaque wears the biretta of the Roman Catholic hierarchy, whereas the hat in the Frick enamel is of the type usually associated with Calvinist ministers, though in this case it does not cover the ears. The cut of the beard also resembles that favored by sixteenth-century Calvinists.

It is plausible that the present enamel was copied after a portrait of Guillaume Farel (1489–1565). Born near Gap in the Dauphiné, Farel taught at the college of Cardinal Lemoine in Paris but was forced to flee France in 1526 after the condemnation by the Paris *Parlement* of the "Bibliens"—the Lutherans of Meaux. He became minister of the reformed church at Montbéliard in Franche-Comté and preached in Switzerland at Neuchâtel, Lausanne, and in the canton of Bern. The identification of the enamel with Farel is based on an engraving of him in Théodore de Bèze's *Icones* of 1580[3] and on another, showing him among a group of Calvinists, published after the death of de Bèze in 1605.[4] Due to the time interval between the enamel and the engravings, the identification remains tentative. If it is correct, Léonard Limousin would have enamelled at least three por-

traits of French Protestant theologians, including the famous one of Calvin done in 1535 and one of de Bèze made at an uncertain date.[5]

Exhibited: London, Victoria and Albert Museum, 1909–12, lent by J. Pierpont Morgan. New York, Metropolitan Museum, Morgan Collection, 1914–16, lent by J. Pierpont Morgan.

Collections: J. Pierpont Morgan, London and New York. Duveen. Frick, 1916.

NOTES

1 J. Breck, in *The Frick Collection Catalogue,* VII, 1955, p. 26.
2 L. Bourdery and E. Lachenaud, *Léonard Limosin,* Paris, 1897, No. 94, pp. 241–42, repr. facing p. 240.
3 The French edition of the *Icones,* entitled *Les Vrais Portraits des hommes illustres en piété et doctrine,* was published by Jean de Laon at Geneva in 1581; for Farel see pp. 123–25.
4 E. Doumergue, *Iconographie calvinienne,* Lausanne, 1909, pp. 197–200, repr. p. 199. The print was made in Amsterdam by Jan Houwens, with explanatory captions in German by H. Bergius Nardenus.
5 The Calvin portrait, contemporary with the preparation for press of the first edition of his *Institutes of the Christian Religion* (1536), appeared in the Spitzer sale, 33 rue de Villejust, Paris, April 17–June 16, 1893, Lot 484, bought for 14,000 francs by Sir Julius Wernher, and is now in the Wernher collection at Luton Hoo, Bedfordshire. The de Bèze portrait was in the collection of Baron James de Rothschild. Jean II Pénicaud enamelled portraits of Luther and Erasmus; these appeared—as works by Léonard Limousin—in the Soltykoff sale, Hôtel Drouot, Paris, April 8–May 1, 1861, Lots 1049, 1050, sold respectively to James de Rothschild for 12,000 francs and to Baron Seillière for 14,300 francs.

Plaque: Odet de Coligny, Cardinal de Châtillon (16.4.19)

$7^7/_{16} \times 5\frac{1}{4}$ in. (19 × 13.4 cm).

Description: Coligny is shown in bust length, his face turned three-quarters to the left, behind a table top of translucent green enamel. The flesh tones are pink shading to light red and gray, the eyes are blue, the hair, beard, and moustache are light brown. He wears a black coat with traces of gilding, a white fur collar shaded with green and gray, and sleeves and biretta of translucent orange shading to red. The background is blue, and the plaque is bordered by gold fillets within a narrow black band.

Condition: The plaque is in good condition except for repairs in the upper right corner and both lower corners, possible further repairs along the outlines of the coat, and some crazing.

Odet de Coligny, Cardinal de Châtillon (1515–71), was the eldest son of Gaspard I de Coligny, Marshall of France. Odet was named Cardinal at the age of eighteen and became successively Archbishop of Toulouse and Count-Bishop of Beauvais. Converted to Calvinism, he was deprived of his ecclesiastical ranks and excommunicated in 1563. He then married Élisabeth de Hauteville and assumed the title of Comte de Beauvais. After fighting in the Huguenot ranks at the battle of Saint-Denis (1567), he fled to England to escape arrest. He was poisoned by his valet as he was preparing to return to France after the peace of 1570.

The identification of the Frick plaque with Odet de Coligny is established by comparison with drawings and paintings by François Clouet and his studio, including: a painted portrait dated 1548 in the Musée Condé at Chantilly, long attributed to Primaticcio but reassigned to Clouet by Charles Sterling; a second portrait and a drawing also at Chantilly; and four other drawings, in the British Museum, London, the Bibliothèque Nationale and Bibliothèque du Protestantisme Français, Paris, and the Uffizi, Florence. The Frick plaque is also close to the likeness of Odet in a group portrait of about 1555 in the Mauritshuis, The Hague, showing him with his two brothers, Gaspard II de Coligny, Admiral of France (1519–72), and François de Coligny, Seigneur d'Andelot (1521–69). Numerous other portraits are known.[1]

It is quite possible that Léonard Limousin enamelled the present portrait directly after the above-mentioned Clouet drawing at Chantilly.[2] Though the two likenesses differ somewhat in total effect, they correspond precisely in many of the particulars—for example in the diagonal line of the right eyebrow, the irregular contour of the lower lip, the folds under the eyes, and even the loops of the frill. As the subject appears to be a few years older in the drawing than in the Chantilly painting of 1548, Léonard may have enamelled his copy some time around 1552, the year in which Rabelais dedicated the fourth book of *Pantagruel* to the "très illustre prince et reverendissime Monseigneur Odet Cardinal de Chastillon."

Exhibited: London, Victoria and Albert Museum, 1903 and 1908–12, lent by J. Pierpont Morgan. Glasgow, Kelvingrove Art Gallery, 1903–08. New York, Metropolitan Museum, Morgan Collection, 1914–16, lent by J. Pierpont Morgan.

Collections: J. Pierpont Morgan, London and New York. Duveen. Frick, 1916.

NOTES

1 F.-G. Pariset and R. de Broglie, *Institut de France: Chantilly, Musée Condé: Peintures de l'école française...XVIe siècle,* Paris, 1970, No. 7. *Musée Condé,* IV, 1973, Nos. 14, 103. L. Dimier, *Histoire de la peinture de portrait en France au XVIème siècle,* Paris–Brussels, 1924–26, II, No. 1390, p. 341, No. 665, p. 161, No. 1341, p. 332 (Cabinet des Estampes, Bibliothèque Nationale, rec. Na 21, fol. 68 vo.), No. 421, p. 105 (Uffizi, No. 14925). *Coligny: Protestants et Catholiques en France au XVIème siècle,* exhibition catalogue, Archives Nationales, Paris, 1972, Nos. 454, 401 (compare Dimier, No. 768, p. 187, and *Oud-Holland,* XLVII, 1930, repr. facing p. 224).

2 *Musée Condé,* No. 103.

Plaque: Antoine de Bourbon, King of Navarre (?) (16.4.18)

Signed, in gold, on the table top at right: LL. 5⅛ × 4¼ in. (13 × 10.8 cm).

Description: The subject is shown in half length behind a table draped in green, his face turned three-quarters to the left. The flesh tints shade from whitish-pink to light red and gray, the eyes are blue, the hair and beard are dark brown, and the moustache is light brown. He wears a coat of black pourpoint, a small white frill at the neck, and a black cap—a costume that became fashionable after 1560. The background is blue flecked with gold. Framing the composition is a band of golden-brown translucent enamel hatched with gold along the top and right side to suggest a light source from below and to the left; outside the brown is a band of black, and this in turn is edged with white.

Condition: The plaque is in good condition apart from repairs at upper right, along the lower edge of the gold band at top, and along a horizontal crack that runs through the drapery at bottom. The gold on the blue background is largely effaced.

When the present plaque was in the Hollingworth Magniac collection,[1] it was conjectured, on the basis of comparison with an enamelled roundel in the same collection[2] as well as with other enamelled portraits,[3] that it represented Antoine de Bourbon and that it had been executed some time after the roundel, about 1560. A date of around 1560 is also given to an enamelled portrait of Antoine de Bourbon in the Musée Condé at Chantilly, though the identification of that work is open to question.[4]

Antoine de Bourbon (1518–62), second son of Charles de Bourbon, Duc de Vendôme, was married in 1548 to Jeanne, daughter of Henri d'Albret, King of Navarre (see Frick No. 16.4.16, p. 109). After the death of his father-in-law, Antoine became in 1555 King of Navarre and Duc d'Albret. From his marriage with Jeanne d'Albret was born Henri IV, King of France.

Exhibited: London, South Kensington Loan Exhibition, 1862, No. 1702, lent by Hollingworth Magniac.

Collections: Hollingworth Magniac, London. His sale, July 2 *et seq.,* 1892, Christie's, Lot 399. Charles Mannheim, Paris.[5] J. Pierpont Morgan, London and New York. Duveen. Frick, 1916.

NOTES

1 In the Magniac sale catalogue, the Frick plaque (Lot 399) is incorrectly said to have been purchased at the sale of Horace Walpole's collection at Strawberry Hill in 1842.

The error stems from a confusion either with Lot 39 in the twentieth day of the Walpole sale—"a small portrait of Anthony king of Navarre, father of Henry IV, king of France, beautifully finished, equal to a fine miniature, Janet"—or with Walpole Lot 33 (see note 2, below). The dimensions of Magniac Lot 399 were given as $4\frac{1}{2} \times 4$ in.; the enamel sold for £210.

2 Magniac sale, Lot 398, from the Walpole sale, Lot 33; compare p.109 of the present catalogue, note 1. After having been shown at the South Kensington Loan Exhibition of 1862 (No.1701), the roundel entered the collection of Alphonse de Rothschild through the Stettiner and Léguillon collections (Léguillon sale, Hôtel Drouot, Paris, December 9, 1895, Lot 16). In L. Bourdery and E. Lachenaud, *Léonard Limosin,* Paris, 1897, No.93, pp.237–40, the subject of the roundel is identified as Henri d'Albret. For successive sales, see E. Lachenaud, *Émaux de Limoges: Collectionneurs du XVIIIe et XIXe siècles,* Ms. at the Musée Municipal, Limoges, V, p.165, repr. p. 165B. The roundel was subsequently in the former Baronne Édouard de Rothschild collection, Paris.

3 Victoria and Albert Museum, London, No. 8416–1863 (from the Soulages sale, London, December 1856) and No.C. 2414–1910 (from the Salting collection). The latter enamel presents a closer likeness. Portraits thought to represent Antoine de Bourbon exhibit approximately the same features: a drooping, thin moustache with curling ends and a shaven chin with a forked, cropped beard.

4 *Musée Condé,* IV, 1973, No.109 (from the Debruge-Duménil sale, Hôtel des Ventes, Paris, January 23 *et seq.,* 1850, Lot 703, and the Soltykoff sale, Hôtel Drouot, Paris, April 8–May 1, 1861, Lot 1043). Bought for 15,750 francs by the Duc d'Aumale, it was shown at the South Kensington Loan Exhibition of 1862 (No.1700). See: J. Labarte, *Histoire des arts industriels au moyen âge et à la renaissance,* Paris, 1864, II, Pl.CXV; Bourdery and Lachenaud, No.2, pp.6–13. On the iconography of Antoine de Bourbon, see also L. Dimier, *Histoire de la peinture de portrait en France au XVIème siècle,* Paris–Brussels, 1924–26, III, Nos. 47–49, pp.252–53.

5 É. Molinier, *Collection Charles Mannheim,* Paris, 1898, No.172, subject not identified.

Plaque: Triumph of the Eucharist and of the Catholic Faith
(16.4.22)

Signed, in gold, on the base of the obelisk at right: LEONARD.L. $7^9/_{16} \times 9^7/_8$ in. (19.2 × 25.1 cm).

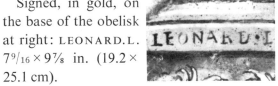

Description: Orthodox Catholicism is personified by Antoinette de Bourbon, Duchesse de Guise, who is carried in triumph in a golden chariot drawn by four white doves amid rosy clouds. Clad in black and white, she holds in her outstretched left hand a gold chalice with the consecrated wafer and in her right hand a cross draped with a wreath and surmounted by the titulus INRI. The chariot crushes beneath its wheels a group of heretics (see below). Standing at center are her husband, Claude de Lorraine, first Duc de Guise, dressed in blue, black, and white and resting his right hand on the hilt of his sword, and her fourth son, Louis de Lorraine, second Cardinal de Guise, in scarlet gown and biretta. At far left, dressed in white and gold except for a black cap and cape, his left hand on the wheel of the chariot, is her eldest son, François de Lorraine, second Duc de Guise. At right, wearing a black biretta and gown and holding a white book, is her second son, Charles de Lorraine, first Cardinal de Guise and second Cardinal de Lorraine. Near him rises a lavender-colored, ivy-wreathed obelisk about which is twined a white scroll with the inverted inscription TE STANTE VIREBO (see below). The landscape background is painted in green, yellow-green, and blue. The flesh tones are enamelled in grisaille stippled with light red.

Condition: The plaque is in generally good condition. There are repairs at all four corners, along part of the left edge, in the gown and doublet of the two central figures, in scattered areas at lower left, and below the obelisk at right. The gold inscriptions identifying the heretics (see below) have all but disappeared, and the gilt patterns on Louis de Lorraine's gown and François de Lorraine's doublet have faded

The House of Guise played a leading role in the political and religious strife in France during the sixteenth century. Claude de Lorraine (1496–1550) and Antoinette de Bourbon (1498–1583) had seven sons and five daughters, one of whom became the mother of Mary Queen of Scots. Their eldest son, François (1519–63), was killed by a Protestant fanatic, and his eldest son, Henri, was assassinated at Blois by order of King Henri III in 1588, together with his younger brother Louis, third Cardinal de Guise. Charles (1524–74), who became Archbishop of Reims in 1538, first Cardinal de Guise in 1547, and second Cardinal de Lorraine in 1550, was a bitter foe of the Protestants; he founded the university at Reims. Louis (1527–78), second Cardinal de Guise, had a jovial character which earned him the nickname "Cardinal bouteilles"; he crowned Henri III in 1575.

The features of Claude de Lorraine and his wife on the Frick plaque are virtually identical to those found on a pair of portraits by Léonard Limousin in the Musée de Cluny, Paris, showing the couple as founders of the monastery of Notre-Dame-de-Pitié near their château at Joinville. The Cluny portraits were acquired from the Hôpital Sainte-Croix at Joinville, which was founded by Antoinette de Bourbon and her son Charles in 1567. The identities of the other three foreground figures on the plaque can be ascertained by comparisons with the following: an enamelled portrait of François de Lorraine in the Louvre, done by Léonard Limousin in 1557; two enamelled portraits of Louis de Lorraine also by Léonard Limousin, one in the Victoria and Albert Museum, London (from the Danby Seymour collection), and the other in the former Baronne Édouard de Rothschild collection, Paris; and a portrait of Charles de Lorraine done in 1572 by the Flemish painter Georges Boba, of which there are three versions, one in bust and two full-length, at Reims.[1]

The twenty heretics crushed by the chariot of the Catholic Faith were originally identified by gilt inscriptions near their heads. The gold, applied after the firing of the enamel, is now almost completely obliterated, but faint traces are still visible under a raking light. These were deciphered by Ritchie in 1939[2] as follows: IEHAN HVS (Jan Hus, the Bohemian reformer); DONATVS (either of two fourth-century heretics); BEZE (Théodore de Bèze, the Calvinist scholar and preacher); ADAMITE (a personification of the primitivizing sect of that name whose beliefs included a return to an Adam-like state of nudity); FRATRICELLI (the name of a heretical branch of the Franciscan order); PRAGE (Jerome of Prague, a follower of Jan Hus); ARIVS (another fourth-century heretic); CALVIN; ANABAPTISTE (personification of a Protestant sect ruthlessly suppressed by the Guise family); VABAPT (apparently a second reference to the Anabaptists); and a fragment ending in the letters VS (possibly, since it accompanies a Turkish head, the conclusion of Aenobarbus, the Latinized name of the sixteenth-century Turkish admiral better known as Barbarossa). Inscriptions for the remaining heads either have left no trace or never existed.

Conspicuously absent among the heretics is Martin Luther, who would be recognizable even if his name had completely faded away. This omission may be due to the fact that Luther was not definitely anathematized until the Council of

Trent in 1563, or perhaps to the alliance in effect between the French monarchy and the Lutheran princes of Germany against the Empire.[3]

The book held in the plaque by Charles, second Cardinal de Lorraine, could represent the thesis in defense of the Catholic dogma of Transubstantiation that he sustained against Théodore de Bèze at the Colloquy of Poissy in 1561.[4] On his deathbed in 1550, Claude de Lorraine had solemnly confessed his faith in the real presence of Christ in the Eucharist and had exhorted his sons to fight for it, with the sword if necessary.[5]

The stage-like setting of the Frick plaque is borrowed from allegorical compositions for which the *Trionfi* of Petrarch—in which the sixth Triumph is that of Faith—and the *Triumphus Crucis* of Savonarola had established a fashion among the emblemata of the Renaissance. Pageants of Religion Triumphant were often performed when French monarchs entered cities.[6] In a relief on the Hôtel de Bourgthéroulde at Rouen, the Trinity is carried in a chariot which is drawn by the four Evangelists and crushes beneath its wheels a group of heretics.[7] The motif of François de Lorraine pushing one of the wheels of the Guise chariot may owe its inspiration to an engraving by Bonifazio Veneziano in which the Fathers of the Church push the wheels of a chariot on which Christ is enthroned.[8] Léonard could also have seen in the Royal collection the Roman cameo, now in the Cabinet des Médailles of the Bibliothèque Nationale, Paris, on which is carved an Imperial charioteer (possibly Licinius) charging over the bodies of his enemies.[9] Representations of the Triumph of Faith analogous to that on the Frick plaque are frequent in sixteenth-century French stained glass.[10]

The immediate source of Antoinette de Bourbon's chariot drawn by a team of four doves is the chariot of Venus in Marcantonio Raimondi's famous engraving *Quos Ego*. Possibly the doves on the plaque have a connotation of peace—that is, peace achieved through victory.[11] The chariot floats on clouds, as do those of the planets in the Italian prints that, copied by French and German engravers, inspired sets of Limoges enamelled plates[12] and were adapted by Léonard Limousin in a series of plaques showing political figures with the attributes of gods and goddesses.[13] Faith holding a crucifix and a chalice with the consecrated wafer was enamelled, after an engraving of Hans Burgkmair, by an anonymous Limoges artist working somewhat in the manner of Couly Noylier.[14]

The motto "Te stante virebo" (While you stand I shall flourish) was added to

124

the emblem of the second Cardinal de Lorraine, an obelisk twined with ivy, after Henri II had named him Chancellor of the Order of Saint-Michel in 1547.[15] The obelisk should properly culminate in a crescent moon. Some time after the death of Henri II in 1559 the Cardinal changed his motto to "Adhaesit anima mea post te" (My soul has clung to thee), which made of the obelisk no longer a royal support for the ivy but a symbol of reliance on God.[16] This is good reason for dating the enamel no later than 1561, the year of the Colloquy of Poissy, which is in all likelihood connected, as Ritchie has proposed,[17] with the commissioning of the present allegorical representation of the Guise family.

Exhibited: London, Victoria and Albert Museum, 1905–12, lent by J. Pierpont Morgan. New York, Metropolitan Museum, Morgan Collection, 1914–16, lent by J. Pierpont Morgan.

Collections: J. Pierpont Morgan, London and New York. Duveen. Frick, 1916.

NOTES

1 For a comprehensive summary of material related to the Frick plaque, including reproductions of the enamels in the Musée de Cluny, the Louvre, and the Victoria and Albert Museum, see A. C. Ritchie, "Léonard Limosin's Triumph of the Faith, with Portraits of the House of Guise," *Art Bulletin,* XXI, 1939, pp. 238–50. See also: L. Bourdery and E. Lachenaud, *Léonard Limosin,* Paris, 1897, Nos. 71–77, pp. 171–90; L. Dimier, *Histoire de la peinture de portrait en France au XVIème siècle,* Paris–Brussels, 1924–26, I, pp. 118–19, Pl. 42, II, Nos. 774, 776–79, pp. 191–92. The plaque in the former Baronne de Rothschild collection is from the collections of Hollingworth Magniac (his sale, Christie's, July 2 *et seq.,* 1892, Lot 250, erroneously described as a portrait of Louis II de Lorraine) and Baron Alphonse de Rothschild.

2 *Op. cit.,* pp. 242–46.

3 In a later propaganda print, a Catholic engraver represented Luther and Calvin riding horses hitched to the chariot of Libera Religio, which crushes under its wheels the insignia of the French monarchy and books of orthodox religious teaching (E. Doumergue, *Iconographie calvinienne,* Lausanne, 1909, p. 156, Fig. 158).

4 See *Histoire ecclésiastique des églises réformées au royaume de France,* ed. G. Baum and E. Cunitz, I, 1883, pp. 493–94. On the conciliatory attitude of the Cardinal de Lorraine toward the "blasphemy" of de Bèze against the real presence of Christ in the Eucharist, see P. F. Geisendorf, *Théodore de Bèze,* Geneva, 1949, pp. 148–51.

5 *Livre I de l'Histoire de la Maison de Guise par Odier en 1647,* Bibliothèque Nationale, Paris, Ms. français 5798, fol. 137.

6 É. Mâle, *L'Art religieux de la fin du moyen âge en France,* Paris, 1908, pp. 302–03, note 1.

7 P. Vitry, *Hôtels et maisons de la renaissance française,* Paris, n.d., II, Pl. LII. The Hôtel de Bourgthéroulde was badly shaken by bombing during World War II, but the Triumph of the Trinity escaped intact.

8 Prince d'Essling and E. Müntz, *Pétrarque,* Paris, 1902, p. 252. The print reflects a lost composition by Botticelli inspired by the *Triumphus Crucis* of Savonarola. It was copied in a stained-glass window for the church of Notre-Dame at Brou, Ain (Mâle, Fig. 143; compare Fig. 140, erroneously attributed to Titian), and in a woodcut illus-

trating Petrarch's *Trionfi* published by Guillaume Roville (or Rouillé) at Lyon in 1550.

9 See *Jahrbuch des deutschen archäologischen Instituts,* XXXVII, 1922, pp. 22–25.

10 Compare for example the window entitled the Three Chariots at Saint-Vincent, Rouen, done about 1522–24, and the Triumph of the Cross window at Saint-Patrice, Rouen, about 1540.

11 Peace, as one of the Beatitudes, is represented with a dove, a shield, and a helmet in a painting of the School of Fontainebleau reproduced by J. Bousquet in *La Peinture maniériste,* Neuchâtel, 1964, facing p. 72.

12 F. Lippmann, *Die sieben Planeten,* Berlin, 1895, Pls. I–IV. B. Rackham, "The Sources of Design in Italian Majolica," *Burlington Magazine,* XXIII, 1913, pp. 193–203. H. Röttinger, *Die Holzschnitte des Georg Pencz,* Leipzig, 1914, Nos. 1–7. P. Verdier, *The Walters Art Gallery: Catalogue of the Painted Enamels of the Renaissance,* Baltimore, 1967, No. 168, pp. 304–07.

13 Twelve of these representations can be recorded: Apollo and Diana (Abbé P. Guilbert, *Description historique des chateau, bourg et forest de Fontainebleau,* Paris, 1731, I, p. 87); Charles IX as Mars, dated 1573 (J. Labarte, *Description des objets d'art qui composent la collection Debruge-Duménil,* Paris, 1847, No. 704); two plaques representing Ceres as Cybele, one at Waddesdon Manor, Buckinghamshire, the other in the former Baronne Édouard de Rothschild collection, Paris; Diane de Poitiers as Cybele, British Museum (Waddesdon Bequest, No. 39); Juno and Venus on a single plaque, in the museum at Brunswick; Juno,

at Waddesdon Manor; and Charles IX as the sun god Sol, dated 1573, Henri III, and Louise de Lorraine as Venus, dated 1574, in the former collection of Baronne de Rothschild. The chariot in the Venus-Louise plaque is the same as that of Antoinette de Bourbon in the Frick plaque.

14 Musée de Cluny, No. 914.

15 M. Dutilleux, "Notice sur... le texte des statuts de l'Ordre de Saint-Michel," *Mémoires de la Société des Sciences morales de Seine-et-Oise,* XIV, 1885. A pyramid with the motto "Te stante virebo" was erected by the Cardinal before the portal of the abbey at Cluny.

16 *Devises héroïques et emblèmes de M. Claude Paradin revues et augmentées de moytié,* Paris, 1614, pp. 93–94; the first edition of Paradin's *Devises héroïques* appeared in 1557. It is possible that the absence of the moon in the Frick plaque alludes to the death of the King, or perhaps to the total eclipse of the crescent moon adopted by Diane de Poitiers as her emblem. Henri's motto "Donec totum impleat orbem" (Until it covers all the earth) implied expectation of the victory of the Church Militant, symbolized by the moon, over the tyrants and heretics. When the King entered Lyon in triumph on September 23, 1548, the decorations included an obelisk surmounted by a three-foot-wide crescent moon bearing his motto and a triumphal arch topped by a figure of Diana with the inscription "Lux aeterna" (Eternal light) on the crescent of her headdress (see *La Magnificence de la superbe et triumphante entrée...,* published by Roville at Lyon in 1549). The Cardinal de Lorraine's emblem, the obelisk twined

with ivy and capped with a crescent moon, was explained by Guillaume des Autelzs (1529–76) in a sonnet which serves as a model of euphuism: "Quel Memfien miracle se haussant / Porte du Ciel l'argentine lumière / Laquelle va, tant qu'elle soit entière / En sa rondeur, toujours, toujours croissant. / Quel sacre saint Lierre gravissant / Jusqu'au plus haut de cette sime fière / De son apui (o nouvelle manière) / Se fait l'apui, plus en plus verdissant? / Soit notre Roy la grande Pyramide / Dont la hauteur en sa force solide / Le terme au ciel plante de sa victoire: / Prince prélat, tu sois le saint Lierre / Qui saintemant abandonnant la terre / De ton soutien va soutenant la gloire."

17 *Op. cit.,* pp. 247, 250.

PIERRE REYMOND

c. 1513–After 1584

Pierre Reymond, a prominent member of a family of enamellers on which information is sparse, occupied a workshop on the Rue des Étaux, or Rue Basse Manigne, in the lower section of the enamellers' district at Limoges. His earliest works are dated 1534. Though he executed a number of religious pieces, he was most active as the head of a studio specializing in the production of covered cups, caskets, saltcellars, plates, dishes, and ewers. The great majority of his compositions were borrowed from engravings by Lucas van Leyden, Albrecht Dürer, Marcantonio Raimondi, and Virgil Solis, from book illustrations by Bernard Salomon and Jacques Androuet du Cerceau, and from ornamental designs by Theodor de Bry and the minor masters of the School of Fontainebleau. Among his principal works is a luxurious enamelled service made about 1560 for Linhard Tucher of Nuremberg. Pierre Reymond served as consul in 1560 and in 1567.

Casket: Old Testament Subjects (16.4.24)

H. 4½ in. (11.5 cm); W. 6½ in. (16.5 cm); D. 4⅝ in. (11.8 cm).

Description: The casket is composed of fourteen enamelled plaques set in a gilt-copper frame. Though several of the scenes are related, there is no apparent plan to the ensemble. The trapezoidal plaques on the gables show respectively a male and a female head of classical type, each within a wreath supported by two putti. The remaining plaques, all rectangular, depict scenes principally from the Old Testament, with identifying inscriptions in Limousin dialect and in Latin. The compositions are painted on a black ground in grisaille, lightly tinted with rose, yellow, blue-green, blue, lilac, and violet. The inscriptions and various details are gilded. On the top of the lid at left, Cain slays Abel with an ass's jawbone before a flaming altar, and the inscription reads COMAN:QVAIN:OVCIT: ABELL (How Cain killed Abel); in the scene to the right, Samson, naked and armed like Hercules with a club, carries off the gates of Gaza, below the inscription SESI:FIGVRO:LE: RESVCITEMAN (This symbolizes the Resurrection). On the front of the lid at left, Tubal-cain and Jubal (TVBAR ET IVBAR) work at an anvil with hammer and tongs while Naamah, the sister of Tubal-cain, strums a gittern; to the right, three angels comfort Daniel in the lions' den as Habakkuk brings him food, with the inscription COMAN:DANIEL.FV [CO]N- FORTE (How Daniel was comforted). On the front of the casket at lower left, two of the

130

spies Moses sent to scout the Promised Land return with a giant cluster of grapes hanging from a staff, and the inscription is COMAN. DES.OMES.PORTION. VNO GRAPO.DE.RASIN (How men carry a cluster of grapes); to the right, Lot is plied with wine by his two daughters, with the inscription COMANT. LOT:VPARTISIPATION.A SES:FILLES (How Lot knew his daughters). On the back of the lid at left, Lot flees the burning city of Sodom with his wife and daughters, here represented as children, as an angel indicates the way, and the inscription reads COMĀ LOC.ET SES ANFANT (How Lot and his children); to the right, around a columnar altar mounted with the Golden Calf, are three men and a woman holding a book, beneath the inscription PANDAN MOISO APORTA.LES COMANDE-MANS (As Moses brought the commandments). On the back of the casket at lower left, two men stand before the altar of Bel while Daniel, represented as a hermit or exorcist, thrusts his cross-staff into the mouth of the dragon worshipped in Babylon, with the inscription COMA DANIEL.DETRVIT LE DRAGON (How Daniel destroyed the dragon); to the right, three naked men burn a heap of books below the inscription LIVRES DE LAR: MAGIC (Books of magic art). On the lower end plaque at left, manna falls like teardrops into a fountain with two basins and is gathered by putti, as Moses, seated in the desert, points with one hand to the Tables of the Law and with the other to the miraculous sustenance; the inscription, this time in Latin, reads HOC:EST:MANA (This is manna). In the lower plaque on the right end, David, holding aloft on a spear the head of Goliath, is met by a procession of maidens and warriors at the gate of Jerusalem; the inscription reads DAVIT: VINCIT:GOLEAS (David conquers Goliath).

Condition: Several of the plaques show losses and repairs at the edges and corners, most notably those on the gables and the front of the lid. On the whole, the casket is in good condition.

The male head crowned with laurel on the right gable of the casket is after a coin showing Constantine the Great glancing heavenward. In the present context, it may have been intended to represent Augustus, in which case the female head on the left gable could be that of the Tiburtine Sibyl.[1]

The plaques of Cain and Abel and Lot and His Daughters are both after engravings by Lucas van Leyden, dated 1529 and 1530 respectively.[2] The female figure to the left of the altar in the Adoration of the Golden Calf is from an engraving of Clio and Urania by Marcantonio Raimondi,[3] and the Burning of the Books[4] derives from the central section of Bandinelli's *Martyrdom of St. Lawrence,* which also was engraved by Marcantonio.[5] The double-basined fountain on the left end of the casket, an allusion to the Fountain of Life, is borrowed from a print by the master of the so-called Tarocchi Cards of Mantegna.[6]

Several of the plaques can be interpreted as allusions to the coming of Christ.

132

The inscription on the Samson plaque refers to the hero specifically as a precursor of the Resurrection. David's defeat of Goliath prefigures Christ's victory over Satan, and Abel's sacrifice of a lamb and his own death parallel the sacrifice of Christ, "the Lamb of God." In the scene of men carrying grapes, the scout at right, wearing a prophet's headdress, personifies the Old Dispensation, while the bareheaded second figure—who, because he walks behind, can see the grapes that symbolize Christ crucified—heralds the New Dispensation;[7] the vat filled with

grapes alludes to the wine press in Isaiah 63:3, another symbol of the Crucifixion. The manna falling in the desert symbolizes the Eucharist.

In medieval iconography Tubal-cain the smith, son of Lamech by his second wife Zillah, personified music, together with Jubal, the inventor of music in Genesis 4:21, who was the son of Lamech by his first wife Adah.[8]

The appearance of the prophet Habakkuk with Daniel in the lions' den and Daniel's slaying of the Babylonian dragon are both recounted in the Apocryphal

Book of Bel and the Dragon. However, the enameller ignored Daniel's promise to King Astyages: "I shall slay this dragon without sword or staff."

The David and Goliath plaque is painted directly below the inscription with a gilded matrimonial knot. The same knot is found on two enamelled plaques in the British Museum, London, one representing the Judgment of Paris and the other an amorous party in a boat. These two plaques were once mounted in a casket together with two other plaques in the same museum, one representing the Rape of Helen, the other the Triumph of Caesar.[9] The Rape of Helen plaque is signed with the gilt letters P. R. The casket to which these four plaques originally belonged must have been the companion piece of the Frick casket. Both no doubt intended as marriage gifts, they are precious examples of the early style of Pierre Reymond on which themes of courtly love were blended with others from the Bible and antiquity in a spirit true to Renaissance culture.

When in the Hollingworth Magniac collection, the present casket was tentatively attributed to the Pénicaud school. At the South Kensington Museum Loan Exhibition of 1862, it was catalogued as probably by Pierre Reymond. Breck correctly maintained the second attribution,[10] which is fully substantiated by the comparison with the four British Museum plaques.

Exhibited: London, South Kensington Loan Exhibition, 1862, No. 1665, lent by Hollingworth Magniac. London, Victoria and Albert Museum, 1901–12, lent by J. Pierpont Morgan. New York, Metropolitan Museum, Morgan Collection, 1914–16, lent by J. Pierpont Morgan.

Collections: Hollingworth Magniac, London. His sale, July 2 *et seq.,* 1892, Christie's, Lot 244, sold to Mainwaring for £278 5s. J. Pierpont Morgan, London and New York. Duveen. Frick, 1916.

NOTES

1 A slightly larger casket in the Toledo Museum of Art (No. 69.290; R. M. Berkowitz, "French Renaissance Enamels," *Museum News,* N. S. XIII, 1970, repr. pp. 8, 9) is decorated with the same Old Testament subjects enamelled in grisaille, but the Burning of the Books is replaced by the *Ara Coeli* vision, in which the Sibyl revealed to Augustus the Virgin and Child in the sun above Rome. The gable plaques on the Toledo casket represent the Lamb of God and Veronica's Veil. The style and details of the subject matter suggest the authorship of Jean II Pénicaud, who painted the

Ara Coeli vision on a plaque in the former Baronne Édouard de Rothschild collection, Paris, and on a badge in the Victoria and Albert Museum, London (No. 8422–63), the latter stamped with the crowned Pénicaud mark. The Frick and Toledo caskets both appeared in the Hollingworth Magniac sale of 1892, as Lots 244 and 243 respectively, the latter sold to Wertheimer for £472 10s. A casket with similar enamelled subjects was exhibited at the Exposition Universelle, Paris, 1900, No. 2787. Compare also a casket formerly in the Dashwood collection painted in grisaille with scenes from the life of Hercules (sale, Sotheby Parke Bernet, November 26, 1976, Lot 36).

2 J. Lavalleye, *Pieter Bruegel the Elder and Lucas van Leyden,* New York, n.d., Nos. 170, 173. A. Bartsch, *Le Peintre-graveur,* Vienna, 1803–21, VII, Nos. 5, 16. On the meaning of the ass's jawbone, which is not mentioned in Genesis, see: M. Schapiro, "Cain's Jaw-Bone that Did the First Murder," *Art Bulletin,* XXIV, 1942, pp. 204–12; P. F. Braude, "Some Implications of Cain's Sacrifice," *Gesta: International Center of Medieval Art,* VII, 1968, pp. 15–28.

3 Bartsch, XV, No. 397. E. Wind, *Pagan Mysteries in the Renaissance,* New Haven, 1958, p. 127, Fig. 38.

4 This curious auto-da-fé may have been meant as a barb against Henry Cornelius Agrippa von Nettesheim's *De occulta philosophia,* the first volume of which appeared in Antwerp in 1531, the following three in Cologne in 1533. Harassed by the Inquisition, Agrippa took refuge in France, where he was arrested by order of François I and

died shortly afterward in 1535. The Semele chimney in the cabinet of François I at Fontainebleau had integrated into its decoration the motif of the burning of the Sibylline Books (S. Béguin, in "La Galerie François Ier au Château de Fontainebleau," *Revue de l'art,* Nos. 16–17, 1972, p. 167).

5 A. Petrucci, *Panorama della incisione italiana: Il cinquecento,* Rome, 1964, Pl. 16. Marcantonio's print after Bandinelli is represented in its entirety in a grisaille enamel signed with the joined letters MP in the Victoria and Albert Museum (C. 2401.1910; H. P. Mitchell, "The Limoges Enamels in the Salting Collection," *Burlington Magazine,* XX, 1911, p. 84). The same enameller signed with an identical monogram a roundel in the Louvre representing a skirmish of cavalrymen (O. A. 2525; J.-J. Marquet de Vasselot, *Catalogue sommaire de l'orfèvrerie, de l'émaillerie et des gemmes,* Paris, 1914, No. 501). According to C. Popelin, the signature MP also appeared on an Adoration of the Magi executed in grisaille in the collection of the Duke of Hamilton, done after a print by Lucas van Leyden (*La Collection Spitzer,* Paris, 1891, II, p. 24, note to No. 13).

6 *Illustrations to the Catalogue of Early Italian Engravings...in the British Museum,* London, 1909, E II 5, 6; compare E I 53. Compare also the fountain in Altdorfer's woodcut *The Holy Family at the Fountain* (H. Tietze, *Albrecht Altdorfer,* Leipzig, 1923, p. 94, repr. facing p. 135). On a plaque mounted into an enamelled casket attributed to Couly Noylier in the former Baronne de Rothschild collection, the Fountain of Life is transformed into a

Fountain of Youth, toward which scamper two putti frightened by a skull held out by an ape. The gable plaques on that casket are decorated, like those on the Frick example, with male and female heads within wreaths held by two putti. The putti resemble those on the Frick casket and wear the same baldrics of coral pearls. The Paris casket must also be an early work of Pierre Reymond.

7 A plaque on a casket in the Victoria and Albert Museum, attributed to the workshop of Pierre Reymond and dated to the early 1540s, shows similar men bearing grapes. There the jovial inscription, LA LIC-QVEVR CEST LE BON VIN QVI REIOVIST MAINT PELERIN (Liquor is the good wine that rejoices many a pilgrim), is in keeping with the other nine subjects, amatory, pastoral, and emblematic, on the casket. The bearing of a cluster of grapes was also enamelled by Pierre Reymond on one of four plaques set into a casket dated 1544 in the Musée de Cluny, Paris. Like the Frick plaque, the Cluny panel is invested with typological overtones: the scout walking second looks ahead, personifying the New Testament, and lays his right hand on the grapes.

8 See P. Verdier, in *Actes du Quatrième Congrès International de Philosophie Médiévale*, Paris–Montreal, 1969, pp. 328 30.

9 Waddesdon Bequest, Nos. 26–29.

10 J. Breck, in *The Frick Collection Catalogue*, VII, 1955, p. 34.

Ewer Stand: Moses Striking the Rock (16.4.25)

Signed twice, in gold, on the back of the rim: P. R. D. 18 in. (45.7 cm).

Description: The obverse of the stand is decorated principally with a circular, frieze-like composition showing the incident of the miraculous waters of Meribah (Exodus 17:1–7; Numbers 20:1–13). In the foreground, the horned figure of Moses strikes the rock in Horeb before the elders of Israel. A slim tree at left indicates the start of a gyrating procession of men and women bearing jars which they will fill at the spring. A dog already laps from the water. In the distance are the tents of Israel pitched in the wilderness. The colors are yellow, orange, red-violet, blue, turquoise, and green, all heightened with gilding; the flesh tones are rendered in an impasto of grisaille tinted with light red. At the center of the stand is a boss decorated with an ideal female head of the traditional Diane de Poitiers type surrounded by concentric rings enamelled with various motifs. The cavetto below the boss is painted with gilt scrolls on a black ground, and a similar treatment appears on the cavetto below the rim. The rim itself is gilded with laurel sprays against a black ground and enamelled in colors with Indian masks, baskets of fruit, grotesque winged figures, sphinxes, and birds in flight or fluttering their wings. On the reverse, the boss is painted with gilt rays surrounded by a starry sky. The principal motifs are: two grotesque caryatid figures wearing Indian headdresses and supporting smoking urns with their outstretched hands;[1] four female figures symbolizing Fame, each holding two trumpets, one long and one short; and two reclining figures, each under a bracket which supports an Indian mask between symmetrical sprays of laurel.[2] One of the reclining figures represents Diana, accompanied by a dog and a stag, and the other probably is intended as the vanquished Eros. Birds, sprays, and two more Indian masks complete the composition, which is executed in gilding and colors against a black background. The cavetto is as on the obverse, and the rim bears a gilt laurel wreath in the style of bookbindings *à la fanfare.*[3]

Condition: The obverse has been skillfully but extensively repaired, most notably within the figures, along the contours of their garments, and along the outer edge of the rim. The upper surface of the cavetto is abraded, and the background of the boss is pitted. The reverse is in fairly good condition apart from abrasion and small scattered repairs.

The iconography of Moses Striking the Rock derives from woodcut vignettes by Bernard Salomon illustrating Claude Paradin's *Quadrins historiques de la Bible,* first published by Jean de Tournes at Lyon in 1553, and de Tournes' *Biblia Sacra,* first issued in 1554.[4] Salomon's woodcuts served as a source of inspiration for countless Limoges enamels (see for example pp. 160, 176, 182, 194, and 198 of the

present catalogue). They were also copied by Pierre Eskrich (called Pierre Vase) in the *Figures de la Bible illustrées de huictains français* and *Biblia Sacra* published by Guillaume Roville (or Rouillé) at Lyon in the 1560s.

The figures bearing jars in Pierre Reymond's adaptation are reminiscent of Il Rosso's fresco *The Sacrifice,* one of a series of historical and mythological allegories painted in the Galerie François I at Fontainebleau (seventh bay north).[5] The motifs that decorate the rim are mainly in the taste of designs engraved by Theodor de Bry after Marten de Vos of Antwerp.

The Fame motif on the reverse of the stand derives from the fresco painted by Il Rosso above the entrance to the cabinet of François I in the middle of the north wall of the Galerie at Fontainebleau. It was engraved by Domenico del Barbiere.[6] The reclining Diana depends from a painting by Primaticcio, which was engraved by the monogrammist L. D. (Léon Davent?) of the Fontainebleau school.[7]

There exist about fifteen ewer stands signed by Pierre Reymond or in his style. Those that are dated fall within the period 1557 to 1566. The great majority are executed in grisaille. The Frick example belongs to Pierre Reymond's return to the chromatic style in his late years.

Exhibited: London, Victoria and Albert Museum, 1907–12, lent by J. Pierpont Morgan. New York, Metropolitan Museum, Morgan Collection, 1914–16, lent by J. Pierpont Morgan.

Collections: Cathedral of Calahorra, province of Logroño, Spain. J. Pierpont Morgan, London and New York. Duveen. Frick, 1916.

NOTES

1 This Pompeian motif derives from Raphael, who introduced it, in imitation of Imperial Roman grotesque decoration, in his frescoes for the Vatican Logge (see P. Ward-Jackson, "Some Main Streams and Tributaries in European Ornament from 1500 to 1750, Part I," *Victoria and Albert Museum Bulletin,* III, 1967, Fig. 3, p. 61). It is found again, together with motifs copied after the stuccoes in the Galerie François I at Fontainebleau, on the reverse of a dish by Pierre Courteys in the British Museum, London (Waddesdon Bequest, No. 31; from the Hollingworth Magniac sale, Christie's, July 2 *et seq.,* 1892, Lot 248).

2 Indian masks are mentioned as early as the 1523 inventory of Margaret of Austria. They were carved on the columns of the episcopal palace at Liège (S. Collon-Gevaert, "L'Art précolombien et le palais des princes-évêques à Liège," *Bulletin de la Société d'Art et d'Histoire du Diocèse de*

Liège, XLI, 1959, pp.73–95) and appeared in France on the tomb of Cardinal d'Amboise in the Lady Chapel of the Cathedral at Rouen (A. Chastel, "Masques mexicains de la renaissance," *Art de France,* No.1, 1961, repr. p.299).

3 Interlaced sprays of laurel were stamped on bindings made for Henri II and Diane de Poitiers, where they accompany Diane's motto "Sola vivit in illo" (C. Paradin, *Devises héroiques et emblèmes,* Lyon, 1557, No. 52). See: H. Bouchot, *Les Reliures d'art à la Bibliothèque Nationale,* Paris, 1888, Pl.XLII; G. D. Hobson, *Les Reliures à la fanfare,* London, 1935, pp.11–12, Fig.9).

4 Claude Paradin, Canon of Beaujeu, dedicated his *Quadrins* to Marguerite de France, Duchesse de Berry, to whom were also dedicated the *Figure del Vecchio Testamento con versi toscani* issued by de Tournes in 1554 for the use of the Italian colony at Lyon. The *Biblia* is more complete than the *Quadrins.* Bernard Salomon, called "le petit Bernard," took his inspiration from the woodcuts illustrating the 1540 edition of the *Biblia Hebraea, Chaldea, Graeca et Latina* of Robert Estienne, the first edition of which (1528) constituted the base of de Tournes' *Biblia Sacra.* The first edition of de Tournes' *Biblia* (1554) had 198 woodcuts, of which twenty still derived from fourteenth- and early fifteenth-century sources. The number of illustrations rose to 231 in 1555, 232 in 1564, and 248 in 1583 (with sixteen added by a different hand). The majolica produced in Lyon during the same period contributed no less than the Limoges enamels to the diffusion of Salomon's compositions. See N. Rondot, *Bernard Salomon,*

Lyon, 1897.

5 For engravings after Il Rosso's *Sacrifice,* see *L'École de Fontainebleau,* Paris, 1972, Nos.308, 432; compare the jar-bearers in engraving No.361, after Primaticcio. The composition on the Frick ewer stand was also used by Pierre Reymond, in a simplified version, on the shoulder of a ewer in the Toledo Museum of Art (No.69.293; R. M. Berkowitz, "French Renaissance Enamels," *Museum News,* N.S. XIII, 1970, repr. p.9). It appears again on the foot of a tazza in the former Debruge-Duménil collection (J. Labarte, *Description des objets d'art qui composent la collection Debruge-Duménil,* Paris, 1847, No.176) and on a grisaille tazza in the former Basilewsky collection (A. Darcel, *Collection Basilewsky,* Paris, 1874, No.325). See also the Frick tazza No. 16.4.38 discussed on p.194.

6 Père P. Dan, *Le Trésor des merveilles de la maison royale de Fontainebleau,* Paris, 1642, p.92. K. Kusenberg, *Il Rosso,* Paris, 1931, pp.64, 79, note 170, p.159, Pl.LXII. *L'École de Fontainebleau,* No.338. The figures of Fame and Victory, painted on a gold ground, framed a carved portrait bust of François I. This decoration and the cabinet itself were destroyed under Louis XVI. The print by Domenico del Barbiere was copied by Virgil Solis (R. van Marle, *Iconographie de l'art profane au moyen âge et à la renaissance,* II, The Hague, 1932, Fig.202, p.176). On the two trumpets of Fame, the longer one designating enduring renown and the shorter one signifying celebrity, see P. Valeriano, *Hieroglyphica,* Basel, ed. of 1575, p.xlvii, under "Tuba."

7 *L'École de Fontainebleau,* No.373. The

same Diana was repeated, in reverse, inside a cup by Pierre Reymond in the Musée de Cluny, Paris (No. 1439; *Fontainebleau: L'Art en France 1528–1610,* Ottawa, 1973, I, Fig. 48, p. 80). The location of Primaticcio's *Diana* at Fontainebleau is unknown. Its engraving inspired three sculptures, including a marble relief in the Musée de Cluny which Alexandre Lenoir claimed to have rescued from Diane de Poitiers' Château d'Anet at the start of the First Empire. See: *L'École de Fontainebleau,* No. 506; *Fontainebleau: L'Art en France,* I, Fig. 52, p. 84; P. du Colombier, *Jean Goujon,* Paris, 1949, pp. 131, 133, Pl. XLIV. Compare also a drawing in the Hector-Martin Lefuel collection (B. Lossky, "Dessins concernant Fontainebleau dans la collection Lefuel," *Bulletin de la Société de l'Histoire de l'Art français,* 1971, pp. 31–44, Fig. 10).

Workshop of
PIERRE REYMOND

Saltcellar in Baluster Form: Amorini and Satyrs (16.4.27)

H. 5½ in. (14 cm).

Description: The upper section of the saltcellar is decorated inside the receptacle with the bust of a man in a Phrygian cap, seen in profile to the right against a black ground dotted with gold, and on the exterior with four seated amorini and four squatting satyrs. On the stem is a frieze of pendent acanthus leaves above two male and two female profile heads in oval white frames. Sportive amorini with animals appear on the foot. The figures are painted in grisaille and flesh tints against black backgrounds decorated with gold. A band of light blue borders the foot, the interior of which is black with gold stars and petal motifs.

Condition: The saltcellar is in good condition. The outer rim is abraded, and there are indications of repairs on the foot, at the juncture of the upper section with the stem (reinforced with a metal pin), and at the juncture of the stem with the foot.

The form of the saltcellar and the decoration on its stem are identical to those of a saltcellar in the former Spitzer collection attributed by Popelin to Pierre Reymond.[1] The shape is in fact closer to that of saltcellars by Jean de Court[2]—see for example Frick No. 16.4.37 (p. 213)—but the latter master does not seem to have employed the decorative themes used in the ornamentation of the present example. The wiry hardness of the *enlevages* is in keeping with the practice followed in the workshop of Pierre Reymond. A similar male head with Phrygian cap is seen in the receptacles of two saltcellars signed P. R. in the Walters Art Gallery, Baltimore.[3]

The squatting figures on the upper section recall the "grotesques accroupis" designed by Jacques Androuet du Cerceau for the pavilion at Charleval and for the front of the terrace of the Château de Verneuil.[4]

Exhibited: London, Victoria and Albert Museum, 1902–12, lent by J. Pierpont Morgan. New York, Metropolitan Museum, Morgan Collection, 1914–16, lent by J. Pierpont Morgan.

Collections: M. Boy, Paris. His sale, May 15–24, 1905, Galerie Georges Petit, Paris, Lot 221. J. Pierpont Morgan, London and New York. Duveen. Frick, 1916.

146

1 C. Popelin, in *La Collection Spitzer,* Paris, 1891, II, No. 104, pp. 50–51; Spitzer sale, 33 rue de Villejust, Paris, April 17–June 16, 1893, Lot 521. The foot of the saltcellar was decorated with two subjects from the *Aeneid* after Marcantonio Raimondi's *Quos Ego* engraving, a favorite source of Pierre Reymond. Compare a saltcellar of the same shape, also attributed to Pierre Reymond, in the Musée Municipal at Limoges (No. 46).

2 When in the Boy collection, the present saltcellar was attributed to Jean de Court.

3 P. Verdier, *The Walters Art Gallery: Catalogue of the Painted Enamels of the Renaissance,* Baltimore, 1967, Nos. 131–32, repr. p. 217, Nos. 134–35, repr. p. 227.

4 H. de Geymüller, *Les Du Cerceau,* Paris, 1887, Figs. 47, 48. Cabinet des Estampes, Bibliothèque Nationale, Paris, Vol. Hd. 197, a drawing in the series *Les Plus Excellents Bastiments de France.* Squatting grotesques are combined with the dragons favored by Jean de Court on the rim of an oval platter by him illustrating the Destruction of Pharaoh's Host in the M. H. de Young Memorial Museum, San Francisco. They also adorn the back of a ewer stand by Pierre Reymond exhibited at the Burlington Fine Arts Club, London, in 1897 (No. 134, Pl. XLVIII). Étienne Delaune designed a squatting satyress in a project for a platter (Cabinet des Dessins, Louvre, No. 26.194; compare RF 1086). On Delaune's projects for Henri II, see B. Thomas, "Die Münchner Harnischvorzeichnungen des Étienne Delaune," *Jahrbuch der Kunsthistorischen Sammlungen in Wien,* LVI, 1960, pp. 7–62. Grotesques of this type appealed particularly to North and Central Italian engravers, among them Nicoletto da Modena, who in 1507 had studied Nero's Domus Aurea in Rome. Pinturicchio was one of the first artists to paint them—for example, in the Baglioni Chapel at S. Maria Maggiore, Spello (N. Dacos, *La Découverte de la Domus Aurea et la formation des grotesques à la Renaissance,* London–Leyden, 1969, Fig. 87). Squatting grotesques are surrealistically caricatured as vases with bent satyr legs on the underside of a cup in the British Museum, London (No. 84,6–18,4).

JEAN REYMOND

d. 1602/03

Jean Reymond and his brother Joseph, who remained active through the first quarter of the seventeenth century, both worked under the influence of Pierre Courteys and both used the signature I. R. Their productions prove difficult to separate, but pieces signed with a fleur-de-lis between the initials probably are by Joseph.

Plaque: The Adoration of the Magi (16.4.28)

11 7/8 × 9 1/2 in. (30.2 × 24.1 cm).

Description: The Virgin, dressed in a blue mantle, sits at right holding the Child on her lap. Behind her stands St. Joseph, wearing a green cloak and red-violet cape over a blue gown, and before her, clad in mulberry brown, kneels an elderly king about to present the Child with a casket. At left, dressed in green and blue and each holding a cup, are a middle-aged king indicating the Star of Bethlehem to the third king, a Negro. The enameller has devoted particular attention to the characters' accessories. The Negro king wears his crown nested in a fantastic hat, and the crowns of the other two kings, one of which lies on the ground, are set in turbans.

Joseph is given two headdresses: a tall cap, and a hat which he holds in his left hand. Both of the foreground kings wear elaborate spurs, and the Negro king rests his hand on the eagle-shaped hilt of his sword. The scene is set before a stable wall which runs parallel to the picture plane and is drawn with a sense for stereometry and geometrical design. Landscape and buildings are seen through a half-ruined arch.

Condition: The plaque shows considerable damage and repair. There are losses in the garments of all of the figures (most notably in the robe of the kneeling king), along much of the top and sides, and at lower left. Various details have been regilt.

The plaque follows the compositional model of an Adoration of the Magi, also with a Negro king, in a Book of Hours of 1525/26 printed by Simon de Colines for Geoffroy Tory.[1] The introduction of a Negro into the Adoration of the Magi derives from North European painting and is met with belatedly in Limoges enamels—for example, in a plaque based on a different model in the Musée de Cluny, Paris,[2] and in one signed by Suzanne Court in the British Museum, London.[3]

150

The same sparkling greens, deep blues, and mulberry-browns reddening to violet that characterize the present enamel are seen on two plaques dated 1571 in the former Bucquet-Bournet de Verron collection, signed I. R.[4] The facial characterizations compare closely with those found on the Last Supper dish signed I. R. in The Frick Collection (see p. 155).

Exhibited: London, Victoria and Albert Museum, 1902 and 1908–12, lent by J. Pierpont Morgan. Glasgow, Kelvingrove Art Gallery, 1903–08. New York, Metropolitan Museum, Morgan Collection, 1914–16, lent by J. Pierpont Morgan.

Collections: Eugen Gutmann, Berlin. J. Pierpont Morgan, London and New York. Duveen. Frick, 1916.

NOTES

1 A. M. Hind, *An Introduction to a History of Woodcut,* London, 1935, II, Fig. 437, pp. 697–98. For various details—for example, the spurs, the more elaborate costumes, and the casket held by the kneeling king—the enameller may also have borrowed from Dürer's *Adoration* woodcut of 1511 (E. Panofsky, *Albrecht Dürer,* Princeton, 1943, II, Fig. 184).

2 No. 917. In his notes on the Cluny Adoration and its companion piece, a Presentation in the Temple, J.-J. Marquet de Vasselot questioned their attribution to Pierre Reymond. A second Adoration in the same museum (No. 914 h), part of an enamelled series illustrating the Life of the Virgin, shows elements of comparison in the group of three figures at center and in the arch opening onto the countryside, and must have been based on the same model as the Frick example.

3 No. 1913, 12–20, 67.

4 The subjects are the Kiss of Judas and Calvary. See G. Migeon, "La Collection Bucquet-Bournet de Verron," *Les Arts,* No. 117, 1911, p. 18, repr. facing p. 16.

Oval Dish: The Last Supper; Jupiter (16.4.31)

Signed, in gold, on the back of the rim: I.R. 15⅞ × 20¼ in. (40.3 × 51.5 cm).

Description: The Last Supper takes place in the porticoed courtyard of a palace with trelliswork leaded glass windows on the first two floors and oeil-de-boeuf windows above. Christ, seated to the right of center with his hand on St. John's shoulder, is offering the bread to Judas, who has been given a halo due to an oversight on the part of the enameller. Judas, still holding the purse, is about to leave. The other Apostles gesture toward him in anger and horror, express amazement, or whisper to each other in a garbled composition vaguely but unmistakably reminiscent of Leonardo da Vinci's fresco. At far left, an attendant brings wine to the table, which is set with bread, plates, a cup, a chalice, and a saltcellar. Christ is dressed in a blue mantle over a purple robe, Judas wears blue over crimson and yellow, and the other Apostles are clad in light and dark blue, violet, green, yellow, and crimson, all painted in translucent enamel over foil and highlighted with gold. The flesh tints are warm, shading to violet, and the hair is pinkish-orange, yellow-gray, or gray. The hanging portion of the white tablecloth is shaded in the folds and covered with a trellis of thin gold lines. The architectural background is violet with gold shadows, and the tiled floor is greenish-black and gold. A blue-green curtain hangs behind Peter, who sits at Christ's left. On the cavetto is a magnificent pattern of arabesques in gold on a black ground, and on the rim are colored motifs very close to those found on the Frick ewer stand by Pierre Reymond (see p.141) and the Frick platter by Martial Reymond (p.165) set against sprays of laurel and other foliage. The design on the back of the dish resembles that on the reverse of Martial Reymond's platter. At center is the figure of Jupiter holding a scepter, naked but for a blue mantle that billows about him as a repoussoir. An eagle spreads its wings at his feet. Jupiter stands within a hanging grotesque niche of Pompeian type flanked by two seated monks with asses' ears reading intently from the tops of twisted supports. To the sides and below are smoking urns, squirrels perched on the volutes of a leafy scroll, two birds, and a cherub mask, all in colored enamels. The black ground is covered with gold sprays of foliage derived from bookbindings *à la fanfare.* The cavetto is decorated with gold scrolls on black, the rim with a laurel wreath. At the top of the rim, in an oval frame, is an imitation cameo or intaglio with a recumbent figure of Diana recalling that on the back of the Frick ewer stand by Pierre Reymond; at the bottom, in a similar setting, is the signature I.R.

Condition: The dish is in fairly good condition. The obverse shows a number of losses in the figures and some crazing in the major areas of translucent enamel, particularly the yellows. The edge of the rim is cracked in several places. The reverse is in generally better condition, though there are losses in Jupiter's mantle and in the hanging drapery below the monk at right, and cracks appear in the niche above Jupiter.

153

The setting of the Last Supper in a palace courtyard reflects the grand manner of staging religious scenes in Italian painting and French stained glass of the Renaissance.[1] A similar composition decorates a rounded enamelled plaque in the Musée des Arts Décoratifs at Lyon, but there the figures differ somewhat: Judas is still seated instead of preparing to leave, and the foreground is occupied by four saints, one holding a baton and a heart, another dressed as an abbot, a third as a bishop, and the last with the attributes of St. Lawrence.[2]

The source of Jupiter on the back of the dish is an engraving (with admixture of etching) by Marcantonio Raimondi or one of his close imitators, transformed into a grotesque by Étienne Delaune.[3] Similar grotesques appear among the designs created by Delaune for goldsmiths, and they recur in a few tapestries, some patterned after Italian models, woven on the looms of Fontainebleau for Henri II and Diane de Poitiers.[4] The medallion figure of Diana derives ultimately from a design by Primaticcio.[5]

Exhibited: London, Burlington Fine Arts Club, 1897, No. 155, lent by the Rev. A. H. Sanxay-Barwell. London, Victoria and Albert Museum, 1904–12, lent by J. Pierpont Morgan. New York, Metropolitan Museum, Morgan Collection, 1914–16, lent by J. Pierpont Morgan.

Collections: Andrew Fountaine, Narford Hall, Norfolk. His sale, June 16–19, 1884, Christie's, Lot 447. The Rev. A. H. Sanxay-Barwell, London. J. Pierpont Morgan, London and New York. Duveen. Frick, 1916.

NOTES

1 For examples of the latter, see a window from the church of Saint-Jean, Rouen, on loan from Queen Elizabeth II to the Victoria and Albert Museum, London, and the window of Christ and St. Thomas in Saint-Germain-l'Auxerrois, Paris. Compare also a relief representing the Last Supper in Saint-Jean, Troyes (M. Beaulieu, "Un Groupe de Sibylles champenoises," *Revue du Louvre,* XIX, 1969, Fig. 11, p. 221).

2 Lambert Bequest, 1850, No. L. 451 (*Catalogue sommaire des musées de la ville de Lyon,* 1887, No. 152). The two saints in the left foreground and the figure of Judas derive from an engraving of 1552 by the monogrammist A over I (F. W. H. Hollstein, *Dutch and Flemish Etchings, Engravings and Woodcuts,* Amsterdam, 1949–, XIII, p. 8).

3 See: A. Bartsch, *Le Peintre-graveur,* Vienna, 1803–21, XIV, No. 253; H. Delaborde, *Marc-Antoine Raimondi,* Paris, 1887, No. 99; A. Robert-Dumesnil, *Le Peintre-graveur français,* Paris, 1835–71, IX, No. 359. On the reverse of a dish of 1567 by Pierre Courteys in the Walters Art Gallery, Baltimore (P. Verdier, *The Walters Art Gallery: Catalogue*

154

of the Painted Enamels of the Renaissance, Baltimore, 1967, No. 151, pp. 275–77), the Raimondesque design is framed in a cartouche simulating scrolled leather, in the style of the first School of Fontainebleau. On a plaque signed I.C. in the Musée de Cluny, Paris (No. 18341), the grotesque version of Delaune was used, but without the squirrels, birds, and cherub mask. Martial Courteys enamelled a Jupiter after the Raimondi-Delaune design on the back of a circular dish with Moses Striking the Rock in the British Museum, London (Waddesdon Bequest, No. 30). The figure also decorates one of the twelve oval bosses on the base of the Frick candlestick by Jean de Court (see p. 210).

4 These tapestries are in the Musée des Gobelins and Musée des Arts Décoratifs, Paris, and the Musée des Tissus et des Arts Décoratifs, Lyon. See: *L'École de Fontainebleau,* Paris, 1972, Nos. 449–52; J. D. Farmer, *The Virtuoso Craftsman: Northern European Design in the 16th Century,* Worcester (Massachusetts) Art Museum, 1969, No. 20.

5 See p. 142 and p. 144, note 7.

Workshop of
PIERRE or JEAN REYMOND

Ewer: The Gathering of Manna; The Destruction of Pharaoh's Host (16.4.26)

H. 12⅝ in. (32.1 cm).

Description: The neck and foot of the ewer are ornamented with spotted and solid-colored cheetahs, flying birds, masks, foliage, and arabesques on a black ground, interspersed with enamelled jewels over foil. On the shoulder is depicted the Gathering of Manna (Exodus 16:14–18) and on the body the Destruction of Pharaoh's Host at the command of Moses after Israel had crossed the Red Sea (Exodus 14:26–28). The colors are green, blue, red-violet, and golden-brown, heightened with gilding; the flesh is rendered in grisaille tinted with light red, and the same process was used to represent the waves of the Red Sea. The handle is decorated on the outside with scrolls and on the inside with petal motifs.

Condition: The ewer is in good condition. There are repairs on the neck and handle, a few cracks inside the neck, and possible further repairs in the outlines of some of the figures and at the junctures of the handle with the lip and body and the body with the foot.

The style and technique are those of the last known works of Pierre Reymond after his return to polychromy. Some of the details are executed in a distinctly painterly fashion: the effect of light and shade on the cuirass of the Egyptian swept before Pharaoh's horses, for instance, is rendered through a combination of greenish-blue and a powdery translucent blue.

The decoration on the neck and foot of the ewer is unusual in Pierre Reymond's production and anticipates a repertory of motifs with which Jean I and Jean II Limousin and Jean and Joseph Reymond were more familiar. Nevertheless, the flying birds are encountered in at least one late work signed by Pierre Reymond—on the rim of the Frick ewer stand with Moses Striking the Rock (see p.141)—and the cheetahs crouching on brackets are not unlike the sphinxes similarly poised on the same stand. The spotted cheetahs on the foot of the ewer are akin to the spotted sphinxes on the rims of two oval dishes in The Frick Collection, the Last Supper by Jean Reymond (p.155) and the Apollo and the Muses by Martial Reymond (p.165); both dishes also show flying birds.

158

The two scenes from Exodus owe their inspiration principally to Bernard Salomon's woodcuts illustrating the *Quadrins historiques de la Bible* and *Biblia Sacra* published in several editions by Jean de Tournes at Lyon[1] and to engravings by Pierre Woeiriot. But extensive cross-pollination from other graphic sources and their adaptation on enamels intervened. The Gathering of Manna is not as close to Salomon's original as is the version that appears on the Frick casket by Pierre Courteys (see p. 187), though it does retain the beautiful motif of the kneeling woman seen from behind, turning her head away from her basket.[2]

Biblical subjects after Salomon's woodcuts are frequent in the productions of Pierre Reymond and Jean de Court, the latter of whom evidenced a partiality for the Drowning of Pharaoh's Host in the Red Sea.[3] Other sources at the disposal of the enamellers include the *Transitus populi per mare rubrum Exodi XIIII* engraved by Hans Sebald Beham in the *Biblicae historiae a Georgio illustratae*[4] and a Crossing of the Red Sea by Pierre Woeiriot in *Figures de la Bible* (1580).[5]

Exhibited: London, South Kensington Loan Exhibition, 1874, No. 746, lent by the Earl of Warwick. London, Victoria and Albert Museum, 1902–12, lent by J. Pierpont Morgan. New York, Metropolitan Museum, Morgan Collection, 1914–16, lent by J. Pierpont Morgan.

Collections: Earl of Warwick. J. Pierpont Morgan, London and New York. Duveen. Frick, 1916.

NOTES

1 For the history of the *Quadrins historiques* and *Biblia Sacra,* see p. 140 and p. 144, note 4.

2 The Gathering of Manna appears on several other works by Pierre Reymond, including: tazze in the former E. Felix and L. Cottreau collections; a plate in the Hermitage Museum, Leningrad (A. Darcel, *Collection Basilewsky,* Paris, 1874, No. 329); a ewer in the Louvre (A. Darcel, *Notice des émaux et de l'orfèvrerie,* Paris, 1867, No. 472); a ewer stand in the Grünes Gewölbe, Dresden; the cover of a tazza, damaged and with the incomplete date 155[?], in the Metropolitan Museum of Art, New York (No. 04.6.5); and a dish that figured in the Sassoon and Rocksavage sale, Christie's, November 26, 1919, Lot 68. The cover of a tazza in the Musées Royaux d'Art et d'Histoire, Brussels, is attributed to Pierre Reymond's workshop (No. 2237/A).

3 At least five platters enamelled by Jean de Court show the Destruction of Pharaoh's Host, including examples in: the Hermitage Museum; the M. H. de Young Memorial Museum, San Francisco; the Los Angeles

County Museum of Art; the Museum of Art, University of Kansas, Lawrence; and the British Museum, London (Waddesdon Bequest, No. 33). Compare a ewer in the Victoria and Albert Museum, London (No. 481–1873), and a tazza in the former Spitzer collection (C. Popelin, in *La Collection Spitzer,* Paris, 1891, II, No. 145, Pl. XVI).

4 Rec. R. A. 14 Rés., Cabinet des Estampes, Bibliothèque Nationale, Paris.

5 Woeiriot's *Figures de la Bible* are catalogued in the continuation by G. Duplessis of A. Robert-Dumesnil's *Le Peintre-graveur français,* Paris, 1835–71, XI, pp. 340–41. Woeiriot's Crossing of the Red Sea (No. 28) reverses the composition of Salomon's woodcut. The motif of the horseman brandishing a banner recurs frequently in sixteenth-century art—for example, in a miniature by Giulio Clovio in the Pierpont Morgan Library, New York (fol. 43 in M. 69).

MARTIAL REYMOND

d. 1599

Little is known of Martial Reymond, son of the enameller Jean Reymond. He signed with the name M REYMOND or, as on the two pieces discussed here, with the initials MR. Typical of his production is the lavish use of gilding and of translucent enamel over foil.

Oval Dish: Apollo and the Muses; Fame (16.4.29)

Signed, in joined gold letters, below the reclining nymph on the obverse: MR. 15⅞ × 21⅜ in. (40.3 × 54.3 cm).

Description: The well of the dish is enamelled with a concert of the Muses presided over by Apollo, who sits at center on a rocky ledge of Mount Helicon playing a viol. From beneath his feet the sacred spring Hippocrene cascades its waters into a reedy basin where a nymph reclines, leaning on an urn. Beyond Apollo, Pegasus stamps his hoofs on the grassy summit. Through the starry sky fly two putti holding wreaths above the Muses, and a third putto extends a wreath from the limb of a tree. The Muses are disposed five to Apollo's left and four to his right. In the first group, Polymnia plays the organ, Melpomene reads from a score, Calliope holds aloft a trumpet, Terpsichore strums a gittern, and Clio clashes the cymbals. In the second group, Erato strikes a tambourine, Thalia rings a triangle, and Urania and Euterpe are each given a viola da gamba.[1] At extreme left are two bearded figures crowned with laurel, possibly representing Homer and Virgil or Tasso and Ariosto. The landscape is green and yellow, with purple rocks and blue water. The garments and the wings of Pegasus are of translucent enamel over foil in shades of blue, turquoise, red-violet, and green, with gold highlights. The flesh tints tend toward gray. The cavetto is gilt with scrolls against a black background, and the rim is decorated with motifs almost identical to those found on the Frick ewer stand by Pierre Reymond (see p. 141) and the Frick platter by Jean Reymond (p. 155). The back of the dish shows Fame holding two trumpets, one long and one short, as on the reverse of Pierre Reymond's ewer stand. Here she wears a dress of transparent blue enamel over foil. Above her is a hanging canopy flanked by snails, beneath her feet is a cherub mask, and to either side are urns, grotesques, and peacocks, all in color against a black ground with gilded motifs. The cavetto is as on the obverse, and the rim is painted with a gold laurel wreath on black.

Condition: The dish is in good condition.

163

A crack and some flaws are visible on the rim, and there are signs of possible repairs in the central scene on the obverse—most notably in the dresses of Urania and Euterpe—and in Fame's dress and the canopy above her on the reverse.

The literary sources for the scene of Apollo and the Muses are twofold. The first incorporates a passage from Antoninus Liberalis' *Metamorphoses* (9), written around A. D. 150, and two passages found in Pausanias' *Description of Greece* (II *Corinth,* xxxi, 9, and IX *Boeotia,* xxxi, 3). When Mount Helicon, in Boeotia, began to ascend to heaven at the rhythm of the Muses' music, Pegasus checked its rise by stamping the ground; where he struck his hoofs, Hippocrene—in Greek, the Horse's Fountain—poured forth its inspiring waters. The second source is the myth of the Castalian spring on Mount Parnassus, above Delphi, as related by Propertius (III, 3). The nymph Castalia, daughter of Achelous, was pursued by Apollo and threw herself into a spring, which took its name after her; the spring was consecrated to Apollo and the Muses, and the sound of its waters was interpreted as an oracle.[2]

The composition on the Frick dish is a close copy of an engraving by Giorgio Ghisi done after a drawing by Luca Penni.[3] Penni's drawing had itself been inspired by a print of Marcantonio Raimondi based on a drawing for Raphael's *Parnassus* fresco in the Stanza della Segnatura at the Vatican. In Raimondi's engraving were incorporated the flying putti which were not included by Raphael in the final fresco.[4]

The theme of the Concert of the Muses enjoyed great popularity throughout Europe during the century between about 1550 and 1650.[5] In France, Parnassus with Apollo and the Muses was painted around 1547 on the vault of the central bay of the Galerie d'Ulysse at Fontainebleau.[6] That fresco is now lost, but it is recorded in an etching by Antoine Garnier after the design by Primaticcio.[7] Parnassus is also the subject of a drawing by Nicolò dell'Abate in the École des Beaux-Arts, Paris, which is close to Luca Penni's composition and was influenced either by an engraving of the latter or by an enamel after it.[8]

Indeed, the very gardens at Fontainebleau, the fountains, and the surrounding forest can be seen as an attempt to realize an actual Parnassus. This mixture of myth and reality took form in an etching of the Muses by Fantuzzi,[9] and it still impressed Père Dan when he wrote his *Trésor* during the reign of Louis XIII.[10]

164

The association of Pegasus with rocks, water, and music had become a theme of Renaissance garden architecture. Luca Penni's drawing took its inspiration in part from a reconstruction of Mount Helicon in a Florentine garden, an ensemble that was imitated at Whitehall in London, at the Tuileries in Paris, and at Alba de Tormes, near Salamanca.[11]

The figure of Fame on the back of the Frick dish derives from a print by Domenico del Barbiere (see p. 142). The canopy and snails are copied after Étienne Delaune, and the grotesque monsters are in the style of Marc Duval. The whole composition recalls a magnificent bookbinding *à la fanfare*.

Martial Reymond painted the same composition of Apollo and the Muses on a dish in the Wallace Collection, London.[12] The subject was also enamelled twice by Pierre Reymond,[13] once by Pierre Courteys,[14] once by Suzanne Court,[15] and twice by Jean de Court.[16]

Exhibited: London, Victoria and Albert Museum, 1901–12, lent by J. Pierpont Morgan. New York, Metropolitan Museum, Morgan Collection, 1914–16, lent by J. Pierpont Morgan.

Collections: J. Pierpont Morgan, London and New York. Duveen. Frick, 1916.

NOTES

1 On the Italian and other sources of the iconography of the Muses, see G. de Tervarent, *Attributs et symboles dans l'art profane, 1450–1600,* Geneva, 1958–59, II, cols. 279–81.

2 See P. Amandry, *La Mantique apollonienne à Delphes,* Paris, 1950. The Castalian oracle had its duplicate at Daphne, a suburb of Antioch. The Daphne oracle was revived by the Emperor Julian the Apostate but became mute in 362. Thenceforth, Christian writers condemned the Castalian sources of inspiration in the name of the Living Waters of the Four Rivers of Paradise (A. Grabar, "Les Quatre Fleuves du Paradis et la source de Castalie," *Bulletin de la Société Nationale des Antiquaires de France,* 1968, pp. 45–63).

3 A. Bartsch, *Le Peintre-graveur,* Vienna, 1803–21, XV, No. 58, pp. 406–07. A copy of Ghisi's print was made by Gaspar ab Avibus and published in 1563, and another copy is anonymous (*idem,* Nos. 58 A and B, p. 407). The composition was also imitated by Étienne Delaune (A. Robert-Dumesnil, *Le Peintre-graveur français,* Paris, 1835–71, IX, No. 309, p. 93; C. Le Blanc, *Manuel de l'amateur d'estampes,* Paris, 1856, II, No. 47). Apollo—or Orpheus—playing a viol was etched after Penni's figure by the mon-

ogrammist L. D. (L. M. Golson, "Landscape Prints and Landscapists of the School of Fontainebleau," *Gazette des Beaux-Arts*, LXXIII, 1969, Fig. 5, p. 98), and the design made its way into the *Livre des grotesques* of Jacques Androuet du Cerceau (H. de Geymüller, *Les Du Cerceau*, Paris, 1887, p. 175). Penni's composition also was copied in a painting now in the Musée Granet at Aix-en-Provence (see note 5, below), carved on a gittern in the former Davillier collection (P. Eudel, *Le Baron Charles Davillier*, Paris, 1883, repr. p. 45), and damascened on an iron shield by Lucio Piccinino (A. Gross, "Vorlagen der Werkstätte des Lucio Piccinino," *Jahrbuch der Kunsthistorischen Sammlungen in Wien*, XXXVI, 1923–25, pp. 148–49).

4 H. Delaborde, *Marc-Antoine Raimondi*, Paris, 1887, p. 110, repr. p. 25. Marcantonio substituted a lyre for Raphael's viola da braccio—an instrument retained by Ghisi. Vasari, describing Raphael's *Parnassus,* integrated the putti that exist only in Marcantonio's print. Similar putti with wreaths hover above Flora in the Fontainebleau painting *The Triumph of Flora* (*L'École de Fontainebleau,* Paris, 1972, No. 130).

5 For a study of this theme, see A. P. de Mirimonde, "Les Concerts des Muses chez les maîtres du nord," *Gazette des Beaux-Arts,* LXIII, 1964, pp. 129–58; the Ghisi engraving and the painting at Aix are Figs. 6, 7. The subject owed much of its success to efforts to reconcile profane music with Christian culture, under the auspices of the Muses. During the sixteenth century instrumental music was widely considered, by Catholic and Protestant theologians alike, as inducive to a dangerous sensuality. Compare: an engraving by Georg Pencz of a garden of delights with the planet Venus and musicians (D. P. Bliss, "Love-Gardens in the Early German Engravings and Woodcuts," *Print Collector's Quarterly,* XV, 1928, p. 108); an etching after Jean Cousin of Venus and Eros on a couch attended by musicians (*L'École de Fontainebleau,* No. 400); and the vignette for the title page of the first novella in Anthoine le Macon's French translation of Boccaccio's *Decameron,* published in Paris by E. Roffet in 1545 (R. Brun, *Le Livre illustré en France,* Paris, 1930, Pl. XIII). See also *The School of Fontainebleau,* exhibition catalogue, Fort Worth and Austin, 1965, pp. 18, 28–29, 67.

6 Père P. Dan, *Le Trésor des merveilles de la maison royale de Fontainebleau,* Paris, 1642, p. 117.

7 *L'École de Fontainebleau,* No. 343.

8 S. Béguin, in *Mostra di Nicolò dell'Abate,* Bologna, 1969, No. 58. Nicolò's drawing was itself engraved in 1569 by Étienne Delaune (*L'École de Fontainebleau,* No. 292).

9 *L'École de Fontainebleau,* No. 307.

10 Dan, *op. cit.,* p. 19: "c'est un autre Parnasse qui entre ses fontaines en a une qui ne cède en rien à celle d'Hélicon, où les Muses et toutes les Grâces que l'antiquité payenne a révérés sous le nom de Divinités bocagères font leur séjour ordinaire."

11 L. Hautecoeur, *Les Jardins des dieux et des hommes,* Paris, 1959, pp. 109–10. Compare a drawing by Antoine Caron representing the reception of the Polish ambassadors in the Tuileries gardens (*Fontainebleau:*

168

L'Art en France 1528–1610, Ottawa, 1973, I, Fig. 171, p. 182, II, p. 137). In a project for a garden, the French architect Salomon de Caus depicted Orpheus playing a cello and taming animals in a grotto within an artificial mountain (reproduced in J. Baltrušaitis, *Anamorphoses,* Paris, 1969, Figs. 43–44, after *Les Raisons des forces mouvantes,* 1615).

12 *Wallace Collection Catalogues: Objects of Art,* London, 1924, No. 268, p. 55.

13 On a platter, without the putti, in the Hermitage Museum, Leningrad (O. Dobroklonskaya, *Painted Enamels of Limoges, XV and XVI Centuries,* Moscow, 1969,

p. 35), and on an oviform vase ascribed to him exhibited at the Burlington Fine Arts Club in 1897 (No. 120, Pl. LIII).

14 On a dish in the Louvre (A. Darcel, *Notice des émaux et de l'orfèvrerie,* Paris, 1867, No. 514; J.-J. Marquet de Vasselot, *Catalogue sommaire de l'orfèvrerie, de l'émaillerie et des gemmes,* Paris, 1914, No. 655).

15 British Museum, Waddesdon Bequest, No. 48.

16 For these see P. Verdier, *The Walters Art Gallery: Catalogue of the Painted Enamels of the Renaissance,* Baltimore, 1967, No. 169, pp. 306–09.

Concave Oval Plaque: Ceres Holding a Torch; Minerva (16.4.30)

Signed, in joined gold letters, below the left foot of Ceres: MR. 14⅛ × 10⁹/₁₆ in. (35.9 × 26.8 cm).

Description: The goddess, crowned with blue-green leaves and flowers, is shown striding forward, a torch in her raised right hand. Her draperies of red-violet, turquoise blue, and green and her billowing mantle of vivid dark blue are painted in translucent enamel over foil, highlighted with gold. The grass is blue-green, the plants are blue, violet, turquoise, and golden-brown, and the sky is of a golden-brown flux shot with gilt rays issuing from clouds of blue and violet. The flesh tints tend toward a harsh gray. The vigorous outlines are in black, and the modelling is hatched or crosshatched and overwashed with gray. The cavetto is decorated with gold scrolls on a black ground, and the rim is painted in translucent enamels and grisaille with masks, grotesque animals, fruit, flowers, birds, and occasional drops imitating jewels. On the reverse, within a gilt laurel wreath, is the buxom figure of Minerva in voluminous blue and red-violet robes. She wears a helmet, a cuirass, and leggings and holds a lance and a baton. The background is black.

Condition: The plaque is in good condition. The enamel on the rim has suffered some injuries, and there are indications of repairs in Ceres' overdress and mantle. Part of the right leg of Minerva has been restored below the knee, but losses are still visible in the top of her legging.

The identification of the figure on the obverse as the earth goddess Ceres is uncertain, but likely. The literary source of the composition would be Ceres' search for her daughter Proserpina as recounted in Ovid's *Metamorphoses* (V, 438–45) and *Fasti* (LV, 561–62). However, the iconographical figure does not correspond to the design of Il Rosso—which was engraved by Caraglio, imitated many times by artists of the School of Fontainebleau, and copied by Jacques Bink and Virgil Solis[1]—in that here the goddess carries a torch but no sickle and is dressed rather than naked.[2] Could the figure be connected with *Cybele at the Gates of Hell,* a lost painting by Toussaint Dubreuil (1561–1602) recorded in 1709 at the château of Saint-Germain-en-Laye?[3]

The fact that the concave oval plaque is decorated in polychrome on both front and back indicates that it may have been intended for mounting in the door of a cabinet. The plaque has a counterpart, with the same signature, in the museum at Brunswick,[4] and another piece from the same decorative set displaying allegorical or mythological figures appeared in the G. Agath sale at Breslau in 1906.[5]

Exhibited: London, Victoria and Albert Museum, 1901–12, lent by J. Pierpont Morgan. New York, Metropolitan Museum, Morgan Collection, 1914–16, lent by J. Pierpont Morgan.

Collections: Madame de La Sayette, Poitiers. Her sale, April 23–28, 1860, Paris, Lot 141. Comte Daupias sale, November 8–10, 1894, Paris, sold for 1,520 francs. J. Pierpont Morgan, London and New York. Duveen. Frick, 1916.

NOTES

1 A. Bartsch, *Le Peintre-graveur,* Vienna, 1803–21, XV, No. 37. J. D. Passavant, *Le Peintre-graveur,* Leipzig, 1860–64, IV, No. 568, p. 117.

2 Persephone (Proserpina), the wife of Hades, herself holds a torch in one of the Triptolemos reliefs in the National Archaeological Museum, Athens (Roman copy in the Metropolitan Museum of Art, New York, No. 14–130–9). She appears naked, holding a torch, and driving a chariot in a Netherlandish woodcut with chiaroscuro (F. W. H. Hollstein, *Dutch and Flemish Etchings, Engravings and Woodcuts,* Amsterdam, 1949–, VIII, p. 121). Ceres holds a torch and a cornucopia in a drawing by Giulio Romano (Louvre, No. 3504) which was engraved (W.

M. Johnson, "Les Débuts de Primatice à Fontainebleau," *Revue de l'art,* No. 6, 1969, Fig. 9, p. 13).

3 The painting was the seventy-third composition described by Bailly in his *Inventaire des tableaux du Roi.*

4 Catalogue of 1891, No. 91, according to a note of E. Lachenaud in the files of the Musée Municipal at Limoges. The obverse of the Brunswick plaque shows a female figure holding a book amid a glory of clouds, and on the back is a male figure, probably Mars, within a laurel wreath.

5 J.-J. Marquet de Vasselot, in his notes at the Louvre, mentions also in this connection three unsigned concave plaques at Brunswick showing the Theological Virtues.

172

PIERRE COURTEYS

c. 1520–Before 1591

Notable among the works of Pierre Courteys are decorative plaques, caskets mounted with scenes from the Old Testament, and enamelled ware much in the manner of Pierre Reymond but executed in a more vigorous and colorful style. His earliest signed piece is a cup dated 1544. According to tradition, twelve exceptionally large plaques by Pierre Courteys dated 1559—nine of them now in the Musée de Cluny, Paris, and three in England—were once part of the polychrome decoration of the Château de Madrid outside Paris; each made up of four smaller units, they represent the Virtues, the Planets, the Roman Charity, and Hercules. The same enameller painted for the chapel of Anne de Montmorency's Château d'Écouen a reredos depicting the Passion of Christ after Dürer.

Casket: Scenes from the Story of Joseph (16.4.32)

Signed, in gold, at the top of the lid near the handle: P.COVRTEYS. H. 9¼ in. (23.5 cm); W. 10⅝ in. (27 cm); D. 6¹¹/₁₆ in. (17 cm).

Description: The casket is composed of seven plaques enamelled with episodes from the Story of Joseph, as recounted in Genesis 39:7 through 45:15. The sequence begins chronologically on the square end plaque at left with the fleeing Joseph leaving his cloak in the hands of Potiphar's wife.[1] On the lunette above, Pharaoh, sleeping naked in a canopied bed with twisted terms forming the posts,[2] dreams of the seven fat and seven lean cattle; they are visible, materializing the dream, through an opening at left, grazing on the banks of the Nile. In the scene on the back of the arched lid, Joseph interprets Pharaoh's dream, making with his fingers the gesture of digital computation;[3] the fat and lean cattle are visible a second time, through an aperture at center. On the front of the lid, Joseph, now Egypt's ruler, rides Pharaoh's chariot, preceded by musicians blowing a bugle and a trumpet as the crowd "cried before him, Bow the knee." On the right lunette of the lid, Jacob sends ten of his sons to Egypt to buy corn, keeping with him Benjamin, the only full brother of Joseph, through Rachel. On the lower back panel, Joseph, represented as an aging man (he was in fact not yet over forty), speaks roughly to his brothers and dismisses them.[4] On the square end plaque at right, Joseph's steward

174

finds in the sack of Benjamin, who accompanied his brothers on their second expedition to Egypt, the sacred vessel that Joseph used for divination, which Joseph had ordered hidden there. The final plaque, at lower front, depicts Judah's supplication for Benjamin, with all the brothers kneeling before the throne of the turbaned Joseph; the tiles of the throne-room floor are gilt with fleurs-de-lis, unlike those in the corresponding plaque on the back of the chest and the plaque at lower left, which have simple four-petal flower motifs. The painting throughout is characterized by strong accents of light and shade. The glowing semiopaque enamels are grayish-blue, green, and red-violet, and the translucent enamels are orange, blue, red-violet, and green. Gilding contributes to the brilliancy of the general effect. The flesh is rendered in grisaille tinted with red and occasionally with cobalt blue. The artist's signature appears at the top left of the aperture in the scene of Joseph Interpreting Pharaoh's Dream. The framework of the casket, which may be original, is of painted and gilded wood decorated with scrolls; the four engaged columns at the corners are coated with white enamel, painted in bister, and pointed up with gold.[5]

Condition: The plaques are in fairly good condition. There are numerous losses and repairs, notably around the handle on the lid, at the edges and corners of several of the plaques, and within the figures, especially along the contours of their garments. Old nail holes appear at the corners of all the plaques except the lunettes, but most of the old nails are missing.

The compositions are adapted from woodcuts by Bernard Salomon illustrating Claude Paradin's *Quadrins historiques de la Bible,* first published by Jean de Tournes at Lyon in 1553, and the *Biblia Sacra* first issued by de Tournes the following year.[6] Pierre Courteys freely revised his models, as indicated by comparing the scene of Joseph Interpreting Pharaoh's Dream on the Frick casket with that on a cup by the same enameller in the Musée des Beaux-Arts at Dijon.[7] The architecture at left in the plaque showing the discovery of Joseph's vessel is taken from Salomon's woodcut depicting the loading of the sacks at the time of the brothers' first visit to Egypt.

Several similar caskets are known illustrating, with few differences, the Story of Joseph, including one in the Metropolitan Museum of Art, New York.[8] Pierre Courteys interspersed episodes from the Story of Joseph with other Biblical scenes on a casket in the Victoria and Albert Museum, London,[9] and the same artist also enamelled the Story of David on a casket in the former Spitzer collection,[10] the Story of Gideon on a casket in the former collection of Vicomte de Tusseau,[11] and the Story of Moses on a casket in the Kunsthaus, Zurich.[12]

176

Exhibited: London, Victoria and Albert Museum, 1901–12, lent by J. Pierpont Morgan. New York, Metropolitan Museum, Morgan Collection, 1914–16, lent by J. Pierpont Morgan.

Collections: Frédéric Spitzer, Paris.[13] His sale, April 17–June 16, 1893, 33 rue de Villejust, Paris, Lot 540. J. Pierpont Morgan, London and New York. Duveen. Frick, 1916.

NOTES

1 The depiction of Potiphar's wife as bare-breasted is not intended as an erotic element, but reflects an iconographical fashion of the sixteenth century. The Marys visiting Christ's tomb on Easter morning are shown naked to the waist in an engraving of a *Missale romanum* published in Paris by J. Kerver in 1583 (fol. 100). Compare the female figures allegorizing the Virtues and the Liberal Arts on Frick saltcellar No. 16.4.41 by Jean Guibert (pp. 229, 230). The story of Joseph fleeing from Potiphar's wife is an archetype of the Triumph of Chastity.

2 The twisted terms, a Fontainebleau decorative motif, are after engravings by Fantuzzi and Jean Mignon. See *L'École de Fontainebleau,* Paris, 1972, No. 408. Compare also Hugues Sambin's *Oeuvre de la diversité des termes dont on use en architecture,* Lyon, 1572.

3 On this gesture, which dates from Scholastic iconography, see O. Chomentovskaya, "Le Comput digital: Histoire d'un geste dans l'art de la renaissance italienne," *Gazette des Beaux-Arts,* II, 1938, pp. 152–72.

4 Compare the lower section of a tazza of 1557 signed I.C. in the Musée de Cluny, Paris (No. Cl. 1440).

5 The framework is identical to those of a casket by Pierre Courteys in the Louvre

enamelled with the Stoning of Achan and the Feast of Belshazzar (No. O.A. 948 a–b; J.-J. Marquet de Vasselot, *Catalogue sommaire de l'orfèvrerie, de l'émaillerie et des gemmes,* Paris, 1914, No. 650) and a casket attributed to a follower of Pierre Courteys in the Walters Art Gallery, Baltimore, enamelled with scenes of the Creation (P. Verdier, *The Walters Art Gallery: Catalogue of the Painted Enamels of the Renaissance,* Baltimore, 1967, No. 160, pp. 288–92).

6 For the history of these two publications, see p. 140 and p. 144, note 4. Pierre Woeiriot, who is recorded in Lyon between 1554 and 1577, engraved five episodes from the Story of Joseph and added two to the series of forty included in the *Figures de la Bible* begun about 1560 and dedicated in 1580 to Charles III, Duc de Lorraine. He contributed ten of forty vignettes to the edition of Flavius' *Antiquities* published in Latin by the heirs of Jacopo Giunti and reissued by them in French in 1568, with all the small vignettes copied after Bernard Salomon's woodcuts. See: A. Robert-Dumesnil, *Le Peintre-graveur français,* Paris, 1835–71, VII, Nos. 6–10, p. 55; G. Duplessis' continuation of *Le Peintre-graveur,* XI, Nos. 12–13, pp. 335–36; N. Rondot, *L'Art et les artistes à Lyon du XIVè au XVIIIè siècle,* Lyon, 1902, pp. 273–87. Joseph and Poti-

phar's wife, Joseph Interpreting Pharaoh's Dream, and the Triumph of Joseph were painted after the same models as the scenes on the Frick casket in three of eight tympana illustrating the Story of Joseph at the Château du Lude, Sarthe; below the tympana are compositions taken mainly from Petrarch's *Trionfi* (D. Bozo, "Les Peintures murales du château du Lude," *Gazette des Beaux-Arts,* LXVI, 1965, pp. 199–218). Joseph and Potiphar's Wife and Joseph Inter-

preting Pharaoh's Dream were also engraved after Salomon's models on two silver-gilt plates, part of a set of twelve signed with the monogram P over M, in the Metropolitan Museum of Art, New York (No. 65.260, 10–1, gift of C. Ruxton Love, Jr.); the plates were published by Y. Hackenbroch ("A Mysterious Monogram," *Metropolitan Museum of Art Bulletin,* XIX, 1960, pp. 18–24) as English, but Hackenbroch subsequently believed she had traced

179

a Strasbourg mark on them. According to Père Dan, there were on the marble mantlepiece in the Cabinet du Roi off the Galerie François I at Fontainebleau two paintings, one depicting the *Cyclopes in Vulcan's Forge* and the other "une histoire représentant Joseph comme ses frères sont venus le visiter en Égypte" (*L'École de Fontainebleau,* No. 150).

7 Trimolet Collection, No. 1304.

8 No. 32.100.264, formerly in the collections of Baronne Mathilde de Rothschild and Col. Michael Friedsam (*Metropolitan Museum of Art: The Michael Friedsam Collection,* New York, 1932, p. 67, Fig. 13 on p. 63). An anonymous casket with the Story of Joseph enamelled after the *Quadrins historiques* was included in the 1965 exhibition Old Masters and the Bible at the Israel Museum, Jerusalem (No. 3, lent by Sidney J. Lamon, New York). The Story of Joseph was also enamelled by Jean Court *dit* Vigier on a casket in the Louvre (Salomon de Rothschild Bequest, 1922) and by Jean de Court on a set of plates in the Louvre, on a casket in the Walters Art Gallery (Verdier, No. 178, pp. 332–34), and on a plate with the Dream of Pharaoh in the City Art Museum of St. Louis. A casket very close to the Frick example was exhibited at the Burlington Fine Arts Club, London, in 1897 (No. 98).

9 Salting Bequest, formerly in the collections of Didier-Petit (sale, Paris, March 15 *et seq.,* 1843, Lot 95), George Field, and Gibson Carmichael (Christie's, May 12, 1902, sold for £ 1,450).

10 C. Popelin, in *La Collection Spitzer,* Paris, 1891, II, No. 123.

11 Exhibited at the Musée Rétrospectif, Paris, 1865, No. 2556. The Spitzer and Tusseau caskets share with the one in the Louvre (see note 5, above) representations of Belshazzar's Feast.

12 O. von Falke, *Alte Goldschmiedewerke im Zürcher Kunsthaus,* Zurich–Leipzig, 1928, No. 117, Pl. 32.

13 Popelin, II, No. 124, p. 58, repr.

Casket: Old Testament Subjects (16.4.33)

Signed, in gold, at the bottom of both scenes on the back of the casket and the lower scene on the  front: PC. H. 8⁵/₁₆ in. (21.1 cm); W. 9¹³/₁₆ in. (24.9 cm); D. 6¼ in. (16 cm).

Description: The casket is composed of seven plaques enamelled with Old Testament subjects mounted into a silver-gilt frame. Though several of the episodes are closely related, there is no apparent plan to the ensemble. The scenes on the front and back of the arched lid are, respectively, the Falling of Quails in the Desert and the Gathering of Manna in the Desert (Exodus 16:13–18; Numbers 11:31–32). The lower plaque on the front shows the institution of the Feast of the Passover in Egypt; around a table set with a roasted lamb and unleavened bread stand the Hebrews, dressed as God commanded "with your loins girded, your shoes on your feet, and your staff in your hand" (Exodus 12:8–11). In the lower plaque on the back, Shaphan the scribe reads to King Josiah from the "book of the law of the Lord given by Moses," which had been discovered in the Temple; the enameller was careful to give the reference on the opened pages of the book: IIII ROIS XXII (Fourth Kings 22, which is Second Chronicles 34 in the King James Bible). In the lunette on the right end of the lid, the angel comforts the bondwoman Hagar, who with her son Ishmael had been cast into the wilderness (Genesis 21:17–18). On the rectangular plaque below, Sennacherib, King of Assyria, is slain by two of his sons (Second Kings 19:36–37), an event that occurred in the time of Tobit, the father of Tobias (Tobit 1). The lunette on the left end depicts Tobias as, obeying the angel, he catches the fish that had sought to devour him (Tobit 6). Below are Tobias and Sarah before their wedding, praying in front of a fireplace in which burn the heart and liver of the fish (Tobit 8); the demon Asmodeus, who, in love with Sarah, had killed her seven previous husbands, is seen through the window at left being bound by the angel to a tree. The deep color scheme of the enamels melts into a sfumato, its sheen obtained by glazings in golden-brown and purple flux. The white preparation shines through, harmonizing the areas painted in cobalt blue, turquoise, red-violet, and golden-brown. The grisaille of the flesh parts is tinted with light red or shaded in violet.

Condition: The plaques are in good condition except for cracks and chips at several of the corners and for possible repairs around the handle, in the group at left on the front of the lid, and along some of the edges, most notably those of the lunettes.

The designs are adapted, like those on the same enameller's casket with the Story of Joseph (see preceding entry), from woodcut illustrations done by Bernard Salomon for Jean de Tournes of Lyon, as well as from prints by Pierre Woeiriot, who was active in Lyon during the period 1554–77.[1] A Gathering of Quails and

Manna after Woeiriot[2] was also enamelled, along with the Passover and other Biblical scenes, on a signed casket by Pierre Courteys in the former Sir Julian Goldsmid collection.[3]

The scene of Shaphan Reading to Josiah, including the Biblical citation, was painted by Pierre Reymond on the body of a ewer in the former Spitzer collection[4] and on an oval platter in the Louvre.[5] It appears again, along with the same

Triumph of Diana that decorates the body of the Frick ewer by Jean de Court (see p. 203), on a grisaille ewer by de Court in the Walters Art Gallery, Baltimore.[6] Three of the principal figures in the Gathering of Manna plaque are found on a casket of 1544 by Pierre Reymond in the Musée de Cluny, Paris.[7] The Story of Tobias is narrated on twelve plaques, attributed to Jean II Pénicaud or the master who signed KIP, mounted into a casket at the British Museum, London.[8]

Exhibited: London, Victoria and Albert Museum, 1901–12, lent by J. Pierpont Morgan. New York, Metropolitan Museum, Morgan Collection, 1914–16, lent by J. Pierpont Morgan.

Collections: J. Pierpont Morgan, London and New York. Duveen. Frick, 1916.

NOTES

1 For Salomon's woodcuts see p. 140 and p. 144, note 4. For Woeiriot see p. 162, note 5, and p. 178, note 6.

2 A. Robert-Dumesnil, *Le Peintre-graveur français,* Paris, 1835–71, VII, No. 17, p. 57.

3 Goldsmid sale, Christie's, June 8 *et seq.,* 1896, Lot 739.

4 The shoulder of the Spitzer ewer shows Moses Striking the Rock, and the body is decorated on one side with Shaphan and Josiah and on the other with the Worthies in the Furnace after a print by Étienne Delaune (impression in the New York Public Library). See: C. Popelin, in *La Collection Spitzer,* Paris, 1891, II, No. 100; C. Eisler, "Étienne Delaune et les graveurs de son entourage," *L'Oeil,* No. 132, 1965, Fig. 21, p. 19. The Biblical citation in the scene of Shaphan reading is not included in Salomon's woodcut.

5 Durand Bequest, 1825. J.-J. Marquet de Vasselot, *Catalogue sommaire de l'orfèvrerie, de l'émaillerie et des gemmes,* Paris, 1914, No. 621.

6 P. Verdier, *The Walters Art Gallery: Catalogue of the Painted Enamels of the Renaissance,* Baltimore, 1967, No. 175, pp. 324–29.

7 No. 921. Compare the cover of a tazza attributed to Pierre Reymond's workshop in the Musées Royaux d'Art et d'Histoire, Brussels, No. 2237 (*Europe humaniste,* exhibition catalogue, Brussels, 1954, No. 363). See also the Frick ewer with the Gathering of Manna (pp. 159, 161, and p. 160, note 2).

8 Waddesdon Bequest, No. 22 (from the Louis Fould collection).

JEAN DE COURT (MASTER I.C.)

Active c. 1555–c. 1585

The only known enamel fully signed by Jean de Court is a portrait dated 1555 in the Wallace Collection, London, showing Marguerite de France, daughter of François I, in the guise of Minerva. Features from that portrait are found again on an oval plaque of Minerva in the Louvre signed I. D. C., *and the latter signature, often abbreviated* I. C. *or occasionally* C. I., *appears on a large number of enamels that obviously all originated in the same studio. It is possible that the enameller Jean de Court was identical with the Jean de Court who from 1562 to 1567 was painter to Mary Queen of Scots, the widow of François II, and who in 1572 succeeded François Clouet as painter to Charles IX. His enamelled production is brilliant but frequently repetitive, perhaps an indication that, like Léonard Limousin, he delegated authority to assistants during his sojourns at the French court. Jean de Court may have been the brother of the enameller Jean Court* dit *Vigier, whose surviving works are relatively few but of the highest quality.*

Plaque: The Adoration of the Shepherds (16.4.34)

Signed, in gold, on the side of the stone podium below the Child: I. D. C. 17½ × 13⅜ in. (44.5 × 34 cm).

Description: In the central foreground the Virgin, clad in a blue mantle over a reddish-purple gown with green sleeves, kneels beside the Child. To the left are the shepherds, wearing rough skins and peasant garb; two of them bear gifts of fruit and a lamb, one leans on a sack presumably filled with grain, and another holds a bagpipe as he converses with a companion. Flanking the Virgin are three angels, one of them holding an olive branch. Joseph, dressed in blue, turquoise, and reddish-purple, sits at right. An old woman kneels in adoration of the Child, who lies on a sheet draped over a bundle of straw. Behind Joseph appear the ox and the ass under a thatched roof with a broken stone column forming one of its supports. The composition is staged on fragments of architecture colored, like the column, in gray-blue.[1] In the background at left, in a verdant landscape livened with touches of yellow, occurs the Annunciation to the Shepherds, and in the central distance nestles the town of Bethlehem, which, with its characteristic Limousin Gothic stee-

ple, resembles the walled city of Limoges. Above, in the golden radiance of the Star, dances a choir of cherubs. The flesh tones throughout range from pinkish-white to salmon red and gray. The garments of the foreground figures and the wings of the cherubs are in transparent enamel over foil, its effect enhanced by rich gilding. At upper left and right, framed by blue and white clouds, are two inscriptions in black letters on gold. The first reads: "*Maria | Heli. P. omnium | foeminarum feliciss. so | la inter virgines foecunda | prit* [for "peperit"] *tot saeculis expec: | tum Salvatorem Me: | um. Anno, Mundi | M M M DCCCC LX | pl. mi.*" The second is: "*Hec eadem, | ut illum mirifice ex | se natum alacriter edu: | cavit ita et grandia fa: | cientem gravia tolerantem | morientem resurgentem, ad | Patrem redeuntem con: | spexit, carum mox | sequūtura fili: | um.*"

("Mary, daughter of Heli [?], most fortunate among women, alone fruitful among virgins, bore My Saviour, awaited for so many centuries, in the Year of the World 3960 plus or minus."[2] "This same, as she joyfully reared Him miraculously born of her, beheld Him doing great deeds, bearing grievous things, dying, rising again, returning to His Father, where she was soon to follow her beloved son.")

Condition: The plaque is in good condition despite a number of small losses and repairs, most notably in the wings of all three foreground angels and some of the cherubs, in the area of the annunciatory angel in the background, in the garments of the seated shepherd at left, along the left and right margins, at the corners, and along the outlines of the Virgin and St. Joseph.

The inventor of the subject was Agnolo Bronzino, who, between 1530 and 1540, painted in Florence for his patron Filippo d'Averardo Salviati the *Adoration* now in the Museum of Fine Arts, Budapest.[3] In Bronzino's painting breathe a quietness of mood and a feeling of harmonious space in an elegiac landscape pervaded with divine light, qualities that were not grasped by those who, directly or indirectly, copied the composition. It was much admired in its own day[4] and was engraved several times, the prints inspiring in their turn copies in oil. An engraving by Giorgio Ghisi (1554), including the same Latin inscriptions, was published by Hieronymus Cock, and an anonymous copy of it was sold in Rome by Antonio Lafreri, who also published in 1568 a reinterpretation of Bronzino's *Adoration* engraved by Cornelis Cort after a painting by Marco Pino.[5] In Cort's print, the canopy of cherubs above the Child has been enlarged, and a sort of orchestra pit has been added below in which stand the bagpipe player and other peasants. Although Jean de Court followed in the main Bronzino's *Adoration* as engraved by Ghisi, he treated the landscape and the glory of clouds in the spirit of Marco Pino's painting as engraved by Cort.

190

The iconography of the Adoration of the newborn Child follows that traditional since the *Revelations* of St. Bridget of Sweden (d. 1373). The Latin inscriptions on the plaque, set within a glory of clouds and rays reminiscent of a painted retable, do not record the good tidings of the Nativity expressed in the song of the angels, but instead praise the divine motherhood of the Virgin. The fluted stone shaft supporting the shed's roof may refer to the ruin of the Temple of Peace at Rome when Christ was born, to the breakdown of the old order, or to the late medieval legend of the column against which the Virgin had to lean before her delivery. The ass, with its head turned away from the Child, is intended to symbolize the rejection of Christ by the Jewish people.

Exhibited: London, Victoria and Albert Museum, 1901–12, lent by J. Pierpont Morgan. New York, Metropolitan Museum, Morgan Collection, 1914–16, lent by J. Pierpont Morgan.

Collections: Charles Mannheim, Paris.[6] J. Pierpont Morgan, London and New York. Duveen. Frick, 1916.

NOTES

1 H. P. Mitchell, who saw the present plaque when it was lent to the Victoria and Albert Museum by Morgan, thought that the gray-blue and gray-green of the enamel were close to the palette of Jean Court *dit* Vigier ("The Limoges Enamels in the Salting Collection," *Burlington Magazine,* XX, 1911, p. 84).

2 The cryptic "Heli. P." may allude to the concept that Mary was, according to grace, the adopted daughter of Heli, father of her husband Joseph (Luke 3:23). See F. P. Dutripon, *Bibliorum sacrorum concordantiae,* Paris, VIIIᵃ, 1880, p. 600, under "Heli." Compare the office for the feast of St. Joachim on August 16, the day following Mary's Assumption; the name of Joachim sometimes appears as "Eliacim." On the year "3960 plus or minus," see *L'Art de vérifier les dates,* Paris, ed. of 1770, p. xii, according to which the date should be 4163.

3 A. Emiliani, *Il Bronzino,* Busto Arsizio, 1960, Pls. 30–32. M. Haraszti-Takács, *The Masters of Mannerism,* Budapest, 1968, No. I. G. Vasari, *Le vite de' più eccellenti pittori, scultori, ed architettori,* ed. G. Milanesi, Florence, 1878–85, VII, p. 596.

4 Vasari, *loc. cit.* R. Borghini, *Il riposo,* Florence, 1584, ed. of 1807, Milan, III, p. 99

5 A. Bartsch, *Le Peintre-graveur,* Vienna, 1803–21, XV, No. 3, p. 385. F. W. H. Hollstein, *Dutch and Flemish Etchings, Engravings and Woodcuts,* Amsterdam, 1949–, V, p. 42, No. 31 (three states). J. Bierens de Haan, *L'Oeuvre gravé de Cornelis de Cort,* The Hague, 1948, pp. 53–54. M. Hébert, retired Curator of the Département des Estampes at the Bibliothèque Nationale, Paris, called the author's attention to Cort's print in the Lieure Collection of her department. Marco Pino's painting is lost, but its *concetto* survives in a drawing at the Louvre (No. 22474); the Bronzinesque model is distorted in the drawing by a dramatization of the religious mood and an emphasis on stage setting (E. Borea, "Grazia e furia in Marco Pino," *Paragone,* No. 151, 1962, pp. 30–33, note 13, Fig. 26a). It is interesting to compare the measurements of the various versions: Bronzino's *Adoration,* 65.3 × 46.7 cm; Ghisi's print, 65.2 × 45.6 cm; Cort's print, 44.7 × 25.4 cm; Jean de Court's enamel, 44.5 × 34 cm. The proportions of the enamel are the same as those of Cort's print without its *bas de page,* the orchestra pit.

6 É. Molinier, *Collection Charles Mannheim: Objets d'art,* Paris, 1898, No. 206, repr. facing p. 46.

Tazza: Moses Striking the Rock (16.4.38)

Signed, in blue, on the underside of the bowl: I.C. H. 4⅜ in. (11.1 cm); D. 10 in. (25.5 cm).

Description: The interior of the shallow bowl is enamelled, like the obverse of the Frick ewer stand by Pierre Reymond (see p. 141), with the incident of the miraculous waters of Meribah. Moses is seen striking the rock at the command of God, who appears above in a glory of clouds. Three elders of Israel look on, as the people slake their thirst, marvel at what has occurred, and hurry to the stream with jars. The subject is painted in semiopaque enamels on a white preparation and in translucent enamels over foil. For the costumes, the lines of the drapery were first drawn on foil, then covered with enamel, and finally, after the enamel had been rendered transparent by firing, drawn again in dots of gold. The principal colors are blue, turquoise, blue-violet, green, and red-violet. The grisaille elements are outlined by *enlevage,* and the flesh tones are modelled with the brush in shades ranging from pink to violet. The composition is framed by a band of gilt arabesques on a blue ground and by a white rim. The underside of the bowl has a blue ground decorated in gold with scrolling arabesques and in grisaille and flesh tints with strapwork, grotesque terminal figures, cartouches, and masks. The foot is painted on the outside with grotesque sphinxes flanking busts of female terms and on the inside with gold fleurs-de-lis and other motifs.

Condition: The tazza has been extensively damaged and repaired, most notably along the left and right edges and at center in the scene of Moses Striking the Rock, along the outer edges of the lip and foot, at the juncture of the stem with the bowl, and inside the foot.

The exterior decoration of the tazza is nearly identical to that of the Frick tazza by Jean de Court with Lot and His Daughters (see following entry) and to that of a tazza signed I. C. in the Walters Art Gallery, Baltimore.[1] The interior of the latter depicts the Battle of Rephidim (Exodus 17:8–13), the episode immediately following the one shown here.

The scene of Moses Striking the Rock derives from a woodcut by Bernard Salomon illustrating the *Quadrins historiques de la Bible* and *Biblia Sacra* published in Lyon by Jean de Tournes.[2] When the present tazza was in the Spitzer collection, it had as a companion piece another tazza signed I. C. painted with the same scene in grisaille.[3] Duplicate versions in color and in grisaille were often produced by the workshop of Jean de Court.[4]

Exhibited: London, Victoria and Albert Museum, 1902 and 1908–12, lent by J. Pierpont Morgan. Glasgow, Kelvingrove Art Gallery, 1903–08. New York, Metropolitan Mu-

194

seum, Morgan Collection, 1914–16, lent by J. Pierpont Morgan.

Collections: Possibly Debruge-Duménil sale, January 23 *et seq.,* 1850, Hôtel des Ventes, Paris, Lot 738. Frédéric Spitzer, Paris. His sale, April 17–June 16, 1893, 33 rue de Villejust, Paris, Lot 564. J. Pierpont Morgan, London and New York. Duveen. Frick, 1916.

NOTES

1 P. Verdier, *The Walters Art Gallery: Catalogue of the Painted Enamels of the Renaissance,* Baltimore, 1967, No. 174, pp. 320–23. Compare also the motif of the female terms between grotesque dragons on the foot of a tazza representing the Crossing of the Red Sea, again signed I.C., in the former Spitzer collection (C. Popelin, in *La Collection Spitzer,* Paris, 1891, II, No. 145, Pl. XVI).

2 Compare the depiction of the same subject on a circular dish by Martial Courteys in the British Museum, London (Waddesdon Bequest, No. 30). For the history of the *Quadrins historiques* and *Biblia Sacra,* see p. 140 and p. 144, note 4.

3 Popelin, Nos. 147, 149. Compare a tazza in grisaille in the former Baroness James de Rothschild collection (E. A. Jones, *A Catalogue of the ... Collection of the Baroness James de Rothschild,* London, 1912, p. 196, Pl. CI).

4 See for example Verdier Nos. 172 (grisaille) and 173 (color), and Verdier No. 174 (grisaille) and its replica in the Wallace Collection, London. Similar duplication is found in various platters painted with the Crossing of the Red Sea.

Tazza: Lot and His Daughters (16.4.39)

Signed, in gold, on the underside of the bowl: I.C. H. 4¼ in. (10.8 cm); D. 9⅞ in. (25.1 cm).

Description: The interior of the shallow bowl shows the intoxication of Lot by his daughters, one of whom offers him a scalloped Venetian cup which the other fills with a good measure of wine from a jar. Beyond them opens the cave in which Lot would lie with his daughters; moss drips from its rocks, and trees grow above. To the right in the middle distance stands Lot's wife turned to salt, and beyond her rises Sodom with fire and smoke erupting from its walls. Near the rim at the top is the gold inscription G. XIX (Genesis 19). Conspicuous among the colors, which also include orange, green, red-violet, and blue-violet, are a vivid blue and a translucent red over foil used to render the flames consuming Sodom. The enamel of the flesh tints is rather thickly applied. The rim is painted on the inside with a band of gilt arabesques on a black ground (verging toward brown where the enamel was applied thinly) and on the outside with a band of egg-and-dart ornament.[1] The decoration on the underside of the bowl and on the foot, both inside and out, is nearly identical to that on the Frick tazza with Moses Striking the Rock (see preceding entry), except that here the ground is enamelled black.

Condition: Apart from small scattered repairs and some abrasion on the rim, the tazza is in very good condition. The stem may have been broken off and reattached.

For the group of Lot and his two daughters, Jean de Court copied mainly from a woodcut by Bernard Salomon illustrating the *Quadrins historiques de la Bible* and *Biblia Sacra* published in several editions by Jean de Tournes at Lyon.[2] For the remainder of the composition he adapted a print by the Dutch engraver Philip Galle (1537–1612), the second in a series showing the power of women for good or evil; the other subjects in the series are *Adam and Eve, Jael Killing Sisera, Samson and Delilah, Solomon Turning to Idolatry,* and *Judith Beheading Holofernes.* Galle's prints do not seem to have survived in any states other than the six impressions now in the Rijksmuseum, Amsterdam.[3] By remarkable coincidence, they were all copied by Pierre Reymond in his late revival of polychromy, and these six enamels are preserved.[4]

It seems probable that Jean de Court had no direct knowledge of Galle's print of *Lot and His Daughters,* but simply pirated from Pierre Reymond's enamel important elements of its design: the cave, the singular overhanging trees with bared roots, the flaming city, and Lot's wife turned to a pillar of salt.[5] He reproduced many details mechanically, without understanding their proper function in the

composition: Lot's wife, for instance, faces absurdly to the right instead of turning back to view the destruction of Sodom, and the torrents of fire rushing through the city gate in Galle's print are here transformed into the winding curves of a low wooden bridge.

Jean de Court enamelled this subject many times—for example, inside the bowl of a tazza in the Louvre[6] and on a ewer in the Taft Museum, Cincinnati.[7]

Exhibited: London, Victoria and Albert Museum, 1902–12, lent by J. Pierpont Morgan. New York, Metropolitan Museum, Morgan Collection, 1914–16, lent by J. Pierpont Morgan.

Collections: Maurice Kann, Paris. J. Pierpont Morgan, London and New York. Duveen. Frick, 1916.

NOTES

1 Compare the outer rim of a dish signed I.D.C. in the Hermitage Museum, Leningrad, representing Moses and the Brazen Serpent (O. Dobroklonskaya, *Painted Enamels of Limoges, XV and XVI Centuries,* Moscow, 1969, pp. 50–51).

2 In the enamel, however, the relative positions of Lot and the seated daughter have been reversed. For the history of the *Quadrins historiques* and the *Biblia Sacra,* see p. 140 and p. 144, note 4.

3 They are not mentioned in volume VII of Hollstein (see note 5, below), but all are reproduced in A. T. Lurie, "Gerard van Honthorst: Samson and Delilah," *Bulletin of The Cleveland Museum of Art,* LVI, 1969, Fig. 2, p. 333.

4 Four, including Lot and His Daughters, are in the Victoria and Albert Museum, London (Nos. 8410-3–1863, from the Soulages collection), and two are in the Walters Art Gallery, Baltimore (P. Verdier, *The Walters Art Gallery: Catalogue of the Painted Enamels of the Renaissance,* Baltimore, 1967, Nos. 137–38, pp. 231–34). Three of the subjects

were also enamelled in grisaille on a saltcellar signed P.R. in the Louvre.

5 The bare breasts of the seated daughter also derive from Galle, who engraved the subject of *Lot and His Daughters* two other times, once after Frans Floris and once after Anthonie van Blocklandt (F. W. H. Hollstein, *Dutch and Flemish Etchings, Engravings and Woodcuts,* Amsterdam, 1949–, VII, p. 74). The story of Lot and the destruction of Sodom, with its elements of eroticism, incest, and annihilation, knew great popularity among the Northern Mannerist painters of the sixteenth century. It was a favorite subject of Pierre Reymond, who used at least three different models (see for example Verdier, Nos. 139–40, pp. 235–43). It was also engraved, together with other subjects after Bernard Salomon's woodcuts, on a set of twelve silver-gilt plates in the Metropolitan Museum of Art, New York (see p. 179, note 6).

6 Durand Collection, 1825.

7 No. 1931.290.

200

Ewer: Triumph of Bacchus; Triumph of Diana (16.4.35)

Signed, in black, on the rear projection of the lip below the junc-  ture with the handle: I.C. H. 11 in. (28 cm).

Description: On the shoulder of the ewer, the infant Bacchus rides a goat accompanied by revelling putti. Two of them strike tambourines, others carry a leopard, a kid, and a flag, and at the head of the procession a putto dressed in a lion's skin frightens three companions with a mask of the type worn in ancient tragedies. The body of the ewer shows Diana seated in a chariot drawn by stags. Behind the goddess crouch the bound figures of Venus and Cupid. The chariot is preceded by nymphs and two winged female heralds blowing trumpets and is followed by hounds and additional nymphs escorting the captive Calypso and two Erotes taken prisoner. The two friezes, separated by a white torus painted with an arabesque, are enamelled in deep shades of orange-yellow, green, blue, purple, and red-violet against a background of midnight blue powdered with gold dots. The flesh is rendered in grisaille tinted with salmon red. The neck is decorated with acanthus, the lip with scrolls both inside and out, the handle with scrolls and petal motifs, and the foot with acanthus, swags, and masks. The interior is enamelled white.

Condition: The ewer appears to be in good condition, but there are signs of possible repairs at all of the junctures, on the foot, and in a few areas on the shoulder and the body.

The Triumph of Bacchus and the Triumph of Diana are adapted from a series of subjects designed about 1546 by Jacques Androuet du Cerceau for the decoration of cups, tazze, ewers, and ewer stands.[1] The other compositions include the Fall of Phaëthon, the Triumph of Amphitrite, and a Shipwreck. Du Cerceau's Triumph of Bacchus is derived from an engraving by J. T. de Bry based perhaps on drawings by Giulio Romano after Roman sarcophagi.[2]

Since the Triumph of Diana had a connotation of chaste love, it was often enamelled on ware intended as marriage gifts.[3] On ewers, it is not uncommon for a Triumph of Diana or a Triumph of Bacchus to decorate the shoulder while the body shows a religious or battle scene. A ewer in the Walters Art Gallery, Baltimore, for example, identical in form and height to the Frick piece and again signed I.C. on the lip, shows the same Triumph of Diana on the shoulder and is decorated on the body with the same scene of Shaphan Reading to Josiah as that used on the Frick casket with Old Testament subjects by Pierre Courteys (see p. 187).[4] In combining two pagan subjects superposed, the Frick piece compares with an unsigned ewer in the former Fountaine collection, the foot of which was also adorned with acanthus.[5]

Exhibited: London, South Kensington Loan Exhibition, 1862, No. 1835, lent by Hollingworth Magniac. London, Burlington Fine Arts Club, 1897, No. 160, lent by Sir Thomas D. Gibson Carmichael. New York, Metropolitan Museum, Morgan Collection, 1914–16, lent by J. Pierpont Morgan.

Collections: Hollingworth Magniac, London. IIis sale, July 2 *et seq.*, 1892, Christie's, Lot 523. Sir Thomas D. Gibson Carmichael, Salisbury. His sale, May 12, 1902, Christie's, Lot 73. J. Pierpont Morgan, London and New York. Duveen. Frick, 1916.

NOTES

1 See: H. de Geymüller, *Les Du Cerceau,* Paris, 1887, Fig. 68, p. 321; P. Verdier, *The Walters Art Gallery: Catalogue of the Painted Enamels of the Renaissance,* Baltimore, 1967, Fig. 33, p. 326. A composition similar to the Triumph of Diana, a print of which is in the Kupferstichkabinett, Berlin, is attributed to the monogrammist L. D. (F. Herbet, "Les Graveurs de l'École de Fontainebleau," *Annales de la Société historique et archéologique du Gâtinais,* XIV, 1896, No. 222, p. 101).

2 G. du Choul, *Discours sur la religion des anciens romains,* Lyon, 1556. Compare: G. Kauffmann, "Poussins letztes Werk," *Zeitschrift für Kunstgeschichte,* XXIV, 1961, pp. 101–27; A. Blunt, *Nicolas Poussin,* New York, 1967, pp. 146–47.

3 A similar Triumph of Diana after du Cerceau decorates a cup made by Jean Court *dit* Vigier in 1556 for the betrothal of Mary Stuart to the future François II (Cabinet des Médailles, Bibliothèque Nationale, Paris; see J. Babelon, in *Bulletin de la Société Nationale des Antiquaires de France,* session of June 5, 1929). The design recurs: on two ewer stands associated with Diane de Poitiers, one exhibited at the Burlington Fine Arts Club in 1897 (No. 67, Pls. XL, XLI) and the other, enamelled by Pierre Reymond in 1558, in the Kunsthistorisches Museum, Vienna (Verdier, Fig. 34, p. 327); on a candlestick in the Abegg-Stiftung, Bern, enamelled by Pierre Reymond in 1577 for the Chaspoux de Verneuil family (A. Faÿ, *Un Chandelier émaillé de Pierre Reymond,* Bern, 1971, No. 40, Figs. 9–12); and on a tazza signed by Pierre Reymond in the City Art Museum of St. Louis (P. Verdier, "Enamels by Pierre Reymond and Jean II Pénicaud," *Museum Monographs,* II, 1970, pp. 101–05). A Triumph of Diana very close to du Cerceau's central group was woven for Diane de Poitiers on the looms of Fontainebleau (L. Golson, "Lucca Penni: A Pupil of Raphael at the Court of Fontainebleau," *Gazette des Beaux-Arts,* L, 1957, Fig. 13, p. 28). On the reverse of a medal of Diane de Poitiers in the Louvre struck after 1548, Diana appears holding a bow and trampling underfoot the nude Eros (P. Erlanger, "Diane de Poitiers—The Myth," *Connoisseur,* CLXIII, 1966, Fig. 8b, p. 86). Elsewhere, the Triumph of Diana is found on a casket in the Charles Stein sale, Galerie Georges Petit, Paris, June 8–10, 1899, Lot 77; on a ewer of 1544 by Pierre Reymond in the Louvre; and on a plaque attributed

to Martin Didier in the Agath sale, Berlin, 1916, Lot 46. The Triumph of Diana and the Triumph of Bacchus decorate two candlesticks in the Metropolitan Museum of Art, New York (Blumenthal Bequest; see p. 211, note 5). The Triumph of Bacchus appears on the cover of a cup by Pierre Reymond in the Wernher collection at Luton Hoo, Bedfordshire (No. 337), and on a saltcellar signed I.C. in the former Spitzer collection (C. Popelin, in *La Collection Spitzer,* Paris, 1891, II, No. 159; compare No. 127, a ewer by Pierre Courteys, and No. 106, a saltcellar by Pierre Reymond).

4 Verdier, 1967, No. 175, pp. 324–29. See also: a ewer by Pierre Reymond in the Eugen Felix sale, Cologne, October 25–30, 1886, Lot 371, decorated with the Triumph of Bacchus and a battle scene; an unsigned ewer with the Triumph of Diana and Moses Striking the Rock in the British Museum, London (No. 1913, 12–20, 44); and a ewer with the Triumph of Diana and the Battle of Rephidim in the former Gustave de Rothschild collection (Exposition Universelle, Paris, 1867, *Histoire du travail,* No. 3003). Compare a ewer signed by Suzanne Court in the Victoria and Albert Museum, London (No. 553–1883), decorated on the shoulder with the Triumph of Ceres and on the body with Moses Striking the Rock after the woodcut by Bernard Salomon (see pp. 140 and 194). A ewer signed I.C. in the Dutuit Collection at the Musée du Petit-Palais, Paris, is shaped, like the Frick and Walters examples, as a *buire,* with its shoulder and body given a slightly depressed oviform structure. Such *buires* were designed by goldsmiths. Compare the drawing by Étienne Delaune reproduced in J. F. Hayward, "The Mannerist Goldsmiths: 2; France and the School of Fontainebleau, Part 2," *Connoisseur,* CLIII, 1963, Fig. 14, p. 15.

5 Fountaine sale, Christie's, June 16–19, 1884, Lot 452.

Pillar Candlestick: Olympian Deities; Labors of Hercules

(18.4.36)

Signed, in gold, inside the foot: I.C. H. 11¼ in. (28.6 cm).

Description: The stem is ornamented with interlaced white strapwork bands enclosing violet, blue, and green rosettes on a dark blue ground patterned with gold arabesques. The principal decoration on the foot, the ground of which is enamelled thinly in black and again patterned with gold arabesques, consists of twelve polychrome paintings on oval bosses representing Olympian gods and goddesses alternating with six of the Labors of Hercules. The subjects are: Jupiter; Hercules and the Nemean Lion; Venus and Cupid; Hercules and the Hydra; Juno; Hercules and the Dragon of the Hesperides' Garden; Minerva; Hercules Bearing the Two Pillars; Mars; Hercules and Cacus; Diana; and Hercules draped in the skin of the Nemean Lion. The colors are blue-green, turquoise, green, and orange, heightened with gold; the flesh parts are painted in grisaille and glazed with a hazy light red. The interior of the foot is patterned with gold fleurs-de-lis and other motifs.

Condition: The stem has been broken off from the base and soldered back. Repaired chips are visible around the reattachment, and a few small chips occur along the white rim of the foot. Several minute losses appear on the oval bosses, and there are indications of minor repairs on the upper stem and on the black ground of the foot. The candlestick is otherwise in good condition.

The form of the candlestick, distinguished by its columnar stem turning bulbous at the base, is that referred to in old French texts as "chandelier à la romaine."[1] Such candlesticks were easily wrought out of copper, with the stem polished on the wheel, the foot hammered and embossed, and the two parts then soldered together. They were intended to hold either wax candles or resin torches.

The gods and goddesses adorning the base of the present example are after prints by Étienne Delaune inspired by Italian designs. The same Jupiter appears on the back of the Frick oval dish with the Last Supper by Jean Reymond (see p. 157), and the same figures of Juno with the peacock and Venus and Cupid are found on the Frick saltcellar with Olympian deities by Jean II Limousin (p. 241). The Labors of Hercules copy prints engraved by Heinrich Aldegrever in 1550 after his own drawings.[2] The candlestick must originally have had a companion piece similarly decorated with alternating figures of Olympian deities and the six remaining Labors of Hercules.

The white bands on the shaft of the candlestick and the gilt sprays covering the ground on both sections represent two kinds of arabesque ornament, the strapwork interlace and the foliated stem, that were introduced to French goldsmiths, bookbinders, and enamellers and to the ceramists of Saint-Porchaire[3] by Francesco Pellegrini. They are exhibited one above the other in his *La Fleur de la science de pourtraicture,* published in Paris in 1530. Pellegrini was employed by Il Rosso at Fontainebleau, and his ornamental patterns were disseminated by the French and Netherlandish decorators working at the court. Étienne Delaune copied them with great gusto. Very close to the ornamentation on the candlestick are designs combining the two kinds of arabesque engraved after Jean Gourmont (d. 1551) and the illustrations by Balthasar Sylvius in his *Variarum protractionum quas vulgo Maurusias vocant* (1554). This "Saracenic" or "Moresque" decoration revived a type of half-geometrical, half-vegetal scroll pattern which, practiced in antiquity and in the Middle Ages by Moslem and Christian alike, found new favor in the early Renaissance, thanks in large part to the damascened brass vessels exported from Venice. The gilt scrollwork, or Granjon arabesque, was increasingly employed by the Limoges enamellers beginning about 1565.[4]

At the South Kensington Loan Exhibition of 1862, the Frick candlestick was shown beside three related pairs of candlesticks also signed I. C. and a fourth pair presumably from the same workshop.[5] Another related pair signed I. C. is in the British Museum, London,[6] and yet another is in the Germain Seligman collection, New York.[7] Two incomplete candlesticks with similar decoration and signed I. C. are in the Louvre,[8] and a pair of which only the bases survive is in the Musées Royaux d'Art et d'Histoire, Brussels.[9] An isolated candlestick attributed to Jean de Court, again incomplete, appeared in the Spitzer sale of 1893.[10]

Pierre Reymond in his late production also used Aldegrever's *Hercules* prints, adapting them to other mythological motifs and to a shorter type of candlestick with a flat foot molded as a torus, a wide concave dish forming a secondary drip pan, and a stem supported by a baluster. It is sometimes difficult to distinguish the work of the two masters when their candlesticks are unsigned.[11]

Exhibited: London, South Kensington Loan Exhibition, 1862, No. 1841, lent by Hollingworth Magniac. London, Burlington Fine Arts Club, 1897, No. 163, lent by John E. Taylor. New York, Metropolitan Museum, Morgan Collection, 1914–16, lent by J. Pierpont Morgan.

Collections: Debruge-Duménil, Paris.[12] His

sale, January 23 *et seq.,* 1850, Hôtel des Ventes, Paris, Lot 739. Hollingworth Magniac, London. His sale, July 2 *et seq.,* 1892, Christie's, Lot 400. John E. Taylor, London. His

sale, July 2, 1912, Christie's, Lot 140. J. Pierpont Morgan, London and New York. Duveen. Frick, 1918.

NOTES

1 H. R. d'Allemagne, *Histoire du luminaire depuis l'époque romaine jusqu'au XIXè siècle,* Paris, 1891, p. 225.

2 A. Shestack, "Some Preliminary Drawings for Engravings by Heinrich Aldegrever," *Master Drawings,* VIII, 1970, pp. 141–48, Fig. 6, Pls. 33a, 35a–37c. The drawings (ten in the Städelsches Kunstinstitut at Frankfurt am Main, two in the Museum der Bildenden Künste at Leipzig) have the same dimensions as the engravings—about 9.5 × 6.9 cm—exclusive of the inscriptions added on the prints. The complete set of thirteen prints—*Hercules Strangling the Snakes* followed by the *Labors*—is reproduced in F. W. H. Hollstein, *German Engravings, Etchings and Woodcuts,* Amsterdam, 1954–, I, pp. 50–51. Aldegrever's *Labors* were engraved on twelve parcel-

gilt spice- or fruit-plates struck with the mark of the hooded falcon, attributed to Thomas Bampton, and the London hallmark for 1567 (J. F. Hayward, "English Silver in the Francis E. Fowler Jr. Museum in Beverley Hills, California: Part 1," *Connoisseur,* CLXXVIII, 1971, pp. 114–23, repr. p. 115).

3 See for example the Frick Saint-Porchaire ewer with interlace decoration and applied reliefs (M. Brunet, in *The Frick Collection: An Illustrated Catalogue,* New York, VII, 1974, pp. 174–80).

4 On the history of these arabesque motifs see: J. H. Hayward, "The Mannerist Goldsmiths: 2; France and the School of Fontainebleau, Part 1," *Connoisseur,* CLII, 1963, pp. 240–45; P. Ward-Jackson, "Some Main Streams and Tributaries in European

Ornament 1500–1750, Part 2: The Arabesque," *Victoria and Albert Museum Bulletin,* III, 1967, pp. 90–103; J. Evans, *A
History of Jewellery,* London, 1970, pp.
86–88.

5 Nos. 1839–40, 1842–43, 1844 45, and 1846–
47. Nos. 1844–45 were given by Anne Payne
Blumenthal to the Metropolitan Museum
of Art, New York (Nos. 39.66.1, 2, see
J. G. Phillips, "Two Limoges Candlesticks," *Metropolitan Museum of Art Bulletin,* XXXIV, 1939, pp. 138–40).

6 Waddesdon Bequest, No. 32.

7 See P. Verdier, *The Walters Art Gallery:
Catalogue of the Painted Enamels of the
Renaissance,* Baltimore, 1967, Fig. 37, p.
369.

8 J.-J. Marquet de Vasselot, *Catalogue sommaire de l'orfèvrerie, de l'émaillerie et des
gemmes,* Paris, 1914, Nos. 683–84.

9 Nos. 2238 a–b.

10 33 rue de Villejust, Paris, April 17–June 16,
1893, Lot 554. See also C. Popelin, in *La
Collection Spitzer,* Paris, 1891, II, No. 139.

11 See for example a pair in the South Kensington Loan Exhibition of 1874, Nos.

764–65, the Earl of Warwick sale, Christie's, July 17, 1896, Lot 23, the Burlington
Fine Arts Club Exhibition of 1897, Nos.
158–59, attributed to Jean de Court, and
the Adda sale, Paris, November 29–December 3, 1965, Lot 181, attributed to Pierre
Reymond. Pierre Reymond copied four
prints from the *Labors of Hercules* on a
saltcellar dated 1555 in the Dutuit Collection at the Musée du Petit-Palais, Paris.
To the comprehensive list of enamelled
candlesticks given by A. Faÿ in *Un Chandelier émaillé de Pierre Reymond,* Bern,
1971, should be added the Seligman "chan-
deliers à la romaine" (see note 7, above),
one of which is decorated with the Labors
of Hercules and the other with the Triumph
of Diana; the same two themes are combined on a candlestick of 1577 by Pierre
Reymond in the Abegg-Stiftung, Bern. On
the further development of Limoges enamelled candlesticks, see Verdier, Nos. 195–96,
pp. 366–69, and Nos. 207–08, pp. 389–91.

12 J. Labarte, *Description des objets d'art qui
composent la collection Debruge-Duménil,*
Paris, 1847, No. 739, p. 600.

Saltcellar in Baluster Form: Bacchic Procession; Putti and Satyrs
(16.4.37)

Signed, in gold, inside the foot: I. C. H. 5⅛ in. (13 cm).

Description: The foot, in the form of a depressed bell, is painted with a continuous Bacchic procession of satyrs, youths, and maidens carrying musical instruments and grapes. Above the revellers runs a laurel wreath, and gold rays emanate from the juncture of the foot with the stem. The latter is decorated below with male and female terms holding garlands and above with a string of ovals imitating the gems or cameos of a goldsmith's model; a white molding separates the two motifs. On the exterior of the upper section, seated putti and satyrs alternate with cherub heads and horned masks. Smaller male heads adorn the rim of the salt receptacle, within which is the head of a man in profile to the right against a black ground dotted with gold. In addition to the opaque flesh tints, which range from salmon pink to gray and give an overall tone of warmth, the colors include translucent enamels of blue-green, blue-violet, deep blue, and golden-orange over foil. The black enamel ground was spread thinly, so that the copper shines through. There is much gilding. The inside of the foot is powdered in gold with fleurs-de-lis and five-petal flower motifs.

Condition: The saltcellar is in fairly good condition. Large areas of enamel are missing from the foot near the juncture with the stem. On the upper section, a triangular loss occurs in one of the masks, and there are indications of repairs in the drapery of one of the putti and in one of the cherub masks and the two adjacent figures.

Two similar, slightly taller saltcellars signed I. C. were in the former Spitzer collection, Paris.[1] There, the putti and satyrs on the upper sections did not alternate, but were kept separate. One saltcellar was decorated on the foot with the Triumph of Mars and Venus, the other with a Triumph of Bacchus after a model different from the one copied by the same artist on Frick ewer No. 16.4.35 (see p. 203).

Another pair of similar saltcellars, from the Soltykoff collection, is in the Louvre, and a single example was in the former John E. Taylor collection, London.[2] In form and height the present saltcellar also closely resembles Frick saltcellar No. 16.4.27, attributed to the workshop of Pierre Reymond (pp. 146–49); the receptacle of that piece is likewise painted with a male head in profile to the right against a black ground dotted with gold, and the exterior of the upper section shows satyrs alternating with amorini.

212

Exhibited: London, Victoria and Albert Museum, 1902–12, lent by J. Pierpont Morgan. New York, Metropolitan Museum, Morgan Collection, 1914–16, lent by J. Pierpont Morgan.

Collections: Charles Stein, Paris. His sale, June 8–10, 1899, Galerie Georges Petit, Paris, Lot 25. J. Pierpont Morgan, London and New York. Duveen. Frick, 1916.

NOTES

1 C. Popelin, in *La Collection Spitzer,* Paris, 1891, II, Nos. 158–59.

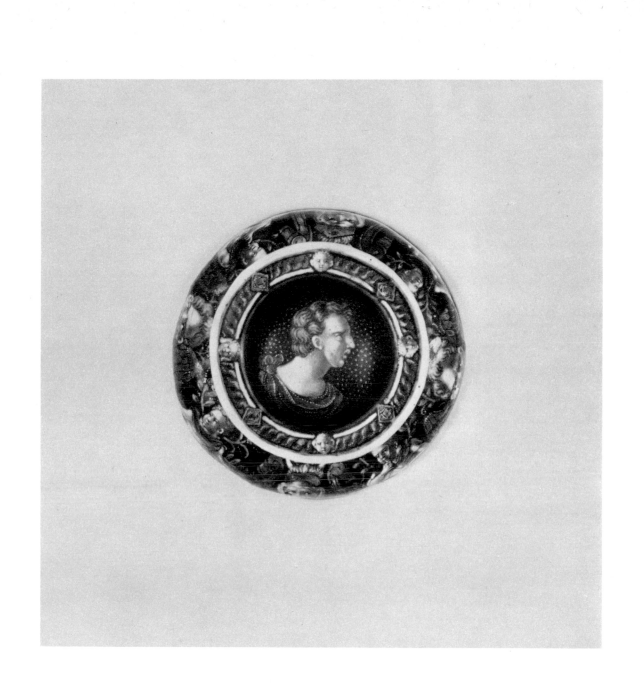

JEAN III PÉNICAUD

Late Sixteenth Century–Early Seventeenth Century

The most enigmatic member of the Pénicaud family, Jean III is probably to be identified with the "Jehan Pénicaud esmalheur" mentioned in documents dating from 1573 to 1606 and with the Jean Pénicaud who served as consul in 1571 and 1578. He may have been the son of Jean II, whose models he reinterpreted, with little originality, in a sketchy, impressionistic manner. The undeserved reputation he enjoyed in the nineteenth century was based on the erroneous attribution to him of enamels actually by Jean II.

Ewer: The Trojan Horse; A Cavalry Combat (16.4.13)

H. 11⅛ in. (28.3 cm).

Description: The upper half of the ewer is decorated in grisaille and gold on a blue ground. On the underside of the spout is a grotesque mask, and on the shoulder, flanked by two oval medallions enclosing respectively a male and a female bust in profile, is a coat of arms within a wreath supported by two putti. The arms are quarterly; one and four, azure, a fesse, with three columns, or; two and three, azure (for gules), a foi parée (two clasped hands), a fesse, argent; above, a shield, azure, and behind the shield a crozier, or. The exterior of the handle and the interior of the neck are enamelled in white. On the lower part of the body are represented the Entry of the Wooden Horse into Troy and a Cavalry Combat. The figures are painted in grisaille, glazed in pale flesh color, against backgrounds enamelled in shades of blue, blue-green, and yellow-green. The foot is decorated with scrolls and alternating masks and bucrania in grisaille on a blue ground. On the stem, both front and back, is the cipher DBYSI within a frame. The interior of the foot is enamelled blue.

Condition: The ewer is in good condition. Some cracks occur inside the neck, there is a small chip on the foot, and the lower parts of the horses and riders in the Cavalry Combat seem to have been coated with varnish. Signs of possible repairs are visible on the spout and at the junctures of the shoulder with the lower body and of the lower body with the foot. A flaw in the white band framing the male bust portrait on the shoulder was caused by slippage of the enamel during firing.

The arms on the ewer are those of Dominique de Vic, son of Emeric (Mery) de Vic, Duc d'Anjou, *Maître des Requêtes* under Henri III (1581), and *Garde des Sceaux* under Louis XIII (1621). Born about 1588, Dominique was named Abbot

216

of Bec-Hellouin at the age of nine and in 1621 became *Conseiller d'État* and member of the *Conseil Privé*. He was made Archbishop of Corinth and Coadjutor to the Archbishop of Auch in 1625, succeeding to the latter's office four years later. After 1625 he substituted on his coat of arms a cross with a double bar for the abbot's crozier found here.[1] The ewer must thus have been fashioned after 1597 and before 1625.

The Entry of the Wooden Horse into Troy is after an etching by Jean Mignon, an engraver of the School of Fontainebleau, who had himself interpreted one of a series of drawings on the Trojan War by Luca Penni.[2] The motif of the Trojans demolishing their city gate because it was too low to admit the horse has been omitted by the enameller, and the family of Priam is here reduced to a frieze of kneeling puppets reaching out in blind supplication.

The Cavalry Combat has often been reproduced alone—for instance, on a tazza in the Victoria and Albert Museum, London, attributed to the school of Jean II Pénicaud,[3] and on another in the former L. Cottreau collection.[4] The second and fourth cavalrymen from the left on the ewer reappear in a hunting scene on the lid of a casket by Pierre Reymond in the Walters Art Gallery, Baltimore.[5] The design of that composition, which is after an engraving by Agostino Veneziano, was also copied inside an enamelled cup formerly in the castle at Goluchów, Poland, attributed by Molinier to Jean III Pénicaud.[6] The same cavalrymen as on the ewer, this time naked, are enamelled on a ewer signed I. C. in the former Spitzer collection.[7]

Though the present ewer is neither signed nor dated, the sense of movement in the forms, a certain distortion in the figures, and the sketchy impasto technique with foamy whites juxtaposed to hard *enlevages* make probable an attribution to Jean III Pénicaud. An unsigned ewer dated 1556 formerly in the Van Gelder collection, of approximately the same height (27.5 cm) and enamelled with the Story of Aeneas in grisaille against a blue background, is in the style of the Pénicaud workshop and may well be an earlier work of Jean III.[8] Similar bust portraits with blurred, foamy outlines set within oval medallions are found on several pieces, including: two tazze in the Louvre attributed by Darcel to Jean III;[9] the cover of a tazza in the Walters Art Gallery attributed to Jean III or Pierre Pénicaud;[10] a candlestick in the Taft Museum, Cincinnati;[11] and the cover of a tazza in the Musées Royaux d'Art et d'Histoire, Brussels.[12]

218

The Trojan War inspired the decoration on a large number of Limoges enamels.[13] During the sixteenth century the Trojan Horse was widely employed as an emblem of deceit, as reflected in the following lines from Guillaume de la Perrière's *La Morosophie:* "Ce grand cheval tant bien fait par dehors / Portoit en soi des Troyens la ruine / Car bien souvent sont pires dans le corps / Qui par dehors nous font plus sainte mine."

Exhibited: London, Victoria and Albert Museum, 1901–12, lent by J. Pierpont Morgan. New York, Metropolitan Museum, Morgan Collection, 1914–16, lent by J. Pierpont Morgan.

Collections: J. Pierpont Morgan, London and New York. Duveen. Frick, 1916.

NOTES

1 See E. Olivier, G. Hermal, and R. de Rotou, *Manuel de l'amateur de reliures armoriées françaises,* Paris, 1925, under "de Vic (Guyenne)" and Pl. 472.

2 Luca Penni, already known for his work in Genoa, was invited to Fontainebleau and was much esteemed in France. Three of his Trojan War drawings are preserved in the Louvre (Nos. 1398–1400); his *Trojan Horse* is reproduced by L. Dimier in *French Painting in the XVIth Century,* New York, 1904, p. 116. Five etchings from Mignon's series after Penni, including the *Trojan Horse,* also survive. See: J. Adhémar, *Bibliothèque Nationale... Inventaire du fonds français: Graveurs du XVIème siècle,* II, Paris, 1938, No. 14, p. 16; H. Zerner, *École de Fontainebleau: Gravures,* Paris, 1969, Nos. 41–45; F. Herbet, "Les Graveurs de l'École de Fontainebleau," *Annales de la Société historique et archéologique du Gâtinais,* XVII, 1901, pp. 75–76, 85; H. Zerner, "Les Eaux-fortes de Jean Mignon," *L'Oeil,* No. 171, 1969, pp. 8–15, Fig. 4.

3 No. 1873–479.

4 Sale, Galerie Georges Petit, Paris, April 28–29, 1910, Lot 62. Similar scenes appear on two plaques in grisaille by Jean III Pénicaud in the Louvre (Sauvageot Bequest, 1856, No. O. A. 965; J.-J. Marquet de Vasselot, *Catalogue sommaire de l'orfèvrerie, de l'émaillerie et des gemmes,* Paris, 1914, No. 500) and on a ewer in bluish grisaille, possibly by Jean III, on loan from the Boston Athenaeum to the Boston Museum of Fine Arts.

5 P. Verdier, *The Walters Art Gallery: Catalogue of the Painted Enamels of the Renaissance,* Baltimore, 1967, No. 133, repr. p. 220.

6 É. Molinier, *Collections du château de Goluchów: Objets d'art,* Paris, 1903, No. 89.

7 C. Popelin, in *La Collection Spitzer,* Paris, 1891, II, No. 143. Compare a ewer in the Louvre painted in grisaille (Marquet de Vasselot, No. 672; Inv. MR 2418) and a ewer signed I.C., decorated with bust portraits on the shoulder and with nude riders

below, loaned to the Manchester Exhibition of 1857 and to the South Kensington Exhibition of 1862 (No. 1814; E. Lachenaud, *Émaux de Limoges: Ventes et collections anglaises,* Ms. at the Musée Municipal, Limoges, repr. p. 51 A).

8 Van Gelder sale, Hôtel Drouot, Paris, June 24–25, 1953, Lot 302.

9 A. Darcel, *Notice des émaux et de l'orfèvrerie,* 4th ed., Paris, 1891, Nos. 235, 236.

10 Verdier, No. 56, repr. p. 116. The bowl of the tazza is painted with a Cavalry Combat after a different model.

11 No. 1931.295.

12 No. 2237. See *Europe humaniste,* exhibition catalogue, Brussels, 1954, No. 363.

13 A Judgment of Paris and four episodes of the Trojan War after Jean Mignon decorate a casket by Pierre Reymond from the Mannheim collection (É. Molinier, *Collection Charles Mannheim: Objets d'art,* Paris, 1898, No. 179, repr.). A plaque of the Trojan Horse after a print by Giovanni Battista Fontana (A. Bartsch, *Le Peintregraveur,* Vienna, 1803–21, XVI, No. 53, pp. 233–34) was part of an unmounted set by Pierre Reymond in the Berlin museum. In the former J. de Lichtenstein collection at the castle of Sebenstein, Austria, were six colored enamelled plaques by Pierre Courteys (55 × 41 cm) illustrating the story of the doom of Troy. See: A. Leroux, "Les Émaux limousins des Musées de Vienne et de Munich," *Bulletin de la Société archéologique et historique du Limousin,* XXXIV, 1887, p. 1; A. Prachoff, *Album de l'Exposition de Saint-Pétersbourg en 1904,* St. Petersburg, 1907, pp. 189–91, Fig. 77; M. Demaison, "Une Exposition rétrospective à Saint-Pétersbourg," *Les Arts,* No. 84, 1908, p. 6, repr. p. 2. The treacherous Sinon, who induced the Trojans to bring the Wooden Horse within their walls, was also enamelled by Pierre Reymond in a simplified oval composition in the Victoria and Albert Museum, London (No. 8414–63). Two convex roundels by Pierre Courteys in the Musée Municipal, Limoges, illustrate the Rape of Helen and the Storming of Priam's Palace, with the addition in the latter subject of figures taken from Il Rosso's fresco in the fifth bay north of the Galerie François I at Fontainebleau.

SUZANNE COURT

Late Sixteenth Century–Early Seventeenth Century

Presumably Suzanne Court belonged, by birth or by marriage, to the family of the enamellers Jean Court dit *Vigier and Jean de Court. The intense coloring that typifies her production links her to the workshop of Jean de Court, but the distinct artistic personality of her draughtsmanship was original enough to be imitated in the workshop of Jean I Limousin.*

Pair of Saltcellars: Scenes from the Story of Orpheus
(16.4.43 and 16.4.44)

Signed, in gold, under the figure of Orpheus on No. 16.4.43  and below the feet of Apollo on No. 16.4.44: s.c. H. 4⁷/₁₆ in. (11.3 cm).

Description: Within the receptacle of each saltcellar is a profile head against a black ground strewn with gold dots, that on No. 16.4.43 representing a bearded and helmeted man facing right, that on the pendant a woman with a diadem facing left.[1] The rim surrounding the receptacle is decorated with four cherub heads in colored enamel linked by a string of gilt disks, and on the upper section of the body are four flesh-colored masks connected by purplish-crimson drapery festooned beneath trophies painted in blue and red-violet. Below the masks is a torus molding with a gilt wreath, and the foot is gilt with a string of small circles above a band of arabesques. The lower section of No. 16.4.43 shows Orpheus seated at the foot of a shady tree, playing his lyre and singing to a group of animals including a lion, a stag, a squirrel, a unicorn, and a monkey perched on a branch. In the midst of his song he is attacked by the frenzied women of the Cicones, who, enraged that he would have nothing to do with mortal women after his return from Hades without Eurydice, rush upon him with spears and stones. At first their missiles, thwarted by the magic of the music, fall harmless at his feet—the moment depicted here. The lower section of No. 16.4.44 is decorated with two independent scenes. One shows the head of the slain Orpheus and his lyre floating in the River Hebrus as three women mourn his loss from the river's bank. The head was carried to sea and to the shore of Lesbos, where a dragon sought to devour it. In the second scene, Apollo turns the dragon to stone. The inhabitants of Lesbos later buried the head, and the soul of Orpheus returned to Hades and to Eurydice. The ground color of both saltcellars is black inside and out, with the interiors thinly enamelled and powdered with gilt fleurs-de-lis and petal motifs. The figures on the lower sections, set against blue-green

16.4.43

16.4.43

fields strewn with tiny gold flowers, are delicately painted in tones of red-violet, blue, and green, contrasting with the flesh tints and their chalky white highlights.

Condition: Except for some faded gilding on No. 16.4.43 and a few minor repairs on the rims and feet of both, the saltcellars are in very good condition.

The scenes were enamelled after woodcuts attributed to Bernard Salomon illustrating the various editions of *La Métamorphose d'Ovide figurée* published by Jean de Tournes at Lyon beginning in 1557.[2] The inclusion on No. 16.4.43 of a unicorn, symbolic of the incarnation of Christ through the Virgin, is justified by the medieval tradition of the *Ovide moralisé,* which viewed Orpheus as a pagan precursor of Christ and saw in the women of the Cicones an image of the Jews who condemned Christ to death.[3]

16.4.44   16.4.44

Exhibited: London, Victoria and Albert Museum, 1901–12, lent by J. Pierpont Morgan. New York, Metropolitan Museum, Morgan Collection, 1914–16, lent by J. Pierpont Morgan.

Collections: No. 16.4.44 was recorded in 1898 in the Mannheim collection, Paris.[4] Both saltcellars were acquired by J. Pierpont Morgan, London and New York. Duveen. Frick, 1916.

NOTES

1 Saltcellars were frequently decorated around 1600 with ideal bust portraits of a couple. See for instance: a pair signed I.L. in the Victoria and Albert Museum, London (No.

647–1893; South Kensington Loan Exhibition of 1862, Nos. 866–67); an isolated example signed I.L. in the Walters Art Gallery, Baltimore (P. Verdier, *The Walters Art Gal-*

16.4.43

16.4.44

lery: Catalogue of the Painted Enamels of the Renaissance, Baltimore, 1967, No. 200, pp. 374–76); and one in the British Museum, London, again signed ɪ.ʟ. (Waddesdon Bequest, No. 43).

2 The events depicted are from Book XI, vv. 1–84. To quote from the Lyon edition of 1564: "Orphée mis en pièces / L'une une pierre et l'autre un dard lui tire / Il meurt chantant mélodieusement" (fol. i 4 vo.); "La langue et lyre d'Orphée / mort sont pleints / Puis à tels pleints que l'une et l'autre entonne / piteusement le rivage répond" (fol. i 5). On the history of de Tournes' editions, see p. 232, note 5.

3 *Ovide moralisé en prose,* ed. C. de Boer, Amsterdam, 1954, pp. 266–69. See also: J. B. Friedman, *Orpheus in the Middle Ages,* Cambridge, Massachusetts, 1970; E. Wind, *Pagan Mysteries in the Renaissance,* 2nd ed., London, 1968, pp. 17–18, 42 ff., 237.

4 É. Molinier, *Collection Charles Mannheim: Objets d'art,* Paris, 1898, No. 207.

JEAN GUIBERT

Late Sixteenth Century–Early Seventeenth Century

Little is certain concerning the life of Jean Guibert. Fifth in line of descent of the Guibert family in Limoges, he is recorded as an enameller in 1613 and died before January 13, 1618. His son François, also an enameller, died in 1684. Jean Guibert the enameller is very probably identical with a goldsmith of the same name listed in 1615 in the parish registers of Saint-Michel-des-Lions, Limoges, and he may also be identifiable with an "escrivain et painctre" mentioned in documents of 1592. The latter once owned the 1521 edition of the De artificiali perspectiva *of Viator (Jean Pelegrin or Pélerin) bound together with the 1537 edition of the* Regole generali di architetura *of Sebastiano Serlio. This two-fold treatise, now in the Bibliothèque Municipale at Limoges, had been the property of a Jean Pénicaud in 1561. Jean Guibert enriched it with drawings in ink and sanguine, three in the Viator and six in Serlio.*[1]

Pair of Saltcellars: Virtues and Liberal Arts with Religion and Justice; The Story of Minos and Scylla (16.4.40 and 16.4.41)

Signed, in gold, inside the receptacle of each saltcellar: I.G. H. 4⁵/₁₆ in. (11 cm).

Description: Each of the hexagonal saltcellars is enamelled on its concave, flaring sides with six allegorical female figures. Those on No. 16.4.40 represent: the three Theological Virtues, Faith holding a crucifix and a book, Hope with an anchor and a hawk, and Charity with two children; two of the Cardinal Virtues, Fortitude carrying a column and Temperance pouring water into a wine cup; and one of the Liberal Arts, Dialectic wielding two snakes emblematic of argumentation pro and contra. The salt receptacle is painted

with a scene of Scylla, daughter of King Nisus of Megara, gesturing from a tower of her besieged city toward the brilliantly arrayed King Minos of Crete, her father's enemy, with whom she had fallen in love. The figures on the sides of No. 16.4.41 represent: Religion with a lantern and a flaming sword; Justice with a balance and a sword; Prudence with a mirror; Poetry with a palm and a scroll; Medicine with a caduceus and a mortar; and Astronomy with an astrolabe, a celestial globe, and a telescope. Prudence might also be interpreted—on the basis of the mirror, an emblem of sight—as one of the visual arts, and the attributes of Poetry could apply as well to Rhetoric or Eloquence. Within the

226

16.4.40

salt receptacle, Scylla gives to Minos the magic purple lock of Nisus' hair, which had protected him and Megara from harm; in possession of it, Minos stormed the city, and Nisus was killed. The colors used on both saltcellars are green, red-violet, orange, turquoise, and light and dark blue, all heightened with gilding. The flesh is painted in grisaille tinted and stippled with red. Translucent enamel on foil was lavishly employed to produce a brilliant effect, notably in the costumes and in the sea and ship on the receptacle of No. 16.4.41. The bands of floral sprays on the rims and feet, painted in gold with the blossoms in jewel-like translucent enamel, are particularly elaborate. The backgrounds are black both inside and out, and the interiors are richly ornamented with gilding.

Condition: Both saltcellars are in very good condition apart from a few minor losses and repairs on the guilloche bands that border the rims and feet.

Despite a few uncertain identifications, the juxtaposition of figures emblematic of the Liberal Arts and the Virtues under the aegis of Religion and Justice is made clear by their source, a group of prints[2] and a series of drawings[3] by Étienne Delaune. Delaune depicted on the frontispiece of the drawings Charles IX distributing crowns to figures representing Philosophy, Jurisprudence, Eloquence, Poetry, Astronomy, Geometry, and Music, in the presence of Piety, who has the attributes of Religion and Charity, and of Justice, who according to Plato is the condition and the summary of all the Virtues. Piety with a cross and book and Justice with a sword and balance stand beside two columns supporting the Royal crown on an enamelled gold medallion commissioned by Catherine de Médicis in 1571 from her goldsmith, François Dujardin.[4]

The scenes depicted in the salt receptacles, taken from Ovid's *Metamorphoses* (VIII, 1–151), possibly were chosen because Scylla, having sinned against Piety, met the retribution of Justice. Scorned by Minos, she was transformed into a ravenous seafowl, forever pursued by the osprey or sea eagle into which her father Nisus had been changed. Both compositions are adapted from woodcuts attributed to Bernard Salomon illustrating various editions of the *Metamorphoses* published in Lyon by Jean de Tournes.[5]

Saltcellars of the present form decorated with allegorical figures usually are signed by or attributed to Jean I Limousin, though some may be by Jean II. The same abnormal thinness of the wrists, and of the ankles of the children shown with Charity, is found also on works by Joseph Limousin. The Frick saltcellars are the first signed works of Jean Guibert that can be put on record. It should be

228

16.4.41

noted in this connection that the scene of Minos and Scylla on No. 16.4.40 also decorates a hexagonal, two-handled cup with similar jewel-like floral decoration in the Musée Municipal, Limoges,[6] and reappears on one of six enamelled plaques with mythological subjects in the Taft Museum, Cincinnati, exhibiting the same characteristics of design and execution.[7]

A saltcellar in the former Debruge-Duménil collection, one of a pair attributed by Labarte to Suzanne Court, was decorated with six figures of Virtues.[8] In the Musée de Cluny, Paris, are a cup decorated with figures of the Liberal Arts and two roundels, one representing Theology with a lantern and a flaming sword and the other Wisdom with a book, that were no doubt originally part of a series.[9]

Exhibited: London, Victoria and Albert Museum, 1902–12, lent by J. Pierpont Morgan. New York, Metropolitan Museum, Morgan Collection, 1914–16, lent by J. Pierpont Morgan.

Collections: J. Pierpont Morgan, London and New York. Duveen. Frick, 1916.

NOTES

1 L. Guibert, in *Bulletin de la Société archéologique et historique du Limousin,* XXXI, 1883, p. 398. E. Ruben, *Catalogue méthodique de la Bibliothèque Municipale de Limoges,* 1863. On Jean Guibert the enameller and the Guibert family (Jacques Guibert was assay master in 1570), see M. Ardant, "François Guibert," *Bulletin... du Limousin,* X, 1860, pp. 77–80.

2 See: A. Robert-Dumesnil, *Le Peintre-graveur français,* Paris, 1835–71, IX, pp. 54–56, 103–04; C. Blanc, *Manuel de l'amateur d'estampes,* Paris, 1856, II, Nos. 156–71, p. 504.

3 See: I. Toesca, "Quelques Dessins attribués à Étienne Delaune," *La Revue des arts,* X, 1960, pp. 255–59; *L'École de Fontainebleau,* Paris, 1972, No. 72. Delaune's drawings are now in the following collections: *Allegory of the Liberal Arts with Charles IX,* Accademia, Venice; *The Triumph of Wisdom* (or *Faith*), *The Temple of the Sciences, Music,* and *Astronomy,* Cabinet des Dessins, Louvre; *Grammar* and *Arithmetic,* Kunstbibliothek, Berlin; *Geometry,* Musée Condé, Chantilly.

4 The medallion, now in the Kunsthistorisches Museum, Vienna, is closely related in design to a woodcut by Olivier Codoré. Two columns inscribed *Pietate* and *Iustitia* dominate an allegorical group presented by the City of Paris to Charles IX on the occasion of his solemn entry in 1571. They were also chosen by Chancellor Michel de l'Hôpital as the device of France, defying the two columns adopted by the Emperor Charles V and the pretension of Philip II to rule the universe. Two columns appear

16.4.40

16.4.41

behind Piety and Justice in a drawing by Antoine Caron illustrating the life of Charles IX. See: Y. Hackenbroch, "Catherine de' Medici and Her Court Jeweller François Dujardin," *Connoisseur,* CLXIII, 1966, pp. 28–33; F. A. Yates, "Charles Quint et l'idée d'Empire," in *Les Fêtes de la Renaissance, II: Fêtes et cérémonies au temps de Charles Quint,* ed. J. Jacquot, Paris, 1960, pp. 94–95, Pl. IV, Figs. 1, 4, 5; J. Guiffrey, *Les Dessins de l'histoire des rois de France par Nicolas Houel,* Paris, 1920, Pl. XXVIII.

5 *La Métamorphose d'Ovide figurée,* first published in 1557 (with an edition in Flemish). An Italian edition, *La vita e Metamorfoseo d'Ovidio figurato,* was published in 1559 and dedicated to Diane de Poitiers. Salomon's prints were pirated in *Johan. Posthii Tetrasticha in Ovidii Metam. lib. IV quibus accesserunt Vergilii Solis figurae.* De Tournes' first edition had 178 woodcuts attributed to Salomon, of which twenty-two had previously appeared in the second part—*Les Traductions*—of the *Oeuvres de Jean Marot*

231

published by de Tournes in 1549. The number of woodcuts eventually rose to 194. The last edition appeared in 1609.

6 On loan since 1875 from the Louvre to the Musée National Adrien Dubouché at Limoges, then to the Musée Municipal; formerly in the Durand collection (No. 45). See: L. de Laborde, *Notice des émaux, bijoux et objets divers,* I, Paris, 1852, No. 559; A. Darcel, *Notice des émaux et de l'orfèvrerie,* Paris, 1867, No. 598. L. Bourdery supported Darcel's attribution of the cup to the workshop of Suzanne Court ("Les Émaux peints à l'Exposition rétrospective de Limoges en 1886," *Bulletin... du Limousin,* XXXV, 1888, pp. 368–69, and *Les Émaux peints,* Limoges, 1888, pp. 90–91). A saltcellar in the Walters Art Gallery, Baltimore, attributed to Joseph Limousin, exhibits certain characteristics closely resembling those of the Frick pair: a background powdered with identical rosettes, figures displaying elongated limbs and abnormally thin joints, and shrubs and hillocks outlined with a hem-like border of connected loops (P. Verdier, *The Walters Art Gallery: Catalogue of the Painted Enamels of the Renaissance,* Baltimore, 1967, No. 194, pp. 363–65).

7 Nos. 1931.514–19. Another episode in the story of Minos—Britomartis, the nymph of Diana, throwing herself into the sea to escape being violated by the King—is enamelled on the back of a pendent mirror by Jean I Limousin in the Toledo Museum of Art (R. H. Riefstahl, "European Jeweled Arts," *Museum News,* N. S. XIII, 1970, repr. p. 59). The subject is adapted from an engraving in a suite by Étienne Delaune illustrating the *Story of Diana,* done after Luca

Penni's cartoons for a set of tapestries commissioned by Henri II for Diane de Poitiers' château at Anet (*L'École de Fontainebleau,* p. 347 and Nos. 455–61; Robert-Dumesnil, IX, pp. 134–36).

8 J. Labarte, *Description des objets d'art qui composent la collection Debruge-Duménil,* Paris, 1847, No. 754. Two other saltcellars decorated with Virtues are in the Wernher collection at Luton Hoo, Bedfordshire (No. 355), and the Louvre (Darcel, No. 388). The latter is pentagonal and depicts the young Louis XIII within the receptacle. A saltcellar in the former Spitzer collection was painted with four Virtues alternating with Spring and Summer (C. Popelin, in *La Collection Spitzer,* II, Paris, 1891, No. 75; Spitzer sale, 33 rue de Villejust, Paris, April 17–June 16, 1893, Lot 491). Because of its violet counterenamel it must be dated rather late in the seventeenth century.

9 Cluny Nos. 909 and 11–272/3. The figures on the cup—inscribed with the names Gramatica, Dimantica, Rhetorica, Artihmet [*sic*], Musica, Geometria, and Astrologia—are painted in a white impasto against a dark blue ground, in the manner of Jean III Pénicaud. Dimantica (assuming the name is not a misspelling) was substituted for Dialectica and is to be considered a duplicate of Astrologia; compare Pontus de Tyard, *Mantice ou discours de la vérité de divination par astrologie,* published by Jean de Tournes and G. Gazeau at Lyon in 1558. The figure of Wisdom on the second Cluny roundel points to a passage in her book, presumably Proverbs 9:1: "Wisdom hath builded her house, she hath hewn out her seven pillars"; the pillars have been con-

232

16.4.40

16.4.41

strued as the Liberal Arts. A third roundel, showing Geometry, formed part of the Leroux Bequest to the Louvre (J.-J. Marquet de Vasselot, *Catalogue sommaire de l'orfèvrerie, de l'émaillerie et des gemmes,* Paris, 1914, No. 709). The Musée de Cluny also possesses seven enamelled plaques, painted partly in grisaille and partly in colors, depicting the Theological and Cardinal Virtues (E. du Sommerard, *Catalogue et description des oeuvres d'art,* Paris, 1883, Nos. 4682–88). The iconographical union of the

Virtues and the Arts and Sciences began in the fourteenth century with the psychomachia—the conflict between the Virtues and their corresponding Vices—stressing the moral value of mastering the Liberal Arts. See for example Giovanni Andrea's *Novella in libros decretalium* of 1354, illuminated by Nicolò di Giacomo, called Nicolò da Bologna (Biblioteca Ambrosiana, Milan, Ms. B 42 inf.), which directly inspired the 1355 *Cantica in qua tractatur de virtutibus et scientiis vulgarizatis* of Barto-

233

lomeo di Bartoli da Bologna (Musée Condé, Ms. lat. et ital. 1426; L. Dorez, *Le canzone delle virtù et delle scienze di Bartolomeo di Bartoli da Bologna,* Bergamo, 1904). Compare the frescoes of Filippino Lippi in the Carafa chapel at S. Maria sopra Minerva, Rome (P. Verdier, in *Actes du Quatrième Congrès International de Philosophie Médiévale,* Paris–Montreal, 1969, pp. 330–31).

JEAN II LIMOUSIN

Active First Half of the Seventeenth Century

Jean II Limousin was the son of the enameller Jean I, who died about 1610 and whose style and signature—the initials I. L. *frequently flanking a fleur-de-lis—were both taken over by his successor.*[1] *The "Jehan Limosin, esmailleur du Roi" who signed an enamelled weathervane at the abbey of Solignac probably was Jean II, as was the Jean Limousin recorded in a document of 1646.*

Concave Oval Plaque: Ninus, King of Nineveh (16.4.42)

$8\,{}^3/_{16} \times 5\,{}^5/_8$ in. (20.8 × 14.3 cm).

Description: Ninus is shown in battle dress astride a brown horse with blue, green, and gold trappings. In his outstretched right hand he holds a golden scepter. His plumed helmet and cuirass are blue, his skirt is green, his mantle red-violet, his open-toed boot purple. The flesh tints are warm, with the shadows delicately hatched in bister. The blue-green grass is strewn with gilt plants, and the blue sky is studded with gold stars interspersed with gilt cyphers consisting of the letter s crossed by a slender diagonal line; at upper left only are additional cyphers of paired vs interlaced to form ws. Toward the top of the plaque is the gold inscription IMPERATOR NINVS. The figure is painted on a white preparation, with the costume in semitranslucent and translucent enamels over foil. The black outlines were obtained by *enlevage,* and gilding was used to point up details and for modelling. Surrounding the composition is a narrow black band edged with gold.

Condition: The plaque is in good condition except for repairs along the borders and in the left hind leg of the horse.

In Greek mythology, Ninus was the eponymous founder of Nineveh. His reign began in 2189 B. C. and lasted fifty-two years. He was the husband of Semiramis, whose story was a favorite subject in the iconography of the early seventeenth century.

The Frick plaque was no doubt originally one of a series showing the conquerors Ninus, Cyrus, Alexander, and Julius Caesar as embodiments of the four great empires of the ancient world, the destiny of which was that each would be overturned by the succeeding. The plaques may have been intended for mounting in a wainscot or a door. The compositions on which the series was based were designed by Marten de Vos and engraved by Adriaen Collaert of Antwerp and, after him, by Gregorius Fentzel of Nuremberg in the first half of the seventeenth century.[2]

The theme of the Four Empires is rooted in the moralizing turn given to comparative history during the late Middle Ages—for example, in the poetry of Eustache Deschamps and Alain Chartier—and comments on Chapter 7 of the Book of Daniel. It was taken up by Montaigne in his *Essais,* by many sixteenth-century Catholic and Protestant theologians, and by Sully in his *Parallèles de César et de Henry le Grand* (1615). Its popularity was due in large part to the success of Sleidan's *De quatuor summis imperiis, babylonico, persico, graeco et romano, libri III,* published at Strasbourg in 1556 and reissued four times until 1565.[3]

Only one companion piece to the Frick plaque can be recorded: the so-called Alexander plaque, which actually represents Cyrus, formerly in the Marlborough collection at Blenheim Palace and now in the Taft Museum, Cincinnati.[4] All four figures—Ninus, Cyrus, Alexander, and Caesar—were carved on the four doors of a cupboard in the former Servier collection, and those of Ninus and Caesar appear on the two doors of the lower section of a cupboard in the Musée des Arts Décoratifs, Paris.[5]

The cypher of the closed s decorating the background of the Ninus plaque appeared as an emblem of loyalty on *jetons* coined by the Protestant House of Béarn in the period 1565–70. It was also an amorous emblem the interpretation of which was "fermesse" (fidelity). The Béarnais cypher was soon adopted by the Catholic supporters of the monarchy, and was much used in France between 1580 and 1640, having been employed by Henri IV, his sister Catherine de Bourbon, his first wife Marguerite de Valois and second wife Marie de Médicis, and his son Louis XIII. The device, which can equally be interpreted as meaning "Spes," the motto of the House of Navarre, or "Sum qui sum," the motto of the House of Bourbon, accompanies signatures on official and private documents and is found on seals, bookbindings, arms, jewels, and enamels.[6]

The interlaced letters AA surrounded by the closed s formed the device of Anne of Austria, who married Louis XIII in 1615. Her cypher appears on a casket in the Victoria and Albert Museum, London,[7] and on a small plaque in the British Museum, London, recording her marriage.[8]

236

Saltcellar: Olympian Deities (16.4.23)

H. 3¾ in. (9.5 cm).

Description: The hexagonal saltcellar is enamelled at the center of the receptacle with a female head in profile to the left and on the concave, flaring sides with figures of gods and goddesses standing on basin-shaped consoles beneath swags of drapery. Reading counterclockwise from the front, the deities include: the bearded and naked Apollo playing a viol; Cupid covering with his right hand the nudity of Venus; Diana holding a spear and a crescent moon; Eros armed with bow and arrow; Mars in battle dress; and Juno holding a rod entwined with a snake, with a peacock at her feet. All face to the left except Apollo. Around the base is a border of ovals. The colors are blue, turquoise, green, orange, red-violet, and grisaille tinted with rose. The black background is interspersed with gilt ornaments, and the inside of the foot is painted with gold fleurs-de-lis.

Condition: The saltcellar is in good condition except for repairs on the rim and along the white enamel borders of the lip and foot.

The figures are after prints by Étienne Delaune,[1] perhaps combined with similar designs by Jacques Androuet du Cerceau. But the enameller has simplified his models. Diana, for instance, is here depicted not running but stationary, nor is she accompanied by two hounds, and the swaggering Mars no longer brandishes a falchion.

The basin-shaped consoles may derive from Hans Burgkmair's engraving *The Double-Headed Eagle,* where the Muses are shown standing in a basin identified as the *Fons Musarum,* with the Liberal Arts below.[2] Bartholomaeus Spranger painted Apollo naked and playing the viol.[3]

The Frick saltcellar must have had a companion piece on which figures representing other deities—perhaps Muses—or personifying the Liberal Arts appeared on identical basin-shaped consoles. A pair of saltcellars in the Victoria and Albert Museum, London, signed I. L. and equal in height to the Frick example, shows deities standing on similar consoles.[4] A saltcellar in the British Museum, London, signed with the same initials and again equal in height, is decorated with deities on the sides and a female head in profile at the center of the receptacle, this time turned to the right;[5] its base and rim are ornamented with ovals like those on the base of the Frick piece. A similar female head and analogous consoles appear on a somewhat larger saltcellar signed I. L. in the Walters Art Gallery, Baltimore, this one decorated with six Muses playing musical instruments.[6] Other pairs of salt-

cellars signed with the same initials include one in the former Fountaine collection at Narford Hall, Norfolk,[7] and another in the Grünes Gewölbe, Dresden.

Saltcellars of this type with concave, hexagonal bodies and figures of deities or Muses usually are given to Jean I or Jean II Limousin, though some are by Joseph Limousin or Léonard II Limousin.[8] In the case of the Frick example, the abnormally thin wrists and ankles of the figures would make an attribution to Joseph Limousin almost as plausible as one to Jean II. The fact that the interior of the base is powdered with fleurs-de-lis is another indication of Jean II's authorship.

Exhibited: London, Victoria and Albert Museum, 1902–12, lent by J. Pierpont Morgan. New York, Metropolitan Museum, Morgan Collection, 1914–16, lent by J. Pierpont Morgan.

Collections: J. Pierpont Morgan, London and New York. Duveen. Frick, 1916.

NOTES

1 A. Robert-Dumesnil, *Le Peintre-graveur français,* Paris, 1835–71, IX, Nos. 360, 363, p. 108, Nos. 416, 418, 419, 420, p. 121, the last three repeated as Nos. 422, 424, 425, pp. 121–22. Similar figures of Venus and Cupid and Juno with the peacock decorate two of the oval bosses on the base of the Frick candlestick by Jean de Court (pp. 210, 211).

2 A. Bartsch, *Le Peintre-graveur,* Vienna, 1803–21, VII, No. 35, p. 213.

3 Kunsthistorisches Museum, Vienna.

4 No. 647–1893; shown at the South Kensington Loan Exhibition of 1862 as Nos. 866–67.

5 Waddesdon Bequest, No. 43.

6 P. Verdier, *The Walters Art Gallery: Catalogue of the Painted Enamels of the Renaissance,* Baltimore, 1967, No. 200, pp. 374–76. Olympian deities after Delaune decorate Walters saltcellar No. 194, pp. 363–65, and the group of Venus and Cupid appears on plaque No. 177, pp. 331–32.

7 Subsequently in the Malcolm sale, Christie's, May 1, 1913, Lot 32, and the J. Rochelle Thomas sale (photograph 2293, Musée Municipal, Limoges).

8 See for example: A. Darcel, *Collection Basilewsky,* Paris, 1874, No. 348; Victoria and Albert Museum, No. C. 2448–1910; Verdier, No. 194; Louvre, Baronne Salomon de Rothschild Bequest, 1922.

ORIENTAL RUGS

The appreciation of Oriental rugs in America has a long and distinguished tradition. Turkish rugs especially have been used as floor or table coverings since Colonial days, and in time American collectors, impressed by their design and color, began acquiring fine examples of Persian, Indian, Caucasian, and Hispano-Moresque as well as Turkish manufacture. The names of such men as Charles T. Yerkes, Joseph L. Williams, Benjamin Altman, William A. Clark, James F. Ballard, John D. Rockefeller, Jr., George H. Myers, Horace Havemeyer, George Blumenthal, and in recent years Joseph V. McMullan are familiar to students and connoisseurs the world over. Thanks to them, some of the finest Oriental rugs in existence are today in American museums chiefly the Metropolitan Museum of Art, New York—and American private collections. Among the most popular rugs imported to America since the 1890s have been the Persian Herat rugs (so-called Isfahans) with predominant floral and arabesque decoration.

PERSIAN HERAT RUGS

During the sixteenth and seventeenth centuries, the finest Oriental rugs were made in Persia—modern Iran. At Tabriz, Kashan (famous for its silk rugs), Herat, Kerman, and Isfahan the court looms established by the rulers of the Safavid dynasty—chiefly Shah Ismail I (reigned 1502–24), Shah Tahmasp I (1524–76), and Shah Abbas I the Great (1586–1628)—produced magnificent pieces, some of them designed by famous court painters such as Sultan Muhammad of Tahmasp's court at Tabriz. Several types are distinguishable, including medallion, compartment, animal, hunting, floral, tree, and garden rugs. With the exception of those made in pairs, no two were alike.

All Persian rugs show a division of the surface into field and border, the latter framed by narrow guard bands and serving to accentuate the pattern of the field by means of contrast in color and design. The distribution of ornament was based on decorative principles developed by Persian illuminators of the fifteenth century. Because most of the rugs were used as floor coverings, the favored principle of composition was symmetry, which took into consideration the spectator's point of view and permitted him to see the design right side up from either end of the rug.

Persian rugs show a well-balanced system of floral scrolls and arabesques which often provide a background for groups of animals or human figures. Many of the motifs were borrowed from China, including the lotus and peony introduced into Persia by the Mongols at the end of the thirteenth century and the Chinese cloud motifs and undulating cloud bands that became an integral part of Persian decoration. The crowning achievement of Safavid rug designers was the combination of different motifs and ornamental devices into innumerable varieties of exquisite patterns. To the Persians these great rugs represented beautiful gardens, a sentiment reflected in the allusions to "a white wild rose," "a garden full of tulips and roses," and the like included in the verses frequently woven into them.

The six Persian rugs in The Frick Collection, all of the floral variety, are of the type commonly known as Isfahans, though they are now generally attributed to the looms of Herat, a celebrated center of rug weaving which in the time of the

Safavids was part of the eastern province of Khurasan. The manufacture of Herat rugs began in the sixteenth century during the reign of Shah Tahmasp. Among the finest earlier Herat products is a magnificent pair of animal rugs, one in the Österreichisches Museum für angewandte Kunst, Vienna, the other formerly in Vienna and now in the Metropolitan Museum of Art, New York. According to tradition this pair, made for Shah Tahmasp, was brought to Vienna in 1698 as a gift of Czar Peter the Great to the Emperor Leopold I.[1] In these and several similar examples,[2] all datable to the second half of the sixteenth century, both field and border are covered by a dense floral pattern against which appear a great variety of animals and birds derived from nature or from Chinese art, shown singly or in combat. Related to this group are other sixteenth-century rugs in which the decoration is entirely floral, though occasionally birds are included—witness the Frick example No. 16.10.1 (p. 255).

Under Shah Abbas in the late sixteenth and early seventeenth centuries the Herat looms continued the manufacture of fine rugs, which are today well represented in the museums and private collections of Europe and America. Establishing Isfahan in central Persia as his capital, Abbas adorned it with elegant mosques and palaces and set up, under court control, state manufactories for the weaving of silk fabrics and of rugs both in silk and in wool. Many of the rugs he presented to foreign rulers, among them Doge Mariano Grimani of Venice, and to such holy shrines of the Shiites as those of Imam Ali at Al-Najaf in Iraq[3] and Imam Riza at Meshed in eastern Persia. Some of these rugs, particularly the woolen ones, show the influence of the Herati pattern but have stylistic traits indicating Isfahan as the manufacturing center.[4]

As the production of rugs in Herat advanced during the seventeenth century, the floral designs and color schemes became gradually bolder, the palmettes and lanceolate leaves larger. Adam Olearius, who visited Persia in 1637 with an embassy from the Duke of Holstein-Gottorp, reported that the handsomest Persian rugs were then made at Herat. The rugs of Herat became very popular and were exported in great quantities to Europe, chiefly to Spain, Portugal, Holland, and England. They are frequently depicted in paintings by Velázquez, Rubens, Vermeer, Van Dyck, and others.

NOTES

1 F. Sarre and H. Trenkwald, *Old Oriental Carpets,* trans. A. F. Kendrick, Vienna–Leipzig, 1926–29, I, Pls. 6–8.

2 *Idem,* Pls. 9, 10. A. U. Dilley and M. S. Dimand, *Oriental Rugs and Carpets,* Philadelphia–New York, 1959, Pl. IX.

3 M. Aga-Oglu, *Safawid Rugs and Textiles: The Collection of the Shrine of Imam Ali at Al-Najaf,* New York, 1941, Pls. I–VI.

4 M. S. Dimand, "The Seventeenth-Century Isfahan School of Rug Weaving," in *Islamic Art in the Metropolitan Museum of Art,* ed. R. Ettinghausen, New York, 1972, pp. 255–66.

Floral Rug, Herat, Second Half of the Sixteenth Century (16.10.1)

21 ft. 10½ in. × 9 ft. 6½ in. (667 × 291 cm). Warp: white cotton, 28 to the in.; weft: white cotton, 3 shoots after each row of knots; knots: wool, Senna, 11 to the in., 308 to the sq. in.

Description: The red field has an allover pattern of a double system of intersecting floral scrolls. Spiralling from the center toward both ends, the stems send out branches and tendrils bearing serrate leaves and palmettes in several sizes interspersed with blossoms and buds. Around the center are grouped four large composite fan-shaped palmettes, each made up of a serrate leaf containing a lobed compartment with a central pomegranate palmette. Toward either end are additional large leafy palmettes arranged symmetrically, and smaller palmettes of differing types follow the directions of the stems.

Wavy Chinese cloud bands are placed symmetrically over the entire field. The green border has an intermittent pattern of arabesque bands ending in large multiple palmettes with central pomegranates, each palmette flanked by two birds of paradise. Both the bands and the ground are overlaid with floral scrolls supporting smaller palmettes and leaves. The white inner guard band has a wavy scroll with palmettes and leaves, and the red outer guard band shows a floral scroll and Chinese cloud bands. Thirteen colors are used: white, yellow, pink, orange, blue, purple, red, brown, light blue, dark blue, light green, green, and blue-green.

Condition: There are scattered small repairs, with one half of the surface showing more wear than the other. The rug was relined in 1963 and was last cleaned and restored in 1973.

The elaborate floral ornament seen here is typical of Persian rugs attributed to the looms of Herat. Adopting the lotus and peony blossoms of China, the Persian artists transformed them into stylized elements known as palmettes, of which they created many varieties. Some are composite in nature, incorporating two or even three motifs—often in the form of large leaves with serrate outlines enclosing either a peony palmette or a stylized pomegranate. Fan-shaped palmettes are the most characteristic Herati motifs, usually large in size and consisting of a frame of serrate leaves around a lobed compartment containing a secondary palmette.

The arabesque border of the Frick rug reappears in several animal and floral Herat rugs datable to the second half of the sixteenth century, including examples in the Österreichisches Museum für angewandte Kunst, Vienna;[1] the Victoria and Albert Museum, London;[2] and the Metropolitan Museum of Art, New York.[3] A Herat rug with a similar border is represented in Ferdinand Bol's *Four Governors of the Leper Hospital,* a painting of 1649 in the Rijksmuseum, Amsterdam.[4]

Collections: Frick, 1916.

NOTES

1 F. Sarre and H. Trenkwald, *Old Oriental Carpets,* trans. A. F. Kendrick, Vienna–Leipzig, 1926–29, I, Pls.9, 10, 16.

2 A. F. Kendrick, *Guide to the Collection of Carpets: Victoria and Albert Museum,* London, 1920, Pl.4.

3 J. Breck and F. Morris, *The James F. Ballard Collection of Oriental Rugs,* New York, 1923, Fig.5.

4 See W. von Bode and E. Kühnel, *Antique Rugs from the Near East,* trans. C. G. Ellis, Brunswick–Berlin, 1958, Fig.83.

256

Floral Rug, Herat, Beginning of the Seventeenth Century (16.10.2)

23 ft. 8 in. × 10 ft. 3¼ in. (721 × 313 cm). Warp: white cotton, 20 to the in.; weft: white cotton, 3 shoots after each row of knots; knots: wool, Senna, 11 to the in., 110 to the sq. in.

Description: The red field has an allover pattern of a double system of intersecting floral scrolls. Spiralling toward the corners and sending out shoots in various directions, the stems bear leaves and palmettes of several sizes interspersed with flowers and buds. At the center they form a lozenge-shaped compartment terminating in four large fan-shaped composite palmettes, each made up of an outer serrate leaf, a lobed medallion, and a central palmette. At either end of the field are similar fan-shaped composite palmettes arranged symmetrically. Smaller palmettes and leaves follow the directions of the stems, which are intersected here and there by Chinese cloud bands. The green border has a floral scroll ending alternately in large composite fan-shaped palmettes and large leafy palmettes, with smaller palmettes, buds, and leaves in between. The inner guard band in yellow and green shows a wavy arabesque scroll with lotus palmettes, and the outer guard band in yellow and orange contains a wavy scroll with palmettes and leaves. Twelve colors are used: white, yellow, orange, pink, red, brown, gray-green, medium green, dark green, blue-green, light blue, and dark blue.

Condition: The entire surface is worn, and the colors have been retouched with dyes in many places. The rug was last cleaned, restored, and relined in 1973.

Herat rugs of this type, with floral decoration only, were introduced in the second half of the sixteenth century and continued in production through the seventeenth. Early examples are in the Victoria and Albert Museum, London;[1] the former J. Paul Getty collection (previously in the Kevorkian collection[2]); and elsewhere. All have the characteristic border of large fan-shaped palmettes alternating with leafy palmettes.

In the time of Shah Abbas I the manufacture of Herat floral rugs increased considerably. The design became bolder—as here—and curly lanceolate leaves, often resembling fly whisks, were added. Several fine rugs of this period are in the Metropolitan Museum of Art, New York;[3] the Islamisches Museum, Berlin;[4] the Heinrich Wulff collection, Copenhagen;[5] and the Corcoran Gallery of Art, Washington.[6]

Collections: Frick, 1916.

NOTES

1 K. Erdmann, *Oriental Carpets,* trans. C. G. Ellis, New York, 1962, Fig. 79.

2 M. S. Dimand, *The Kevorkian Foundation: Collection of Rare and Magnificent Oriental Carpets,* New York, 1966, Pl. III.

3 Erdmann, Fig. 80.

4 *Idem,* Fig. 81.

5 K. Erdmann, *Seven Hundred Years of Oriental Carpets,* Berkeley—Los Angeles, 1968, Pl. XV.

6 "Carpets for the Great Shah: The Near-Eastern Carpets from the W. A. Clark Collection," *Corcoran Gallery of Art Bulletin,* II, October 1948, Pl. VI.

Floral Rug, Herat, First Quarter of the Seventeenth Century (16.10.4)

24 ft. 1½ in. × 9 ft. 4 in. (735 × 285 cm). Warp: white cotton, 20 to the in.; weft: white cotton, 3 shoots after each row of knots; knots: wool, Senna, 11 to the in., 110 to the sq. in.

Description: The red field has an allover pattern of floral scrolls made up of two intersecting systems. The curling stems issue from a central lozenge which ends in four composite palmettes and proceed to cover the field symmetrically, repeating the motif of the central lozenge with its surrounding composite palmettes. The intervening spaces are covered with shoots which send off small lotus palmettes, rosette blossoms, and lanceolate leaves. Chinese cloud bands accompany a number of the larger palmettes. The green border has an intermittent floral scroll ending in large composite leafy palmettes containing alternately lotus palmettes and pomegranates. Between the large palmettes the stems bear small palmettes and leaves, and occasionally they end in large lanceolate leaves. Both the green inner guard band and the red outer guard band have a wavy floral scroll with rosettes and leaves. Ten colors are used: white, yellow, pink, red, brown, light blue, dark blue, light green, green, and blue-green.

Condition: The rug was last cleaned, restored, and relined in 1973.

Similar in style and size to the preceding example, this rug shows, in addition to the usual Herat pattern, many Chinese cloud bands and a number of lanceolate leaves in the field. Related rugs include two in the Satterwhite Collection of the J. B. Speed Memorial Museum, Louisville, Kentucky;[1] one in the former collection of Dr. Alsberg, Berlin;[2] and one in the Corcoran Gallery of Art, Washington.[3]

Collections: Frick, 1916.

NOTES

[1] M. S. Dimand, *A Guide to an Exhibition of Oriental Rugs and Textiles: Metropolitan Museum of Art,* New York, 1935, Fig. 7.

[2] W. von Bode and E. Kühnel, *Antique Rugs from the Near East,* trans. C. G. Ellis, Brunswick–Berlin, 1958, Fig. 86.

[3] "Carpets for the Great Shah: The Near-Eastern Carpets from the W. A. Clark Collection," *Corcoran Gallery of Art Bulletin,* II, October 1948, Pl. VII.

Floral Rug, Herat, First Half of the Seventeenth Century (16.10.3)

8 ft. 3¾ in. × 4 ft. 7 in. (253 × 140 cm). Warp: white cotton, 24 to the in.; weft: white cotton, 3 shoots after each row of knots; knots: wool, Senna, 12 to the in., 144 to the sq. in.

Description: The red field has a symmetrical allover pattern of floral scrolls which spiral out from a central lozenge toward the four corners and bear palmettes of various types and sizes interspersed with rosettes and leaves. At each corner of the lozenge is a large composite fan-shaped palmette consisting of three sections: a series of serrate leaves framing a compartment which in turn contains a lotus or pomegranate palmette. A similar group of composite palmettes appears at either end of the field, and sections of large palmettes occur along the edges. Chinese cloud bands arranged symmetrically complete the decoration. The blue-green border has a wavy floral scroll ending in large composite fan-shaped palmettes similar to those in the field alternating with small palmettes and leaves connected by stems. Both the white inner guard band and the red outer guard band have a wavy scroll with small rosette blossoms. Nine colors are used: white, yellow, pink, red, light blue, dark blue, green, dark green, and brown.

Condition: The rug is much worn and has been retouched in many places with color dyes. It was last cleaned and restored in 1937.

Similar rugs are in various collections, including one in the Henry Francis du Pont Winterthur Museum, Winterthur, Delaware,[1] and another in the Metropolitan Museum of Art, New York.[2] Two others figured in the Hagop Kevorkian Foundation sale of 1970.[3]

The smaller Herat rugs usually have a central composition of four large fan-shaped palmettes, with the design repeated at each end of the field. Surviving examples of this type date from the beginning to the middle of the seventeenth century.

Collections: Oscar Hainauer, Berlin. Duveen. Frick, 1916.

NOTES

1 A. U. Dilley and M. S. Dimand, *Oriental Rugs and Carpets,* Philadelphia–New York, 1959, Pl. XII.

2 M. S. Dimand, "The Seventeenth-Century Isfahan School of Rug Weaving," in *Islamic Art in the Metropolitan Museum of Art,* ed. R. Ettinghausen, New York, 1972, Fig. 10.

3 Sotheby's, December 11, 1970, Pt. II, Lots 16, 17.

Floral Rug, Herat, Middle of the Seventeenth Century (16.10.5)

8 ft. 1 in. × 4 ft. 11½ in. (246 × 151 cm). Warp: white cotton, 28 to the in.; weft: white cotton, 3 shoots after each row of knots; knots: wool, Senna, 12 to the in., 168 to the sq. in.

Description: The red field is decorated with a double system of intersecting floral scrolls arranged symmetrically and developing into the corners. In the center is a group of four small lotus palmettes flanked by two large composite fan-shaped palmettes, the latter each consisting of a ring of serrate leaves framing a compartment with a central peony palmette. Toward either end of the field is a similar pair of fan-shaped palmettes, and sections of related palmettes appear along the edges. The longitudinal axis shows in addition a series of small palmettes, two larger fan-shaped palmettes, and Chinese cloud bands, and the remaining field carries spiral stems bearing a variety of small palmettes, blossoms, leaves, and cloud bands. The blue-green border has an intermittent floral scroll ending in composite leaf palmettes alternating with fan-shaped palmettes identical to those near the center of the field. Between these motifs are stems with lotus or peony palmettes and leaves. The inner guard band in yellow and blue and the outer guard band in red both contain a wavy scroll with rosettes and leaves. Ten colors are used: white, yellow, pink, orange, red, brown, light blue, dark blue, green, and blue-green.

Condition: The rug is badly worn. It was last cleaned and repaired in 1937, when the colors were retouched.

This rug resembles the preceding example in style and size but is a later version.

Collections: Frick, 1916.

Floral Rug, Herat, Middle of the Seventeenth Century (16.10.6)

26 ft. ¾ in. × 11 ft. 3 in. (794 × 343 cm). Warp: white cotton, 24 to the in.; weft: white cotton, 3 shoots after each row of knots; knots: wool, Senna, 10 to the in., 120 to the sq. in.

Description: The red field is covered with a double system of floral scrolls issuing from a small lobed medallion at the center and sending out stems into the corners. Along the longitudinal axis the stems bear large composite fan-shaped palmettes, and to either side of the axis the spiralling tendrils support additional palmettes of various sizes, flowers, buds, lanceolate leaves, and small leaves. Chinese cloud bands, placed symmetrically, intersect the scrolls. The green border has an intermittent floral scroll ending in large composite palmettes each flanked by a pair of large lanceolate leaves. The intervening spaces contain stems with rosette blossoms, buds, and small leaves. The yellow inner guard band shows a series of arabesque devices, and the red outer guard band has a floral scroll with rosettes and leaves. Ten colors are used: white, yellow, orange, red, brown, light blue, dark blue, yellow-green, green, and dark green.

Condition: The surface is worn throughout and repaired in several places, and the colors have been retouched with various dyes. A section has been cut away near one end. The rug was last cleaned, restored, and relined in 1971.

Large lanceolate leaves in the field and border are characteristic of seventeenth-century Herati rugs, appearing first in the time of Shah Abbas and continuing through the century. Paired lanceolate leaves framing palmettes occur in the field and border of several rugs in the Österreichisches Museum für angewandte Kunst, Vienna, and other collections.[1]

Collections: Frick, 1916.

NOTES

1 F. Sarre and H. Trenkwald, *Old Oriental Carpets,* trans. A. F. Kendrick, Vienna–Leipzig, 1926–29, I, Pls. 13–15. W. von Bode and E. Kühnel, *Antique Rugs from the Near East,* trans. C. G. Ellis, Brunswick–Berlin, 1958, Figs. 87, 88. K. Erdmann, *Oriental Carpets,* trans. C. G. Ellis, New York, 1962, Fig. 87. "Carpets for the Great Shah: The Near-Eastern Carpets from the W. A. Clark Collection," *Corcoran Gallery of Art Bulletin,* II, October 1948, Pls. V, IX.

MUGHAL RUGS OF INDIA

Like the Mughal school of painting, Mughal rug weaving was of Persian origin. During the sixteenth century not only Persian rugs but also Persian weavers were imported to India. According to the historian Abul Fazl, the Emperor Akbar the Great (reigned 1556–1605) "caused carpets to be made of wonderful variety and charming textures; he has appointed experienced workmen, who have produced many masterpieces. The carpets of Iran and Turan are no more thought of, although merchants still import carpets from Jushagan, Khuzistan, Kirman, and Sabzavar. All kinds of carpet weavers have settled here, and drive a flourishing trade. These are found in every town, especially in Agra, Fathpur, and Lahore."

As can be determined from contemporary paintings, the products of the court looms under Akbar were influenced by Persian floral rugs, especially those of the Herat variety. Gradually during the rule of Akbar's son and successor, Jahangir (1605–28), the Hindu weavers introduced into rug design naturalistic plants, landscapes, and figure subjects peculiar to India. The Mughal style of rug weaving, chiefly in the northern city of Lahore, became fully developed during the reign of Shah Jahan (1628–58). Persian influence diminished considerably, and many rugs from this period are decorated with naturalistic plants and trees unknown to the Safavid rug designers. The technical perfection of the Hindu weavers frequently surpassed that of their masters, while their color schemes were enriched by many delicate nuances and by shading, which the Persian rug weavers never used at all. Two of the rugs in The Frick Collection are Mughal and can be attributed to the period of Shah Jahan.

Tree Rug, Mughal, First Half of the Seventeenth Century, Period of Shah Jahan (16.10.7)

7 ft. 5½ in. × 6 ft. 3½ in. (227 × 192 cm). Warp: cotton, 50 to the in.; weft: cotton, 2 shoots after each row of knots; knots: wool, Senna, 23 to the in., 575 to the sq. in.

Description: The wine-red field has a design of trees arranged in three horizontal rows, each row growing from a chain of conventionalized patches of ground. In the bottom tier, cypresses alternate with a type of blossoming tree often seen in Mughal textiles and paintings. In the two upper tiers, trees with flowers resembling irises alternate with leafy trees rendered naturalistically. Between the trees grow flowering plants, among them tulips and carnations. The wine-red border is decorated with a Mughal version of a Persian floral scroll bearing large carnations and lotus palmettes separated by branches with lilies and tulips. Chinese cloud motifs appear in several places. The light green inner and outer guard bands have similar wavy scrolls with blossoms and leaves, and both are bordered by narrow stripes of cream-yellow. Twelve colors are used: white, cream-yellow, tan, pink, salmon red, wine red, light green, olive green, green, blue-green, light blue, and dark blue.

Condition: The rug is fragmentary (see below) and shows many repairs. It was skillfully restored in London in the 1880s, and was last repaired in 1929, at which time it was also relined.

This tree rug, made up from several sections of a larger rug with a tree pattern, comes from the tomb mosque of Shaikh Safi in the Persian city of Ardebil, and was most probably the gift of Shah Jahan (1628–58). Exhibiting all the characteristic features of Mughal rugs made on the court looms of Lahore, it represents the Indian version of the Persian landscape or tree rug, a type popular under the Safavids. One of the earliest extant Persian examples is in the Joseph Lees Williams Collection at the Philadelphia Museum of Art.[1]

Tree patterns are often included in the composition of garden rugs, in which plots of various sizes are separated by streams and canals. One of the most magnificent surviving garden rugs was discovered in 1937 in a sealed storeroom of the palace at Amber, India.[2] The naturalistic style of its trees and flowering shrubs indicates that it was made at Isfahan in the time of the Persian ruler Shah Abbas I (1586–1628). The Amber rug and similar pieces[3] had a great influence on the rug industry of Lahore in the time of Shah Jahan.

Of special importance in connection with the present example is a Persian rug in the Islamisches Museum, Berlin,[4] decorated with four rows of flowering trees

274

accompanied by birds. Also deserving of mention are two rugs in the Metropolitan Museum of Art, New York, both datable to the beginning of the seventeenth century, one, with a central medallion, in the Joseph V. McMullan Collection[5] and the other in the James F. Ballard Collection.[6]

Collections: Tomb mosque of Shaikh Safi at Ardebil. Acquired in the 1880s by Vincent Robinson & Co., London. Charles T. Yerkes, New York. His sale, April 8, 1910, American Art Association, New York, Lot 215. Duveen. Frick, 1916.

NOTES

1 F. Sarre and H. Trenkwald, *Old Oriental Carpets,* trans. A. F. Kendrick, Vienna–Leipzig, 1926–29, II, Pl. 13.

2 M. S. Dimand, "A Persian Carpet in the Jaipur Museum," *Ars Islamica,* VII, 1940, p. 93.

3 See for example: W. von Bode and E. Kühnel, *Antique Rugs from the Near East,* trans. C. G. Ellis, Brunswick–Berlin, 1958, Fig. 104 (the so-called Wagner carpet, now in the Burrell Collection of the Glasgow Art Gallery and Museum); M. Beattie, *The Rug in Islamic Art: Exhibition at Temple Newsam House,* Leeds, 1964, Pl. 6.

4 Bode and Kühnel, Fig. 101.

5 J. V. McMullan, *Islamic Carpets,* New York, 1965, Pl. 17. M. S. Dimand and J. Mailey, *Oriental Rugs in the Metropolitan Museum of Art,* New York, 1973, Fig. 112, p. 82; see also Fig. 139, p. 125.

6 J. Breck and F. Morris, *The James F. Ballard Collection of Oriental Rugs,* New York, 1923, Fig. 10. Dimand and Mailey, No. 41, p. 111, Fig. 111, p. 81.

Floral Rug, Mughal, First Half of the Seventeenth Century, Period of Shah Jahan (16.10.8)

6 ft. 4 in. × 3 ft. 10 in. (193 × 117 cm). Warp: silk, 58 to the in.; weft: silk, 3 shoots after each row of knots; knots: wool, Senna, 24 to the in., 696 to the sq. in.

Description: The dark red field has an all-over pattern of flowering plants arranged in rows and rendered naturalistically. Two large lilies of different types dominate the composition, accompanied at either side by smaller flowers including primroses, lilies, poppies, and roses. The blue-green border has a row of roses, tulips, lilies, and other plants familiar in Indian rug design. The yellow inner and outer guard bands carry respectively a floral scroll with blossoms and leaves and a row of cloud bands and cloud motifs. Thirteen colors are used: white, yellow, pink, red, dark red, light purple, dark purple, light brown, light green, olive green, dark green, blue-green, and dark blue.

Condition: The rug is fragmentary (see below) and shows many repairs. It was last restored in 1922, at which time it was also relined.

The present rug is a fragment of a much larger garden rug made in the Royal factory at Lahore. Naturalistic plant decoration of the type seen here was introduced into Mughal art during the reign of the Emperor Jahangir (1605–28), who was very fond of the flowers of Kashmir, a region he once described as "the garden of eternal spring." Popular during his reign was the fashion of decorating the borders of miniature paintings with rows of flowering plants, among them tulips, violets, poppies, primroses, jonquils, several varieties of lilies, and roses.

The use of such borders continued during the rule of Jahangir's son and successor, Shah Jahan (1628–58). The architecture of this period—witness the Taj Mahal at Agra—as well as its silks, brocades, and rugs were frequently decorated with flowering plants. On rugs they appeared at first only in the borders,[1] but later they covered the whole field.[2] Some of these so-called garden rugs, including a group formerly in the collection of the Maharaja of Jaipur and now in the Jaipur Museum, were made especially to frame fountains of palaces built by Shah Jahan.

Collections: Duveen. Frick, 1916.

NOTES

1 F. Sarre and H. Trenkwald, *Old Oriental Carpets,* trans. A. F. Kendrick, Vienna–Leipzig, 1926–29, II, Pl. 57.

2 M. S. Dimand, *The Kevorkian Foundation: Collection of Rare and Magnificent Oriental Carpets,* New York, 1966, Pls. XII, XIII.

278

ENGLISH SILVER

PAUL DE LAMERIE

1688–1751

The son of Huguenot émigrés apparently of the minor French nobility, De Lamerie was baptized in the Walloon church at Bois-le-Duc ('s Hertogenbosch) in the Netherlands and was with his family in London by 1691.[1] At the age of fifteen he was apprenticed to the Huguenot silversmith Pierre Platel.[2] De Lamerie registered his first mark in February of 1712 from Windmill Street near Haymarket,[3] took his first apprentice three years later,[4] and in 1717 married Louisa Juliott, by whom he would have six children. In 1732 he entered his second mark from "Weedmill" Street, and in 1739, when he fashioned the écuelle discussed below, he entered his third from "Garard" Street, where he had moved the previous year. De Lamerie's earliest known piece is a double-banded caster with the date-letter for 1711/12, which he matched with a smaller pair dated 1713/14.[5] Among his many notable works are an elaborate wine cistern made for the Duke of Sutherland in 1719/20,[6] a series of commissions including a surtout and a set of dressing plate executed for the Rt. Hon. George Treby between about 1720 and 1725,[7] the celebrated Walpole salver of 1728/29 with engraving probably by William Hogarth,[8] and an inkstand and highly sculptural ewer and dish ordered by the Goldsmiths' Company of London.[9] He worked in addition for George II[10] and for the Imperial court of Russia.[11] De Lamerie's obituary in the London Evening Post *of August 6, 1751, described him as "particularly famous in making fine ornamental Plate, and . . . very instrumental in bringing that Branch of Trade to the Perfection it is now in."[12] He also produced some undecorated ware,[13] and he appears to have been the only English goldsmith of Huguenot extraction to fashion an appreciable amount of church plate.[14]*

Silver-Gilt Écuelle, 1739/40 (16.7.2)

H. overall 6¾ in. (17.2 cm); H. at handles 3½ in. (8.9 cm); H. of bowl at rim 2¾ in. (7 cm); D. at rim 6 1/16 in. (15.4 cm); L. overall 9¾ in. (24.8 cm). Stamped, on the bottom of the bowl and on the bezel of the cover to

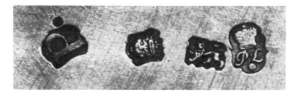

the left of the opening for the ladle: the initials P·L with a crown above and a device below, the mark of Paul De Lamerie, and the lion passant; and on the bowl only: the date-letter *d* for 1739/40 and the leopard's head crowned.

Description: The low, circular bowl of the écuelle has a flat bottom, curved sides, an everted lip, and a rather heavy molded rim which is probably applied. Attached to the bowl with open scrolls below the rim are two hollow horizontal handles, their upper surfaces overlaid with cast vine leaves, tendrils, and grapes and their sides swirling to form a hollow voluted shell at each tip. On the front and back of the bowl, flanked by wide, very shallow fluting, are shaped panels decorated with branches of lightly veined leaves in low relief on a matted ground, one showing broad leaves rising to the left, the other narrower ones slanting right; the top of each panel curves downward to accommodate a small impressed flower. At either side of the bowl similar flutes flank matted panels showing in one case a lily-like plant rising to the right, in the other a leafy branch slanting left; above these panels is a tooled shell. Between the panels are four sets of indentations in the

form of paired thumbprints. Along the bottom of the bowl runs a cast floral skirt or baseband centering on a large double blossom at front and back and continuing below at the sides to form four short scroll legs which terminate in patterned cup feet (see *Condition*). The écuelle's raised cover has a broad curving rim decorated against a tooled background with eight large elliptical panels between eight small roundels, the former filled with vegetables and foliage partly applied and spilling over onto the molded edge, the latter containing alternately a flower and a bud. The central section of the cover, which is circled by a narrow band of tooling and adorned with eight long matted panels overlaid with leaves, curves gently downward and then steeply upward to form a finial with a flat molded top, upon which rests a trussed bird. The rim and bezel are cut at one side with an arched opening for the handle of a ladle (see p. 291).

Condition: The écuelle is in very good condition. The gilding seems thin, but none of the silver is exposed. The cupped feet, which are attached to the legs somewhat irregularly, may have been added when the accompanying plate was made in 1797/98 (see p. 294).

The term écuelle designates a shallow bowl usually having two horizontal handles and a raised cover surmounted by a finial. French in origin, the form is encountered frequently in French silver but rarely in English, where its closest equivalent is the one-handled porringer. A conventional écuelle made in London in 1704/05 by De Lamerie's master, Pierre Platel, has two flat, pierced handles and a flat cover with a concave rim, cut-card ornament on the top, and a turned finial.[15] A pair from 1721/22 by De Lamerie's Huguenot contemporary David Willaume have almost vertical sides, solid handles in the form of shells, and low domed covers with gadrooned edges and leaf-and-ball finials.[16]

The present écuelle, markedly French in style and form, is unique in De Lame-

rie's known production, where indeed there appears to be nothing else even remotely resembling it. Particularly noteworthy are its innovative baseband with feet and its hollow, partially open handles, features that not only enhance its appearance but also serve to insulate the contents of the bowl more effectively than the solid handles and accompanying plates (see p. 294) often found in French examples. Also unusual is the carefully notched cover.

The floral baseband is akin to those on two kettle stands by De Lamerie dated 1737/38 and 1745/46 in the Sterling and Francine Clark Art Institute, Williamstown, Massachusetts.[17] By way of contrast, there is in the same museum a circular bowl by De Lamerie dated 1735/36 which is of approximately the same size as the present piece but has a plain molded foot, hinged bail or swing handles, and a low domed cover with no notch at the rim.[18]

The riot of vegetables and herbs on the cover and the trussed game bird on the finial—apparently a red grouse[19]—tend to confirm that the écuelle was meant to hold porridge, defined in the 1728 edition of Bailey's *English Dictionary* as "a liquid Food of Herbs, Flesh, &c."[20] That it was not intended for broth—Bailey's "Liquor in which Flesh is boiled"—is further indicated by the perforated bowl of the ladle that accompanied the écuelle when it was acquired and appears to have been made for it (see p. 291). In conjunction with the vegetables and game bird the flowers on the baseband might seem incongruous, but that the skirt is contemporary with the bowl is confirmed by the shaped indentations made for it above the feet. The shells at the tips of and underneath the handles could also be considered an anomaly, though shells appear on a De Lamerie coffee jug of 1738/39, as well as on a sideboard dish made two years earlier.[21] Also common in De Lamerie's production are grapes like those on the handles of the écuelle, framed compartments like those on the cover, and designs executed on matted panels.

An elliptical tureen by De Lamerie dated 1736/37 in the Metropolitan Museum of Art, New York, has the raised cover of the Frick piece, and its full-round finial in the form of a lion passant gardant is similarly sculptural.[22] Its shell decoration is somewhat reminiscent of that under the écuelle's handles but less realistic.

The omission of the present piece from Phillips' comprehensive monograph on De Lamerie published in London in 1935 is probably due to its having been acquired by Henry Clay Frick some twenty years earlier. So far as is known, the écuelle has never been exhibited at The Frick Collection.

Collections: Duveen. Frick, 1916.

NOTES

1 On De Lamerie's life and work, see P. A. S. Phillips' definitive biography, *Paul De Lamerie, Citizen and Goldsmith of London,* London, 1935. As proved by Phillips' reproductions (pp. 18, 24, 28, 35, 37, 112), De Lamerie included the capitalized "De" in his signature, though he ignored it in his maker's marks. Common practice today is to make it lower case or eliminate it.

2 The apprenticeship was recorded by the Worshipful Company of Goldsmiths on August 6, 1703: "Memorand[um] that I, Paul de Lamerie, son of Paul de Lamerie [born Paul Souchay de la Merie], of yᵉ parish of St. Annes, Westminster, Gent, do put myself apprentice to Peter Plattell, Citizen and Goldsmith of London, for the term of seven years from this day." Platel had been made free in 1699. Shortly afterward he fashioned a famous gold ewer and dish for the Duke of Devonshire.

3 The mark consisted of the first two letters of his surname, LA, with a crowned star above and a fleur-de-lis below, in the manner of French goldsmiths' marks. In March of 1732, well after the sterling standard had become legal again in 1720, De Lamerie entered a new mark for the lower quality, using a similar design with the initials P.L.

4 Phillips (p. 23) records thirteen apprentices, the last of whom, Samuel William Hodgson, was at De Lamerie's death transferred to William Cripps.

5 Phillips, Pl. I. The London date-letter changes on May 29th of each year.

6 J. F. Hayward, *Huguenot Silver in England, 1688–1727,* London, 1959, p. 7. Phillips, Pl. VIII.

7 Phillips, Pls. XXXI–XXXIV, Figs. 12–19 between pp. 46 and 47.

8 C. Oman, *English Silversmiths' Work, Civil and Domestic,* London, 1965, Fig. 118. Phillips (pp. 47–49, 86–90, Pls. LX, LXI) discusses the possible collaboration between De Lamerie and Hogarth, who engraved the goldsmith's coat of arms, and their common use of Jean Bérain's designs.

9 Phillips, Pls. CXXXIII–CXXXV. De Lamerie was among those chosen by the Goldsmiths' Company in 1740/41 to make plate for their Guild Hall replacing that which had been melted in the financial troubles of the seventeenth century. He also served as Company Warden. His inkstand incorporated a bell given the Company in 1667 by Sir Robert Vyner, Crown Goldsmith.

10 A gilt basin and ewer were commissioned by the King in 1746 for the christening of his son, the Earl of Lincoln. They have not been traced.

11 Phillips, Pls. XV, XLIII, XCV, XCVI.

12 *Idem,* p. 38.

13 Hayward, p. 7.

14 C. Oman, *English Church Plate, 598–1830,* Oxford, 1957, p. 152, note 2.

15 Hayward, Pl. 69 a.

16 K. C. Buhler, in *The Campbell Museum Collection,* Camden, New Jersey, 2nd ed., 1972, No. 1.

17 *Paul De Lamerie,* exhibition catalogue, Williams College, Williamstown, 1953, repr. chronologically.

18 *Idem.*

19 Information from Dr. Philip Wiedel, New York, November 8, 1973.

20 N. Bailey, *An Universal Etymological English Dictionary,* London, 4th ed., 1728.

21 Phillips, Pls. CXXI, CIV.

22 *Idem,* p. 99, Pl. CVIII.

PAUL DE LAMERIE, Attributed to

Silver-Gilt Ladle, c. 1739 (16.7.1)

L. 9¼ in. (23.5 cm); D. of bowl 2¾ in. (7 cm).

Description: The front of the cast, slightly curved handle has at its rounded tip a maned lion's head above a shell, with a leafy tendril trailing from the base of the shell halfway down the tapering, grooved stem. On the reverse the handle is decorated above with a segmented rat-tail against a feather-like background and at the base with a shell that widens for attachment to the circular bowl. The nearly straight sides of the bowl curve inward to a flat center on which is elaborately engraved and pierced the cypher AC surmounted by an engraved ducal coronet, its midband also pierced. Set symmetrically around the cypher are six areas in the form of irregular trapezoids delicately chased and pierced with tiny crosses. The high polish of the bowl and stem contrast with the extensive matting on the relieved surfaces of the handle.

Condition: Apart from the loss of gilding on some of its raised ornament, the ladle is in very good condition.

When the écuelle by Paul De Lamerie discussed in the preceding entry was acquired in 1916, it was accompanied by the present unmarked ladle and by the plate signed ı s described in the entry that follows.[1] In *The Frick Collection Catalogue* of 1956 the ladle was listed preceding the écuelle as the work of an anonymous eighteenth-century English silversmith, with the notation that "there is no relation between the designs of the two objects."[2] Though the ladle does indeed introduce motifs not found on the écuelle, it nevertheless seems safely attributable to De Lamerie on several grounds: first on account of its fitting so snugly through the shaped notch in the écuelle's cover, which it does at precisely the point where the trailing tendril terminates; second by reason of the similarity between the matting on its relieved surfaces and that used extensively on both bowl and cover of the écuelle; and third because its design elements recur on many other works struck with De Lamerie's mark.

The lion mask, for example, while its peculiar grimace does not appear to have been duplicated exactly, is related to the masks found frequently in De Lamerie's oeuvre, where the trailing vine and the shell also are familiar. A pair of ladles at Woburn Abbey made in 1737/38 for the fourth Duke of Bedford, again unmarked

291

but confidently attributed to De Lamerie by Grimwade, have similar shells joining the handles to the circular bowls, and the bowls themselves are elaborately pierced with the Duke's cypher.[3] A ladle of 1738/39 has a bowl in the form of a shell and a handle tipped with a voluted shell like that on the handles of the Frick écuelle.[4]

The symmetrical cypher AC—which on account of its being pierced can be read identically from front and back—appears to have been adapted from a contemporary book of monograms, Samuel Sympson's *A New Book of Cyphers* published in London in 1726.[5] De Lamerie's ingenuity added the bellflower to the central area, which is somewhat empty in Sympson's version. The A also varies slightly, and De Lamerie's engraved scrolls are executed with a bit more verve.

Collections: Duveen. Frick, 1916.

NOTES

1 All three were encased in an elaborate fitted box clearly made expressly to house them. The box appears to date from the nineteenth century.

2 *The Frick Collection Catalogue,* XI, 1956, p. 41.

3 A. Grimwade, "Family Silver of Three Centuries," *Apollo,* LXXXII, 1965, p. 502, Fig. 5 on p. 500.

4 P. A. S. Phillips, *Paul De Lamerie, Citizen and Goldsmith of London,* London, 1935, Pls. CXXIII, CXXIV.

5 The cypher appears on Pl. 1. That the book remained a standard is indicated by the list of seventy-two engravers who subscribed to a new edition, among them George Bickham, whose own *The Universal Penman* appeared between 1733 and 1741.

LONDON MONOGRAMMIST I S

Silver-Gilt Plate, 1797/98 (16.7.11)

H. ¾ in. (1.9 cm); D. 7¹⁵/₁₆ in. (20.2 cm). Stamped, on the back of the rim (see below): the unidentified maker's mark I S, the date-letter B for 1797/98, the lion passant, the king's head, and the leopard's head crowned.

Description: The broad, slanted rim of the circular plate is decorated with a molded edge and eight panels of vegetation alternating with as many roundels, all in imitation of the rim on the cover of the Frick écuelle by Paul De Lamerie (see p. 285). The flat inner surface of the plate has along its circumference four curved panels with matted outlines separated by four petalled circles with recessed centers spaced to fit the écuelle's feet.

Condition: The plate has retained its gilding and is in very good condition. An X-mark scratched inside one of the petalled circles corresponds to a similar mark on the base of the écuelle near one of the feet and probably was added to indicate the proper placement of the two pieces.

The plate is an interesting instance of a later and lesser artist attempting to copy elements of a great work but producing a somewhat banal one. Dismissed as of anonymous and "much later" authorship in *The Frick Collection Catalogue* of 1956,[1] the piece in fact bears both maker's mark and date-letter, though all five marks are almost lost in the intricacies on the reverse of one of the panels with grapes and an adjacent roundel. The same craftsman who made the plate may have added the patterned cup feet to De Lamerie's écuelle.

Collections: Duveen. Frick, 1916.[2]

NOTES

1 *The Frick Collection Catalogue,* XI, 1956, p. 42.

2 For the known history of the plate, see p. 291 of the present catalogue and note 1 on p. 292.

WINE COOLERS

Silver vessels for chilling bottled wine in ice or ice water before serving have been produced in England at least since the late seventeenth century. The larger, usually elliptical examples, such as the huge one made for the Duke of Portland in 1682/83,[1] are generally differentiated as wine cisterns, a term used in an inventory of 1701 to describe a vessel fashioned that year by the Huguenot silversmith Philip Rollos for the Duke and Duchess of Marlborough: "one large Cesterne Curiously Enchaced wt. 1944 oz. 4 dwt."[2] The designation wine cooler—or ice pail—is commonly reserved for vessels intended to hold individual bottles, frequently within a removable liner surmounted by a separate collar. Among the earliest surviving English examples of this type is a cooler made by David Willaume for the Duke of Devonshire in 1698.[3] Paul De Lamerie is known to have produced a wine cistern in 1719/20 and another, now in the Hermitage Museum, Leningrad, seven years later,[4] but there seems to be no small or single wine cooler of his fashioning.

The English vessel was undoubtedly of French derivation. A pair of late seventeenth-century Parisian *seaux à rafraîchir* (or *seaux à glace*) formerly in the Puiforcat collection lack liners,[5] as do a closely similar pair in the Untermyer collection, New York, made in London by William Lukin in 1716.[6] Both pairs are octagonal on a splaying foot, whereas the majority of coolers, including the above-mentioned Willaume example of 1698, are circular.

An insight into the role of the wine cooler at table during the eighteenth century is provided in a letter written by George Washington in 1789: "Of plated ware may be made I conceive handsome and useful Coolers for wine *at* and *after* dinner. Those I am in need of viz. *eight* double ones (for madeira and claret the wines usually drank at dinner) each of the apertures to be sufficient to contain a pint decanter, with an allowance in the depth of it for ice at bottom so as to raise the neck of the decanter above the cooler; between the apertures a handle is to be placed by which these double coolers may with convenience be removed from one part of the table to another. For the wine *after* dinner *four* quadruple coolers will be necessary each aperture of which to be the size of a quart decanter or quart bottle for four sorts of wine."[7]

One of Washington's double coolers, with separate bottle racks, has long been at Mount Vernon, and a similar four-bottle cooler was returned there in 1972. A pair of silver-gilt double coolers of a different type, each with a simple vertical partition bisecting its elliptical bowl and no apparent provision for holding the bottles upright, was made by Benjamin Smith and Digby Scott in 1805/06.[8]

The eight wine coolers in The Frick Collection—a set of four fashioned by William Pitts in 1802/04, a pair by Paul Storr dated 1811/12, and a pair by Benjamin and James Smith also from 1811/12—are more or less similar to one another in size, in overall form, and to a lesser degree in decoration. Each is conceived as a thistle-shaped urn with a projecting molded rim, two handles at the sides, vine decoration on the upper body, acanthus leaves on the calyx, and a low, splayed foot with moldings above and below. All are intended for a single bottle and have removable liners and collars.

NOTES

1 C. J. Jackson, *An Illustrated History of English Plate, Ecclesiastical and Secular,* London, 1911, I, Fig. 264, p. 253.

2 A. G. Grimwade, "Silver at Althorp," *Connoisseur,* CLI, No. 608, 1962, p. 81, Fig. 1 on p. 82.

3 Jackson, I, Fig. 288, p. 271. M. Clayton, *The Collector's Dictionary of Silver and Gold of Great Britain and North America,* New York–Cleveland, 1971, p. 339.

4 P. A. S. Phillips, *Paul De Lamerie, Citizen and Goldsmith of London,* London, 1935, Pls. VIII, XLVIII. The Hermitage cistern bears the arms of Nicholas, fourth Earl of Scarsdale. See also J. F. Hayward, *Huguenot Silver in England, 1688–1727,* London, 1959, Pl. 24; compare Figs. 20–24.

5 Puiforcat sale catalogue, Galerie Charpentier, Paris, December 7–8, 1955, Lot 98, Pl. XXI, bought before the sale.

6 Y. Hackenbroch, *English and Other Silver in the Irwin Untermyer Collection,* New York, 1963, Pls. 50, 51, p. 28.

7 See K. C. Buhler, *Mount Vernon Silver,* Mount Vernon, Virginia, 1957, p. 50.

8 A. G. Grimwade, *The Queen's Silver: A Survey of Her Majesty's Personal Collection,* London, 1953, Pl. 42, p. 98.

WILLIAM PITTS

Recorded 1769–1818

Pitts was the second son of Thomas Pitts, of Air Street, Piccadilly.[1] Thomas had been apprenticed in his youth to Charles Hatfield and then to David Willaume, Jr., and was made free in 1744, but no entry of his mark is found until he apprenticed his oldest son to himself in 1767. William was apprenticed to his father two years later. He entered his first mark as a plateworker in 1781 from St. Martin's Street, Leicester Fields, and was made free in 1784. His second mark was registered in 1786 from Litchfield Street, Soho, and a third, entered in 1791, showed him in partnership with Joseph Preedy at the same address. In 1795 the two moved to Newport Street, St. Ann's, Soho. Four years later Pitts entered another mark, this time alone, at Little Wild Street, Lincoln's Inn Fields, where he fashioned the wine coolers discussed below. In 1805, the year he entered his fifth mark from James Street, Lambeth Marsh, he took as apprentice his son William, Jr. (1790–1840), who was to become a sculptor of some note. The elder Pitts counted among his clients the Royal family and produced a number of pieces for Windsor Castle. In 1809 he added a central plaque representing "Jupiter taking vengeance upon the earth" to a sideboard dish made by John Wisdom of London in 1714, and nine years later he fashioned a matching dish, both of them now in the Royal Pavilion at Brighton. Pitts was still at James Street in 1818 when John Childers was apprenticed to him and he was listed as "silversmith and chaser."

Set of Four Silver-Gilt Wine Coolers, 1802/04 (15.7.3–15.7.6)

H. 9¾ in. (24.8 cm); D. at rim 8⅞ in. (22.5 cm); W. at rams' horns 9¾ in. (24.8 cm); D. of base 5¼ in. (13.3 cm). Stamped, on the base of each urn (indistinct on No. 15.7.6) and on the underside of the collar and the outside of the liner of Nos. 15.7.3 and 15.7.4: the initials WP, the mark of William Pitts; on the bezel of the collar and the outside of the liner of Nos. 15.7.5 and 15.7.6: the initials R·G, the mark of Robert Garrard; on the base of Nos. 15.7.3 and 15.7.5: the date-letter G for 1802/03; on the base of

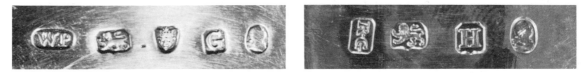

Nos. 15.7.4 and 15.7.6 and on the liners of all four coolers: the date-letter H for 1803/04; on all three sections of each cooler: the lion passant and the king's head; and on the bases only: the leopard's head crowned.

Description: Each cooler consists of three separable sections: a circular, thistle-shaped urn set on a low, splayed foot; a seamed, cylindrical liner (reinforced at the lip with a narrow flat band) which nests within the bowl of the urn and is held slightly above its flattened bottom by a flange; and a flat collar which fits over the top of the liner and secures it by a bezel. The bowl has an applied rim of cast ovolo molding with egg-and-dart decoration. Below the rim at either side is a cast handle in the form of a ram's head, with its ears freestanding, its beard descending to the top of the calyx, and its double-curved horns each affixed to the rim at three points. Festooned between the rams' ears and a knotted ribbon set below the rim at front and back are four applied garlands of vine leaves and grapes in high relief. The swelling calyx is decorated with eight broad, boldly-veined leaves (see below) terminating alternately in pointed and rounded tips. Slightly below the juncture of the bowl with the foot is a cast ovolo with a pattern of small leaves. The foot itself appears to be hammered, joining a cast band of leaves and berries above the angled vertical base. Engraved on each face of the bowl, somewhat crowded beneath the garlands, are greyhound supporters, collared and lined, flanking a coat of arms: gules, a fess between six mullets, argent. Atop the scrolled escutcheon is an earl's coronet and below is the motto LE ROY ET L'ESTAT. Engraved twice on each collar is a crest: out of a ducal coronet, or, an ash tree proper, again surmounted by an earl's coronet.

Condition: Apart from the loss of most of their gilding, the coolers are in good condition. Incised faintly inside each section are numbers ranging from 1 to 4, added evidently to associate the urns with their proper fittings.

The arms and crest on the coolers are those of the Ashburnham family, with the addition of the earl's coronet. Assuming that they were engraved at the time the pieces were fashioned and not added later, the set must have been made for John, second Earl of Ashburnham (1724–1812), or for his son George, third Earl (1760–1830).[2] The coolers appeared in the Ashburnham sale of 1914, at which time they were described as weighing 510 oz.[3]

The mark R·G in a rectangle on the liner and collar of two of the coolers clearly shows the association of William Pitts with Robert Garrard, who in 1792 had been made a partner of John Wakelin in the prominent firm that was founded earlier in the century by George Wickes and would eventually become Garrard & Co. Apparently Garrard acted as Pitts' agent, for according to Grimwade "the Pitts were not in the retail business as far as any of the evidence goes and were entirely workers to the trade as is, of course, supremely demonstrated by the

15.7.5

Garrard ledger entries."[4] It should be added in this connection that some of Pitts' Windsor Castle plate, including dishes of 1810 and 1812, was billed not by Garrard but by Rundell, Bridge and Rundell.[5]

Though the bases of two of the coolers are stamped with the date-letter for 1802/03 and the other two with the letter for the following year, it is probable that all four urns were made in quick succession during 1803, inasmuch as the date-letter changes on May 29th of each year. The liners all bear the later date. It seems safe to conclude that, despite its being incised with the number 4 (see *Condition*), the first urn to be produced was No. 15.7.5, which not only bears the earlier date-letter but also is the only one on which the leaf ornament of the calyx is embossed rather than applied.

Collections: Earls of Ashburnham. Ashburnham sale, March 25, 1914, Christie's, Lot 110. Frick, 1915.

NOTES

1 For biographical information on William Pitts, see A. G. Grimwade, "The Garrard Ledgers," *Proceedings of the Society of Silver Collectors,* paper read April 10, 1961, and *London Goldsmiths, 1697–1837,* London, 1976, p. 626.

2 *The Frick Collection Catalogue,* XI, 1956, p. 43.

3 Information from A. G. Grimwade, letter to the author dated May 21, 1973.

4 *Idem.*

5 E. A. Jones, *The Gold and Silver of Windsor Castle,* Letchworth, 1911, p. 114, Pl. LVIII.

PAUL STORR

1771–1844

Born into the London branch of an old Yorkshire family, Storr was apprenticed in 1785 to Andrew Fogelberg.[1] Seven years later he and William Frisbee entered a mark of their initials in a square, and shortly afterward Storr entered a mark of his own, the first of at least eleven.[2] In 1801 Storr married Elizabeth Beyer, daughter of a neighboring pianoforte-maker, and by 1811 he was a partner in the firm of Rundell, Bridge and Rundell,[3] recipients of numerous commissions from George III. In the latter year Storr was called upon by the Mayor on behalf of the Mansion House to add candelabra and an elaborate base to an epergne made in 1738/39 by Paul De Lamerie.[4] He also produced for the Mansion House dinner plates and meat dishes copying originals by De Lamerie,[5] and in 1816 he was commissioned by the Earl of Lonsdale to add a plinth to a silver-gilt surtout De Lamerie had executed in 1748/49.[6] Storr withdrew from Rundell, Bridge and Rundell in 1819 and moved to Harrison Street. In 1833 he formed an alliance with John Mortimer at New Bond Street, and in 1838, the year before Storr retired, he and Mortimer were listed as "Goldsmiths and Jewellers to Her Majesty." Among Storr's first truly sculptural works was a gold christening font of 1797/98 made for the Duke of Portland,[7] its figures said to have been modelled from designs by the sculptor John Flaxman. Storr's many Royal commissions include a pair of candelabra and the so-called Theocritus Cup designed by Flaxman, a silver-gilt dish designed by the painter Thomas Stothard, and a sculpted figure of George III in Garter robes.[8]

Pair of Silver-Gilt Wine Coolers, 1811/12 (14.7.9 and 14.7.10)

H. at rim 10⅞ in. (27.6 cm); H. including rams' horns 11¼ in. (28.6 cm); D. at rim 9¼ in. (23.5 cm); W. at horns 10½ in.

(26.6 cm); D. of base 5⁹/₁₆ in. (14.1 cm). Stamped, on the base of each urn, on the underside of the collar, and on the outside of the liner: the initials P.S, the mark of Paul Storr, with the date-letter Q for 1811/12 and the lion passant; on the partly freestanding vine leaves and on the lowest grape of each festoon: the lion passant; on the base and the

305

liner: the king's head; and on the base only: the leopard's head crowned and, in minute letters, the inscription RUNDELL BRIDGE ET RUNDELL AURIFICES REGIS ET PRINCIPIS WALLIAE LONDINI FECERUNT.

Description: Though close in form, decoration, and composition to the preceding wine coolers by William Pitts, the present pair exhibit a number of noteworthy modifications. On these the upper part of the bowl is cast, seamed at each side, and applied to a guilloche band at the top of the calyx. The rams' heads have shorter beards, and their horns curve back over the top of the ovolo rim, which is somewhat narrower and more elaborately decorated. The fuller ribbon bows, set tangent to the rim, are partly freestanding, and the vine festoons, which here descend over the top of the guilloche band, are partly soldered and partly bolted to the body, with a bolt at each grape cluster. The calyx is cast with eight swirling acanthus leaves separated by rising tendrils that terminate alternately in upright cornucopias and pendent grape clusters. The ovolo at the top of the foot is gadrooned, and below it is a shallow torus molding. The cast band of leaves and berries above the added vertical base is interrupted at front and back by a flower and at each side by two crossed ribbons. The hammered collar curves steeply downward, and the liner, which flares slightly at the top and shows no seam, has a recessed base with an inner band at the lower edge which fits within a vertical flange at the bottom of the bowl.

Condition: The coolers are in good condition. Virtually all of their gilding is lost except for traces inside the bowl, on the bottom of the liner, under the foot, and in a few of the recesses of the applied reliefs.

RUNDELL BRIDGE

ET RUNDELL AURIFICES

REGIS ET PRINCIPIS

WALLIAE LONDINI FECERUNT

Among the principal pieces Storr fashioned for the Royal family were an enormous wine cistern of 8,000 oz. and the so-called Warwick Vase ice pails, produced at costs of £8,500 and £3,470 respectively.[9] Another large wine cistern of 1,707 oz. 4 dwt. is in the form of an elliptical bowl set on a splayed foot; but for its lack of handles it resembles in outline a punch bowl of 1798/99.[10]

In his monograph on Storr, Penzer lists among the ice pails by him sold at Christie's thirty-five pairs, seven sets of four, and one set of six, ranging from a model of 1798/99 in the form of a hooped barrel to one of 1834/35 with acanthus leaves, vines, and goat's-mask handles.[11] A set of four coolers of 1803/04 at Woburn Abbey, Bedfordshire,[12] have straight sides curving in above a splayed foot, handles in the form of snakes, and a frieze of vine ornament interrupted by

14.7.9

a framed Bacchus mask, all distinctly reminiscent of the Frick coolers of 1811/12 by Benjamin and James Smith (see following entry). A silver-gilt pair of 1809/10 have similar bodies on a lower foot and the unusual addition of domed covers for fruit bowls.[13] From the same year are a pair on footed stands, with a lower body akin to that of the present coolers.[14] A silver-gilt pair of 1810/11 in the Victoria and Albert Museum, London, the design for which is attributed to Flaxman, have the Royal arms applied and an added coronation medal of William IV and Queen Adelaide.[15] Four pails of 1817/18 are decorated all over with grapes.[16]

Very close to the present coolers are a set of eight dated 1812/14 in the collection of Lord Sackville.[17] Unlike the Frick pair, however, the Sackville set are decorated with grapes on the collars of the liners.

Collections: Frick, 1914.

NOTES

1 On the life and work of Storr, see N. M. Penzer, *Paul Storr: The Last of the Goldsmiths,* London, 1954. Fogelberg was presumably of Swedish origin. At the time Storr was apprenticed to him, he was a partner of Stephen Gilbert, who had served his own apprenticeship under Edward Wakelin of the firm that was to become Garrard & Co.

2 For Storr's marks, see Penzer, pp. 81–83.

3 C. Oman (*English Church Plate, 597–1830,* Oxford, 1957, p. 153) remarks of this partnership that "both Paul Storr and John Bridge, who directed the artistic side of the great Regency firm of Rundell, Bridge and Rundell, took trouble to produce original designs for communion plate, although such work formed a very small part of their business." In his foreword to Penzer's monograph (p. 8) Oman also notes Storr's "almost unerring talent for designing and making simple plate for everyday use."

4 Penzer, p. 154, Pl. XXXVIII. The new stand bears the City Arms in relief, Storr's marks, and the name of Rundell, Bridge and Rundell.

5 *Idem,* p. 170, Pl. XLVI.

6 A. G. Grimwade, *The Queen's Silver: A Survey of Her Majesty's Personal Collection,* London, 1953, Pl. 17.

7 Penzer, p. 100, Pl. XI.

8 *Idem,* p. 134, Pl. XXVIII, p. 158, Pl. XL, p. 178, Pl. L, p. 226, Pl. LXXIV. The date of the figure of George III, given by Penzer as 1833/34, is corrected by Grimwade (Pl. 48) to 1812/13.

9 Penzer, pp. 27–29. For the ice pails, see also E. A. Jones, *The Gold and Silver of Windsor Castle,* Letchworth, 1911, p. 208.

10 Penzer, p. 190, Pl. LVI, p. 102, Pl. XIII.

11 *Idem,* pp. 247–81, *passim.*

12 *Idem,* p. 116, Pl. XIX. See also A. Grim-

14.7.10

wade, "Family Silver of Three Centuries," *Apollo,* LXXXII, 1965, p. 505, Fig. 9 on p. 502.

13 Penzer, p. 132, Pl. XXVII. This pair proved sufficiently useful to be matched in 1813/14 and again in 1817/18 (p. 276).

14 *Idem,* p. 136, Pl. XXIX.

15 *Idem,* p. 152. Pl. XXXVII.

16 *Idem,* p. 200, Pl. LXI.

17 *Idem,* p. 160, Pl. XLI.

14.7.10

BENJAMIN and JAMES SMITH

Partners 1809–1812

Benjamin Smith was born in Birmingham in 1764. He and his younger brother James worked there in association with Matthew Boulton until Benjamin left around 1801 for London, where in 1802 he entered his first mark with that of a partner, Digby Scott.[1] Among the many items at Windsor Castle produced by Smith and Scott are a pair of tureens dated 1803/04, a pair of candelabra from the same year, two large cruets of 1805/06, most of the Windsor soup and dinner plates, a number of bread baskets, twenty sauceboats in two sizes, and twenty-four small cups or bowls.[2] Smith entered a mark on his own in 1807 and a third mark in 1809, this time together with James, who appears to have remained until then with Boulton. The production of the brothers' partnership includes eight sugar vases at Windsor Castle dated 1809/10[3] and a very similar vase dated 1810/11 in the Victoria and Albert Museum, London, identified as part of the Duke of Wellington's ambassador's service.[4] In 1812 Benjamin entered another new mark on his own. At the Victoria and Albert Museum by him alone are a gilt candelabrum of 1816/17 and the Wellington Shield of about 1822, both made for presentation to the Duke from the merchants and bankers of the City of London.[5] Most of Benjamin Smith's work, like much of Paul Storr's, was done for the firm of Rundell, Bridge and Rundell, which in all likelihood provided designs to both artists; their work often shows striking similarities.[6] Neither Digby Scott nor James Smith appears to have signed any work independently.[7]

Pair of Silver-Gilt Wine Coolers, 1811/12 (15.7.7 and 15.7.8)

H. 10¼ in. (26 cm); D. at rim 9¼ in. (23.5 cm); D. of base 5⁵/₁₆ in. (13.5 cm). Stamped, on the base of each urn, on the bezel of the collar, on the outside of the liner, and on the upper surface of the frame: the

initials BS over I·S, the mark of Benjamin and James Smith, with the lion passant; on all but the frame: the date-letter Q for 1811/12; on all but the collar: the king's head; and on the base only: the leopard's head crowned.

Description: The coolers are similar in general form to those described in the two preceding entries, but there are marked variations in the decoration, and the number of

312

15.7.7

separable sections is here increased to four by the addition of a flat frame of two concentric circles set under the collar to secure the top of the liner. The collar curves upward near the center, and its opening is bordered by an applied vertical band of small stylized leaves. The everted lip, broader in relation to the width of the body than those on the preceding coolers, bears an applied ovolo molding with egg-and-dart decoration below an edge of beading. In place of the festoons on the upper bodies of the other examples is a wide horizontal cast band of spiralling vine tendrils, leaves, and grapes interrupted at front and back by a Bacchus mask in a circle and flanked above and below by a narrow band repeating the leaf ornament on the collar. The somewhat more functional handles each consist of two opposed snakes, intertwined and ajouré, set at forty-five degree angles to the bowl, to which they are affixed by their heads immediately above the shallow curve of the calyx. The calyx itself is decorated with eight acanthus leaves riveted on. The cast ovolo at the top of the foot repeats the egg-and-dart design on the rim, and the cast band above the vertical base bears pendent acanthus leaves. Both body and foot show hammer marks, and the former has a center point on the base. The cylindrical liner is seamed and has a recessed bottom. Engraved on each face below the mask, surmounted by a helmet and leafy scrolls, is an impaled coat of arms: dexter, vert a chevron ermine between three lions rampant, on the chief erminoise, three fountains; sinister, argent a cross couped gules between three crescents azure. Twice on the collar and once on the outside of the liner is a crest: a demi-tyger erminoise holding between its forepaws a fountain.

Condition: The coolers are in good condition. They have lost much of their gilding, but the remaining traces are more extensive than those on the preceding examples.

The heraldry on the coolers was identified in *The Frick Collection Catalogue* of 1956 as follows: "The dexter arms and the crest...were granted on March 2, 1810, to 'Joseph Burn, late Joseph Teasdale, of Lincoln's Inn Square, Middlesex, and of Orton in the County of Westmoreland, who by Royal License of the 11th of March 1802 took the surname of Burn in compliance with the will of John Burn of Orton aforesaid, dated the 22nd of January 1801. He was in fact the illegitimate son of this John Burn (born 1743, died 1802, son and only child of the Reverend Richard Burn, LL. D., of Winton, co. Westmoreland, Vicar of Orton, Chancellor of the Diocese of Carlisle) by Isobel, daughter of Daniel Teasdale, of Orton, yeoman. At the same time Joseph Burn's wife Eulalia, daughter of Joseph Vila, late of Barcelona in Spain, gentleman (whom he married there in 1806 and again in Orton in 1808) had a grant of the arms shewn on the sinister side of the wine cooler....'"[8]

A cooler of the same design and date and bearing the same arms was reproduced by Jackson in 1911 with no maker given and the owner identified only as "Mr. Jonathan Smith."[9] Among the pieces at Windsor Castle by Benjamin Smith and Digby Scott are six ice pails of 1803/04 and the pair of double wine coolers of 1805/06 mentioned on p. 300. Ice pails with stands were produced by the partnership of Benjamin and James Smith.[10]

Collections: Frick, 1915.

NOTES

1 On Benjamin and James Smith, see A. G. Grimwade, *London Goldsmiths, 1697–1837,* London, 1976, pp. 661–62, 664. For Matthew Boulton, see C. J. Jackson, *English Goldsmiths and Their Marks,* London, 2nd ed., 1921, p. 400. See also N. M. Penzer, *Paul Storr: The Last of the Goldsmiths,* London, 1954, p. 58.

2 E. A. Jones, *The Gold and Silver of Windsor Castle,* Letchworth, 1911, *passim.* For the candelabra see p. 154, Pl. LXXVIII, and for the cruets p. 223.

3 *Idem,* p. 164, Pl. LXXXIII, No. 4. According to Penzer (p. 182), one of the eight was made by Benjamin Smith alone in 1808/09 and the rest by the partners in the ensuing year.

4 C. Oman, *English Silversmiths' Work, Civil and Domestic,* London, 1965, Pl. 195.

5 *Idem,* Pls. 201, 206, made to the order of Green, Ward and Green. Oman also illustrates Thomas Stothard's design for the shield (Pl. 205), as well as the Waterloo Vase of 1825/26 (Pl. 209), its plinth made the same year by Robert Garrard.

6 Grimwade, p. 662.

7 Jackson (p. 226) tentatively lists a joint mark of DS BS IS for Digby Scott and Benjamin and James Smith, citing plate at Windsor Castle, but Jones lists neither the mark nor the triple partnership.

8 *The Frick Collection Catalogue,* XI, 1956, p. 44, citing a communication from the *Richmond Herald* dated March 15, 1956.

9 C. J. Jackson, *An Illustrated History of English Plate, Ecclesiastical and Secular,* London, 1911, II, Fig. 1029.

10 Jones, p. 146, Pl. LVII, and erratum on p. xi.

INDICES

INDEX OF ENAMELLERS

INDEX OF ENAMELLED SUBJECTS

Note: The page numbers are those on which the subjects are first identified.

PORTRAITS

PORTRAITS, UNIDENTIFIED

SAINTS

(For saints traditionally depicted in representations of the Adoration, the Last Supper, the Passion, the Deposition, the Pietà, the Entombment, and the Death of the Virgin, see the appropriate listings under the heading Scenes from the Life of Christ and of the Virgin.)

SCENES FROM THE LIFE OF CHRIST AND OF THE VIRGIN

SCENES FROM THE OLD TESTAMENT

325

UTENSILS

INDEX OF SILVERSMITHS

CONCORDANCE OF CHANGES OF ATTRIBUTION AND TITLE

Folio Catalogues of 1955 and 1956	*Present Catalogue*
ANONYMOUS Silver-Gilt Plate	LONDON MONOGRAMMIST I S Silver-Gilt Plate, 1797/98
ANONYMOUS ATELIER Casket: Heads of Roman Emperors in Wreaths	NOYLIER, Couly II Casket: Heads of the Caesars within Wreaths
ANONYMOUS ENGLISH, Eighteenth Century Silver-Gilt Ladle	DE LAMERIE, Paul, Attributed to Silver-Gilt Ladle, c. 1739
ANONYMOUS LIMOGES ATELIER Concave Oval Plaque: A Roman Emperor	LIMOUSIN, Jean II Concave Oval Plaque: Ninus, King of Nineveh
ANONYMOUS MASTER Plaque: The Seven Sorrows of the Virgin	MASTER OF THE PASSION, Attributed to
LAMERIE, Paul [Jacques de] Silver-Gilt Porringer	DE LAMERIE, Paul Silver-Gilt Écuelle
LIMOSIN, Léonard Plaque: Portrait of a Bearded Man	LIMOUSIN, Léonard Plaque: Guillaume Farel (?)
LIMOSIN, Léonard Plaque: Portrait of a Lady	LIMOUSIN, Léonard Plaque: Louise de Pisseleu, Madame de Jarnac

LIMOSIN, Léonard
 Plaque: Portrait of a Nobleman

LIMOSIN, Léonard
 Plaque: Portrait of
 Antoine de Bourbon

LIMOSIN, Léonard
 Plaque: Triumph of the Faith

LIMOSIN, Léonard II
 Saltcellar: Olympian Deities

MASTER I.C. or I.D.C.
 Saltcellars: Scylla in Love with
 Minos; Six of the Virtues; Scylla
 Brings Evidence to Minos of Her
 Father's Death

ORLÉANS TRIPTYCH, Atelier of the
 Triptych: The Crucifixion;
 Saint Barbara; Saint Catherine
 of Alexandria

PÉNICAUD, Jean I, School of
 Triptych: Christ Carrying the Cross;
 The Crucifixion; The Deposition

PÉNICAUD, Jean I, School of
 Triptych: Christ Carrying the Cross;
 The Crucifixion; The Pietà

PÉNICAUD, Jean I, School of
 Plaque: The Martyrdom of a Saint

PÉNICAUD, Nardon, Atelier of
 Large Triptych: Six Scenes from
 the Passion of Christ

LIMOUSIN, Léonard
 Plaque: Guy Chabot, Baron de Jarnac

LIMOUSIN, Léonard
 Plaque: Antoine de Bourbon,
 King of Navarre (?)

LIMOUSIN, Léonard
 Plaque: Triumph of the Eucharist
 and of the Catholic Faith

LIMOUSIN, Jean II

GUIBERT, Jean
 Pair of Saltcellars: Virtues and
 Liberal Arts with Religion and
 Justice; The Story of Minos and Scylla

MASTER OF THE BALTIMORE AND
ORLÉANS TRIPTYCHS

PÉNICAUD, Nardon, Workshop of

PÉNICAUD, Jean I

PÉNICAUD, Jean I

PÉNICAUD, Nardon
 Double Triptych: Scenes from
 the Passion

329

PÉNICAUDS, School of the
  Ewer: The Trojan Horse;
  A Cavalry Combat
	PÉNICAUD, Jean III

REYMOND, Jean or Joseph Oval Dish: The Last Supper	REYMOND, Jean

REYMOND, Pierre
  Ewer: The Destruction of Pharaoh's
  Host; The Gathering of Manna
	REYMOND, Pierre or Jean, Workshop of

REYMOND, Pierre Plaque: The Adoration of the Magi	REYMOND, Jean
REYMOND, Pierre Saltcellar in Baluster Form	REYMOND, Pierre, Workshop of